"Fast Sailing and Copper-Bottomed"

Aberdeen Sailing Ships and the Emigrant Scots
They Carried to Canada 1774–1855

"FAST SAILING AND COPPER-BOTTOMED"

*Aberdeen Sailing Ships and the Emigrant Scots
They Carried to Canada 1774–1855*

LUCILLE H. CAMPEY

NATURAL HERITAGE BOOKS
TORONTO

Published by Natural Heritage/Natural History Inc.
P.O. Box 95, Station O, Toronto, Ontario M4A 2M8
www.naturalheritagebooks.com

Cover illustration taken from *Aberdeen from the South-east, 1836*,
lithograph by John Hay, from an original drawing by J. W. Allen.
Courtesy of the City of Aberdeen Art Gallery and Museums Collections

Design by Blanche Hamill, Norton Hamill Design
Edited by Jane Gibson
The text in this book was set in a typeface named Bembo.

Printed and bound in Canada by Hignell Printing Limited

Canadian Cataloguing in Publication Data

Campey, Lucille H.
Fast sailing and copper-bottomed : Aberdeen sailing ships and the emigrant
Scots they carried to Canada, 1774–1855 / Lucille H. Campey.

Includes bibliographical references and index.
ISBN 1-896219-31-4

1. Highlands (Scotland)—Emigration and immigration—History. 2. Canada—Emigration and immigration—History. 3. Scots—Canada—History. 4. Sailing ships—Scotland—Aberdeen—History. 5. Harbors—Scotland—Aberdeen—History. 6. Aberdeen
(Scotland)—History. I. Natural Heritage/Natural History Inc. II. Title.

FC106.S3C28 2002   971'.0049163   C2002-901454-9   F1035.S4C28 2002

ONTARIO ARTS COUNCIL
CONSEIL DES ARTS DE L'ONTARIO

THE CANADA COUNCIL | LE CONSEIL DES ARTS
FOR THE ARTS | DU CANADA
SINCE 1957 | DEPUIS 1957

Natural Heritage / Natural History Inc. acknowledges the financial support
of the Canada Council for the Arts and the Ontario Arts Council for our
publishing program. We also acknowledge the financial support of the Government
of Canada through the Book Publishing Industry Development Program (BPIDP)
and the Association for the Export of Canadian Books.

CONTENTS

Tables and Figures

PREFACE

Today Aberdeen is an importance centre of North Sea oil production. Shipping and trade have long dominated the city's industry and commerce. When the world famous clipper-bowed ships were first developed, in 1839, Aberdeen's already high reputation in shipbuilding reached new heights. Breaking speed records on their long journeys to collect tea and opium from China, Aberdeen clippers were the epitome of dazzling design and sound construction. This book is concerned, not with them, but with the stout and sturdy Aberdeen ships of this same era, which went off to Canada to collect timber. They gave emigrant Scots wishing passages to Canada an affordable sea crossing and thus facilitated the growing exodus from the northeast of Scotland and parts of the Highlands. These sailing ships attracted little attention and when the steamship arrived in the mid-1850s their time abruptly came to an end. But for about 50 years emigrants from many parts of Scotland relied on Aberdeen ships to transport them safely to Canada.

I first encountered Aberdeen's fast sailing and copper-bottomed vessels in late eighteenth and early nineteenth century shipping advertisements, which were published in the *Aberdeen Journal* and in the *Inverness Journal*. These were just announcements of intended departures from Aberdeen or ports in the Highlands to destinations in Canada. I had next to ascertain whether any emigrants actually crossed on the Aberdeen ships named in the newspapers. But because Aberdeen ships were also being used to take emigrants to Canada from the Highlands and Hebrides, I needed to broaden the geographical coverage of my research beyond Aberdeen itself.

Using Scottish customs records and newspaper shipping reports, I found a great deal of previously unpublished data on emigrant crossings, both from Aberdeen and ports in the Highlands. And having identified the ships, I located details of their owners, agents and captains from the *Aberdeen Shipping Registers.*

This is a totally different approach to what has been done previously. Most studies of emigrant shipping have concentrated on anecdotal descriptions and the inadequacies of early nineteenth century passenger legislation. There are well-documented accounts of miserable crossings on substandard ships. But by simply dwelling on these we get an unduly biased and negative picture. An objective assessment requires knowledge of the overall standard of services achieved on most crossings, not just the handful which went horribly wrong. Passenger legislation is also a dubious basis for a study of emigrant crossings. While it did eventually become enforceable and relevant to the needs of emigrants, during the sailing ship era, legislation gave little protection to emigrants. The prime deterrent against unscrupulous practices was the shipowner's desire for repeat business. His repeated success in attracting emigrants would indicate that he had consistently provided good ships and a good service. Thus it was important to locate data on ship ownership patterns and this took me to the Aberdeen City Archives, where the *Aberdeen Shipping Registers* are stored.

Upon reaching my destination I went up a long staircase, past the portraits of former Lord Provosts of Aberdeen. On the way down the stairs later in the day I met the same stern-faced gentlemen, but then I could put faces to names. They were former members of Aberdeen's business community, with some owning shares in the ships which took emigrants to Canada. I found myself thinking that if men such as this had been behind Aberdeen's shipping services, emigrants would have been in very safe hands. A hunch only at that stage but it later became a firm conclusion. I found enormous continuity in the shipping services provided by individual owners like William Duthie and Donaldson Rose. Far from being rogues in search of a quick profit, men like them were in business for the long term. I found also that they employed experienced sea captains on Atlantic routes and provided emigrants with a consistently high standard of ship. Thus their repeat business was built on the high standard of service they offered emigrants.

Of course the sea voyage was just the first step in a long process of relocation. There were pressures to leave Scotland and there were factors which attracted emigrants to their particular destinations. Here again I have departed from the position taken by many researchers, who would have us believe that emigration was caused solely by expulsions and destitution. While the reasons why people left Scotland need to be thoroughly assessed, we must also consider what effect events in Canada had on an emigrant's choice of destination. For instance, New Brunswick and Nova Scotia had received large and early capital investment in their timber industries from Scots. That was a crucial factor in the late eighteenth and early nineteenth century influx of Highlanders to the eastern Maritimes. From the 1830s western Upper Canada also had particular advantages to emigrant Scots. It was a time when the Huron Tract was being opened up to settlers and when men with money and a desire to promote colonization were buying up large tracts of land to found new settlements. Groups from Aberdeenshire and different parts of the Highlands formed distinctive settlements which, because of their rapid growth and success, drew successions of friends and relatives to them over long periods.

Thus whole Scottish communities relocated themselves in Canada. A desire for better economic prospects had influenced their decision to emigrate, but many also wanted to retain some aspects of their Old World lifestyle when they got there. And they came from many walks of life. There were many poor labourers and people of very limited means, but also included in their number were University graduates, sons of Aberdeen lawyers, prosperous merchants and wealthy farmers. It was not by any means an influx of just the poor and dispossessed. Their strongly held religious beliefs and values helped them through many early difficulties. But in the end the process of assimilation would fragment their communities and eventually even their settlement names would be lost. But the profound sense of Scottishness which they brought with them, as pioneer settlers, lives on to this day in the Maritimes and Ontario. Our Pipe Bands, traditional dancing, Highland games, commemoration of Robert Burns' birthday and innumerable Scottish societies are all living reminders of the culture and traditions which these settlers brought to Canada. This book salutes their achievements and tells their story.

ACKNOWLEDGEMENTS

Many years of preparation have gone into this book. Working at Archives and Libraries in the Maritimes of Canada, in Scotland and at the British Library and Public Record Office in London, I have reason to be grateful to the many people who helped me to find my way through the various sources used in the preparation of this book. I wish to particularly record my thanks to Siobhan Convery of the Aberdeen City Archives, who tracked down so much useful data for me on Aberdeen shipbuilders. I am also indebted to John Edwards, Keeper (Science and Maritime History) of the Aberdeen Maritime Museum for sending me so much useful data on Aberdeen-built ships and for his help in locating illustrations.

I thank Dr. Marjory Harper of Aberdeen University, who supervised my doctorate and who continues to provide me with much valued help and encouragement. I would also like to acknowledge the help given to me by staff at Aberdeen University, both from the Queen Mother Library and the Manuscripts and Special Collections Department. I am grateful too for the help I received from staff at Aberdeen's City Library. I am also indebted to Karen Wagner, Archivist at the Wellington County Museums and Archives, for her knowledge of what was available by way of illustrations for the Aberdeenshire settlements in Upper Canada.

I thank my friend Jean Lucas for her helpful comments on the initial manuscript. But most of all I thank my husband Geoff, for his enthusiastic support, computer skills and good sense. Without him this book would not have been possible. It is dedicated to him with much love.

Abbreviations

ACA	Aberdeen City Archives
AH	*Aberdeen Herald*
AJ	*Aberdeen Journal*
DC	*Dundee Courier*
DCB	*Dictionary of Canadian Biography*
EC	*Elgin Courier*
HCA	Highland Council Archives
IC	*Inverness Courier*
IJ	*Inverness Journal*
JJ	*John O'Groat Journal*
LL	*Lloyd's List*
MC	*Moray, Nairn and Banff Courant*
NBRG	*New Brunswick Royal Gazette*
NLS	National Library of Scotland
PANS	Public Archives of Nova Scotia
PAPEI	Public Archives of Prince Edward Island
PRO	Public Record Office
PEIG	*PEI Gazette*
PP	*Parliamentary Papers*
QG	*Quebec Gazette*
QM	*Quebec Mercury*
SM	*Scots Magazine*
SRO	Scottish Record Office

"FAST SAILING AND COPPER-BOTTOMED"

Aberdeen Sailing Ships and the Emigrant Scots
They Carried to Canada 1774–1855

1. The Exodus Takes Shape

"I am thoroughly convinced that the emigration will soon be general in this country—two hundred and fifty sailed the other day from Fort George and three hundred and eight of the MacDonalds of Glen Garry and the neighbouring districts from Fort William. Not less than eight or ten vessels are hired this season to carry off emigrants. Eight hundred and forty people sailed from the Isle of Lewis in July."[1]

Writing in 1773, this "gentleman from Strathspey" correctly predicted that emigration from Scotland to North America was on the increase. Agricultural changes, a worsening economic situation, together with a growing belief in the opportunities to be had in North America, led unprecedented numbers from both Lowland Scotland and the Highlands to seek a better life abroad. The two hundred and fifty emigrants, who left Fort George in September 1773 were, in fact, part of an even larger contingent, which included people from Ross-shire, Sutherland and Caithness. They were numbered among the seven hundred and seventy-five emigrants from the north of Scotland, who had gone to Stromness in the Orkney Islands where they had been collected by three vessels and taken to New York and other North American destinations.[2] What had begun as a trickle years earlier, was now a flood. Having made their way to Glasgow in the following year, over 100 emigrants from Strathspey sailed on the *George* of Greenock to New York and, a year later, large numbers from this same area left from Stornoway on the *Clementina* for Philadelphia.[3] By the end of May 1775, some 700 emigrants, mainly from the North Highlands, had sailed for North America in one of four vessels and there were many others to follow.[4]

The emigrants who left from Fort George, in the Moray Firth, had been taken by boat to Stromness to board ocean-going vessels which would take them on to North America. However this routing was a rare occurrence. People wishing passages to North America would normally have sailed directly from Cromarty, situated on the other side of the Firth. Because of its sheltered position and excellent harbour, Cromarty was highly accessible to the large ships from northeastern ports like Aberdeen which were involved in Atlantic trade.[5] However, it was the west side of Scotland, not the east, which lost most people to the late eighteenth and early nineteenth century exodus to North America. The east of Scotland showed less enthusiasm for emigration until Upper Canada became more developed and that was not until 1830.

Aberdeen, an east coast port, might seem an inappropriate choice for a study of emigrant shipping services. Yet Aberdeen did have a considerable Atlantic passenger trade, doing so long before its own people expressed any interest in joining the exodus to British America. This was because of the central role which its shipowners played, initially, in providing vessels to emigrant Scots. Before 1820 Aberdeen vessels made most of their emigrant collections on the west side but later, as the exodus from the northeast grew in scale, they acquired their passengers much closer to home. So a study of the Aberdeen vessels which carried emigrants essentially tracks the overall Scottish exodus, beginning with the west, which initially dominated, and ending with the northeast which only later developed a major transatlantic trade.

This study concentrates on the emigrant Scots who sailed on Aberdeen-registered vessels. Their destinations in British America were influenced by Aberdeen's Atlantic trade links which date back to the eighteenth century. The volume of trade, while insignificant at first, mushroomed from 1811, during the Napoleonic Wars, as duties on Baltic timber were suddenly raised. Because the punitive tariffs on Baltic timber remained in force for some fifty years, this produced a long-term changeover in supplies from the Baltic to British America. And, as

Aberdeen's timber trade with British America grew, more of its vessels crossed the Atlantic and the search was on to find emigrants to fill spare shipping capacity. It became a highly competitive trade as shipowners, particularly those on the east coast, with the greatest distance to cover, increasingly sought emigrants for their vessels' westward journeys.

Aberdeen shipowners had been well used to locating emigrants for Atlantic crossings from the 1770s. They relied on agents to locate emigrants in the Highlands and by the 1820s their agents' advertisements become regular occurrences in Inverness newspapers.[6] From the mid-1830s, when emigration from its own catchment area began to increase and shipowners could rely on a locally based Atlantic passenger trade, Aberdeen's ranking as an emigrant port rose to becoming second only to the Clyde.[7] And because its shipping volume dedicated to Atlantic trade was sizeable but not so unwieldy as to prohibit a detailed analysis, as would have been the case with the much busier Clyde ports, Aberdeen gives us the ideal base from which to study emigrant shipping.

During the sailing ship era Atlantic services were geared to trade, not passengers. It would not be until the second half of the nineteenth century, with the advent of specialist steamships, that passengers could expect consumer-friendly services. Before then crossings were haphazardly run and, although there were some regulations governing space and food, the lack of any enforceability meant that they could be widely ignored.[8] Previous studies have tended to concentrate on overcrowding, food shortages and the spread of disease. The perception is of rotting hulls barely able to cross the Atlantic without sinking and of miserable emigrants in peril for their lives. But in looking at the shipping services which operated from Aberdeen, it soon becomes obvious that the facts do not support such negative imagery. The *Lloyd's Shipping Register,* a source still in use today, is a salutary reminder that anecdotal meanderings are a poor substitute for hard facts. It tells us that the emigrants who travelled on Aberdeen ships sailed on good quality vessels, often the best available.[9]

Through *Lloyd's List* we can reconstruct the Atlantic crossings made by individual vessels to and from Aberdeen.[10] Scottish Customs Records and other sources reveal the timber cargoes carried on eastward journeys while newspaper shipping reports record the numbers of passengers taken on

Aberdeen from the South-east, 1838, lithograph by John Hay, from an original drawing by
J.W. Allan. *City of Aberdeen, Art Gallery and Museums Collections.*

westward journeys.[11] And, through the *Aberdeen Shipping Registers,* which
give the captains' names and the length, breadth and depth dimensions of
vessels, it can be explained why some vessels were far more successful than
others in attracting emigrants. Experienced captains were like magnets,
attracting the bulk of the passenger trade, as were vessels which offered
greater then average height to the steerage passengers who were accommodated in the hold.[12]

The Atlantic crossing was only the first step in a long process of relocation. Emigrants hoped to find suitable land in areas with good prospects.
That, after all, was one of the prime positive reasons for emigrating. Here
the focus is on the settlement locations in British America of the emigrants who sailed on Aberdeen ships. Most originated from Aberdeenshire and the surrounding area while a good many also originated from
the Highlands, especially Sutherland and Caithness. Very few of them are
known by name. The passenger numbers listed in shipping sources identify from which ports they left, while late nineteenth century census data

tells where they settled.[13] Contemporary observers like the Glasgow Colonial Society missionaries describe early Scottish communities in the Maritimes and Upper Canada, while the Quebec Immigration Agent gives his impressions on how emigrant Scots looked on arrival and their settlement destinations in Upper Canada.[14] But before tracing the part played by Aberdeen ships in the exodus from Scotland to British America, it is necessary to go back to the late eighteenth century, when the zeal to emigrate was first gaining momentum.

Our gentleman from Strathspey witnessed the great surge in emigration from the north of Scotland just as it had reached a peak in the mid-1770s. This displacement of Scots, which was mainly to the colonies of North Carolina, New York and Georgia, came to an abrupt but temporary halt in 1775, with the onset of the American War of Independence. The war ended in 1783 with the defeat of the British and the establishment of independence for the Americans. Following the war, tens of thousands of civilians and former soldiers and officers, who had remained loyal to the British side during the war, fled from the United States and became relocated in British America. Receiving financial help from the British government, around 35,000 to 40,000 Loyalists went to the Maritimes region and just under 2,000 Loyalist families to Upper Canada.[15] Although not all remained as permanent settlers, major footholds were established which acted as a spur to follow-on emigration. Included in the large numbers of Loyalists, who had been relocated, were a good many Scots. They came from all walks of life, but there were some who were to have a particularly strong influence on events in British America.

A great many of the merchants who flocked to Montreal, Quebec, Halifax and Saint John, immediately after the American War, were part of the Loyalist influx of Scots who brought their expertise and business contacts with them from the southern colonies. Making an early and major contribution to British American commerce and industry, they were amongst the first to recognize the opportunities to be had from the North American timber trade. Joined by other merchants from Scotland, immediately after the war ended, they provided British America with much-needed capital and economic direction and in doing so helped to facilitate trade between both countries.[16] The rapid growth in shipping dedicated to the timber trade, led to more Atlantic crossings from Scotland, benefiting emigrant Scots, who now had access to regular and more affordable transport. The new shipping routes spawned by the growing timber trade, which were in place by the turn of the century, thus gave Scots important travel opportunities when forest clearance and colonization were at a very early stage of development.

Scots had also been especially well-represented in the various regiments which had fought in North America. Because they qualified for free land once their service had been completed, many eventually became settlers. Men from all parts of Scotland served in the Seven Years War (1756–63), the American War of Independence (1775–83) and later in the War of 1812–14, but Highlanders were to be found in greatest numbers. The really major movement of ex-military personnel occurred just after the American War in the mid-to-late 1780s, when large numbers of Highlanders were resettled at government expense in Glengarry, Upper Canada, the Pictou area of Nova Scotia and at Chatham in Argenteuil County, Lower Canada.[17] Many were former members of the Royal Highland Emigrant Regiment (the 84th), raised just before the American War, who had been recruited in the United States as well as in the Maritimes.[18] Once settled, their communities acquired a strong Highland identity which was reinforced by subsequent arrivals from the Highlands.

Emigration resumed again in 1784, with the ending of the American War, but on a very different basis. Although statistics are incomplete, the trends show that Scots increasingly dominated the late eighteenth century influx to British America [19] But whereas before the outbreak of the American War in 1775, people had emigrated from both the Lowlands and Highlands, after the war ended, in 1783, most emigrants originated from the Highlands and Islands. Emigration had its greatest appeal in the crofting districts of the north and west Highlands and in the Western Isles, regions which had been particularly badly hit by the economic and agricultural changes sweeping through the country. Their location on the Atlantic side of the country also helped since it gave easy access to the vessels, which by then, were leaving the Clyde for North America. Although the Clyde led the way in offering regular Atlantic crossings, it was not long before the trade links between both countries encompassed east coast ports like Aberdeen. By 1801 some

Aberdeen ships were being diverted to the Western Isles and west coast of Scotland to collect emigrants bound for British America.

The transformation to larger farms and introduction of commercial sheep-farming in the Highlands and Islands had brought grievances and uncertainties which influenced many to emigrate. With the help of affluent tacksmen and proprietors, with land to colonize, major settlements were established in Prince Edward Island even before the outbreak of the American War.[20] This was a conscious decision to opt for the preservation of a traditional way of life and the independence which comes from owning land. The pull of the successfully settled Highlanders who had gone before drew each new group into the same distinctive geographical areas and the very existence of these strong Highland footholds also enhanced Highlander success rates as pioneer settlers. As the government began to realize, contented immigrants rarely return home but instead send encouraging reports back to their families and friends. By the turn of the century, as wave after wave of emigrants left Scotland for British America, it seemed that a run-away force had been unleashed.

Initially, the exodus took place against a backdrop of feverish opposition. Emigration was seen as harmful in that it would deprive the nation of people who would otherwise be in its workforce or be military recruits. It was a hostile climate for the shipowners and emigration agents who provided emigrants with their transport across the Atlantic. They needed to be astute propagandists, able to counteract the negative publicity that their work generated. And the emigrants themselves needed to have a steely determination to trust in the positive feedback they were getting from their families and friends since all around them were reports of doom and foreboding about their prospects abroad. But, with the ending of the Napoleonic Wars in 1816 and the severe economic depression which came in its wake, opposition waned.

With diminishing job prospects and the increasing hardship being experienced throughout Scotland, emigration began to broaden its appeal. Although most areas of Scotland were losing people to British America, it was from the cotton industry heartlands near the Clyde and the kelp producing regions of the Highlands and Islands that the exodus primarily occurred. For a decade, from 1816, large numbers of redundant handloom

Thurso from Holbern Head, colour engraving by William Daniell published London, June 1, 1820. Sutherland and Caithness emigrants sailed for Canada from Scrabster in Thurso Bay from as early as 1815. Very large numbers left from this port in the 1840s and 1850s. *Copyright Royal Commission on the Ancient and Historical Monuments of Scotland.*

weavers and labourers from Lanarkshire and Renfrewshire, who originated mainly from Glasgow and Paisley, relocated themselves as farmers in the Rideau Valley region of Upper Canada.[21] With the decline in kelp production from the mid-1820s, which brought extreme destitution to areas of the Western Isles, whole estates were cleared and entire communities left for Cape Breton, Prince Edward Island and Upper Canada.[22] Meanwhile clearances from 1811, occuring on the Sutherland estate to make way for sheep farms, contributed to the growing exodus from the Highlands to eastern Nova Scotia.[23] The exodus from Sutherland continued until 1822, then resumed again in 1830, when new opportunities in Upper Canada stimulated a major outflow of emigrants to Zorra, in Oxford County, which was sustained until the late 1840s.[24] And during the Highland Famine years, from 1846 to 1856, emigration levels rose even further, with a great many of the emigrants being given financial assistance by their landlords.

But it was only from the 1830s that emigration had broadened its appeal to encompass most of Scotland. The emerging popularity of Upper Canada together with the onset of a severe economic depression helped to stimulate a dramatic growth in emigration from the northeast of Scotland. This marked the beginning of a sustained period of emigration to Upper Canada from the port of Aberdeen which lasted for some twenty five years. Founding their "Aberdeenshire colony" of Bon Accord in 1835, Aberdeenshire emigrants achieved great success. Attracting large numbers, their settlement contributed to the high concentrations of Scots who would later settle in Wellington County.[25]

We now look back to the early days of Aberdeen's Atlantic passenger trade, trace its growth across Scotland and follow the emigrants, carried on Aberdeen ships, to their settlements in British America. But before we delve into the way in which shipping services functioned we should spare a thought for the people who crossed the Atlantic at this time. Imagine yourself in the bustling harbour scenes during the final stages as passengers prepared to leave. The accommodation and provisions had to be inspected and names had to be checked from lists to ensure that the correct numbers were on board. In this highly charged atmosphere families were coming to terms with the almost certain knowledge that these were final departures. Because return journeys were prohibitively expensive, most would never again see loved ones in Scotland.[26] These emigrants were outstanding pioneer settlers but, in recognizing their achievements, we should also remember their hardships and qualities of self-reliance and determination. As their ships left the harbour they faced the daunting prospect of a sea voyage and the uncertainties which awaited them in the forest clearings which would become their new homes.

11. Early Atlantic Crossings, 1774–15

"To be sold by public roup upon Friday, the 26th instant, by 6 o'clock in the evening, within the Lemon Tree Tavern of Aberdeen: The Galliot *Perseverance* of Aberdeen, of the burden of 112 tons per register, as she presently lies in the harbour of Aberdeen. The vessel is well found and in good condition and the rigging and materials almost entirely new, having lately undergone a thorough repair."[1]

This advertisement, printed in 1811, was a forerunner of events to come. The *Perseverance* clearly did find a buyer. In just three years time she would call at Cromarty to collect emigrants on her way across the Atlantic. She would, according to an advertisement in the *Inverness Journal* sail "direct for Pictou with passengers" and because "the greater part of them already are engaged" the advice was to book early.[2] In fact the *Perseverance* did four Atlantic crossings in all during the period from 1814 to 1818, each time taking emigrants from either Cromarty or the Western Isles to Halifax and Pictou, Nova Scotia, or Quebec. Not remarkable in itself, but given that she was a relatively small, foreign-built vessel, captured in wartime (a prize made free) and of uncertain age and origin, this vessel's repeated usage seems to reflect badly on the passenger transport services available at the time.[3] We might also wonder why an Aberdeen-registered vessel was chosen to collect Western Isle emigrants. Clyde vessels were far closer and crossed the Atlantic with far greater frequency. Yet on two occasions the

Perseverance, leaving from the northeast side of Scotland, was diverted a considerable distance to the west, to Stornoway and Skye, to collect passengers.[4]

Because of its location on the less-favoured east side of the country, Aberdeen's Atlantic trade initially was relatively small. Meanwhile, the Clyde had already built up major trade links with North America by the late eighteen century. With the shorter distance involved, it had been economic for shippers to get their timber supplies from forests in the eastern Maritimes ever without the incentive of punitive tariffs. The Clyde had been getting North American timber from as early as 1790—some twenty years before the tariff on Baltic timber was suddenly increased. This was also a time when, in the west Highlands and Islands, interest in emigration to the northern colonies had reached fever pitch. In 1802, all but five of the just over forty ships which arrived in British America from Scotland had come from the Clyde. Only one vessel sailed from Aberdeen and only four came from Leith. Most of the nearly 3,000 emigrants who sailed to Prince Edward Island, Pictou, Cape Breton and Quebec, that year, arrived on Clyde-registered ships.[5] Thus Clyde importers and shipowners had a twenty year head start, both in building up their trade links with the northern colonies and also in locating emigrants willing to buy passages on their ships.

The Napoleonic Wars (1803–1815) completely transformed this situation. The Clyde lost its near monopoly and by 1816 all major Scottish ports were trading with British America and offering space on their vessels to emigrants wishing to cross the Atlantic. But, while the Clyde could readily attract emigrants to its ports, Aberdeen could not. With emigrants mainly leaving from the west, a location on the east side of the country was hardly going to stand a chance. The simple fact was that, if Aberdeen shipowners were going to get fares from emigrants on Atlantic crossings, they had to send their ships to the emigrants, and most were to be found in the West Highlands and Islands. So for a few years, they did precisely this. However, before exploring Aberdeen's role as a provider of ships to emigrants, it is necessary to go back to the earliest days of Aberdeen's trade with North America. Although small, this trade was still significant.

From as early as the mid-eighteenth century Aberdeen vessels regularly took woollen and linen goods to the southern colonies and the West

Indies and returned with tobacco, sugar and rum. The British American colonies to the north were anxious to export their vast quantities of timber, but their great distance from Britain made their products prohibitively expensive. Thus, at the time, Aberdeen's importers had little reason to use North America as a timber source. But when, in 1811, there was a steep rise in the tariffs paid on Baltic timber, Aberdeen's traditional suppliers, the situation changed radically. The tariffs, brought in during the Napoleonic Wars, transformed, with a stroke of a pen, the volume of trade between the northern colonies and Britain. British America ceased to be a provider of just fish and skins and became a major exporter of timber. So, from 1816, in common with other major British ports, British America became Aberdeen's principal timber supplier. That would be the situation for some 40 to 50 years.[6]

Emigrants, seeking a new life in the northern colonies, wanted affordable shipping across the Atlantic. Timber importers wanted to recover the extra costs of sailing greater distances. Little wonder that the two interest groups joined forces. The two-way flow in people and timber, first established at the Clyde, set a precedent for other major Scottish ports when they too eventually obtained their timber from British America. In many ways, the timber importers could be likened to the British merchants who recruited indentured servants for American employers during the mid-to-late eighteenth century. In return for their labour for a fixed number of years, usually up to seven, indentured servants would get a free passage and help with further employment or entitlement to land at the end of the expiry period. Ships took them out on their westward journeys to the colonies and returned with tobacco and other produce. Their final American destination was of course determined not by the personal preference of the individuals concerned but by the direction of trade and the colonial servant demand.[7]

Although, only small numbers of people were involved, this interlocked system gave shippers the means to offset the relatively high costs of transporting cargoes across the Atlantic by taking passengers on their westward journeys. This principle was to be the driving force behind the shipping services which were later offered to the emigrant Scots. But first it was indentured servants who were being sought. William Durwood, a merchant from Aberdeen was recruiting people wishing indentures in Quebec from as early as 1775. He wanted: "young women of good character, capable of undertaking house-keeping in genteel families in Quebec, also three tailors, three shoemakers, and two house carpenters all properly recommended and thoroughly masters of their business."[8] Recruits would sail on the *John and Jean*, a vessel, which in the previous year had taken 59 settlers and indentured servants from Aberdeen to Halifax.[9]

As the American War was nearing its end in the mid-1780s, there were further signs that Aberdeen merchants were seeking out experienced and skilled tradesmen wishing indentures in British America. Alexander Smith Jr., "a merchant below the town house, Aberdeen" wanted "tradesmen, labourers and young women of good character who may find it inconvenient to pay" and would wish to be indentured on the "reasonable terms" which he apparently offered. All would be taken to Halifax in 1784 on one of three ships, the *Jean,* the *Lucy* and the *Betsey,* but leave from Greenock, not from Aberdeen.[10] However, Andrew Robertson from the Brewery in North Street, together with merchants from Portsoy (near Banff), Banff and Montrose did have indentures to offer which came with passages from Aberdeen. It was, said his advertisement, "masons, house carpenters, blacksmiths, labourers and maid servants" who were particularly wanted at Halifax and Port Roseway, Nova Scotia.[11] He offered places on the "well known copper-bottomed brigantine the *Mercury*" which would leave Aberdeen in mid-July and call at Portsoy and Cromarty in early August to collect any further passengers. Another brig, the *John,* also provided passages in 1784 from Aberdeen and Cromarty to Halifax and Shelburne, Nova Scotia.[12] Given that, at the time, a cabin fare was 14 guineas and a steerage place was £7, it is not surprising that indenture schemes like these found takers.

The demand for indentured servants declined in the late 1780s and the growing preference from shippers was for paying passengers. While a trickle of skilled tradesmen continued to leave Scotland for Halifax and Quebec to work under the indenture scheme, people were leaving by the hundreds from the Highlands and Islands in search of a better life as pioneer settlers. Shipowners could make far more profit by attracting fares from these emigrants than from servant recruitment fees. The key hurdle for emigrants, though, was the high cost of transatlantic travel. Fares did decrease later, when the shipping volume had expanded to meet the needs of the growing timber trade between Britain and North America, but before then these costs were prohibitively high.

The first large exodus from Scotland, which began in the late eighteenth century, continued until 1803. The combination of the onset of the Napoleonic Wars in 1803 and the introduction of new passenger legislation that year, which led to a sharp increase in transatlantic fares, caused a considerable but short-lived diminution in emigrants numbers.[13] While there was very little interest in emigration before 1816 from Aberdeenshire and the surrounding area, enthusiasm ran high in the Highlands and Islands. Aberdeen shipowners, with interests in Atlantic trade could find plenty of paying passengers here, most of whom wanted to be taken either to Prince Edward Island or eastern Nova Scotia.

The two hundred or so Roman Catholic Highlanders from west Inverness-shire who sailed, in 1801, to Pictou on the *Dove* of Aberdeen had the dubious distinction of being associated with Hugh Dunoon, one of the most reviled emigrants contractors of his day. As disease swept through his vessel there was considerable loss of life. The Highland Society of Edinburgh's devastating critique of severe overcrowding on Dunoon's ships, which they likened to conditions on slave ships, had electrifying consequences, one of which was the introduction of tougher legislation.[14] The plight of emigrants from this same area, who sailed from Fort William on the *Good Intent* of Aberdeen, that same year, is not known.[15] A few years later, in 1806, some 37 people from Skye travelled to Prince Edward Island on the *Isle of Skye* of Aberdeen.[16] She was a first-class vessel and was more like the standard of shipping which would come to be associated with emigrant travel.

Apart from their recruitment campaigns for indentured servants, Aberdeen merchants had little reason to advertise Atlantic crossings to their local population. Vessels which actually took passengers across the Atlantic directly from Aberdeen were a rarity in the early 1800s. The *Emerald* and *Fairfield,* sailing to Quebec in 1806 and 1810 respectively, are two examples but each took only a tiny number of cabin passengers.[17] A particular selling point of the *Fairfield* was that she "carries a large cargo in

Aberdeen Harbour from Balnagask (The North Pier) 1840. *City of Aberdeen, Art Gallery and Museums Collections.*

proportion to her tonnage on an easy draught of water, shifts light and has the character of fast sailing."[18] But at this time there was simply no great interest, from this part of Scotland, in the prospect of emigration.

The year 1811 was a turning point in Aberdeen's trading links with British America. That year, for the first time, sizeable amounts of timber arrived from the Maritimes and lesser amounts from the St. Lawrence region. Napoleon's blockade of the Baltic in 1807 had led to a major shift in timber purchasing. Because Britain's timber importers would only invest capital in new forest ventures on a long term basis, they demanded and got a doubling of the already high duties on Baltic timber, effectively pricing it out of the market. Thus a short disruption in wartime gave colonial economies their first real prospect of sustained economic growth. In spite of widespread and repeated complaints within Britain over the high cost of timber, the protective tariffs remained in place until 1860.[19]

For those contemplating emigration, the rapid growth in regular Atlantic crossings was a significant development since shippers had to compete on price, and there was now a greater choice of vessel and destination. But few responded initially. Scottish Customs Records show that when the *Ploughman, Malvina, Mary, Spring* and *Centurion* set off from Aberdeen in 1811 to collect their timber cargoes, they took, between them, just over 100 passengers (Table 1). Apart from the 12 people, who were a ships' crew on their way to Quebec, most were travelling to either Pictou or Halifax.[20] And only 73 people left Aberdeen in the following year, with most travelling to Halifax.[21] The picture changed little in 1813 and 1814, when a total of just over 100 emigrants sailed from Aberdeen to Halifax.[22] In 1815 eleven vessels, between them, took about 160 emigrants from Aberdeen to Quebec, Halifax, Pictou and various timber ports in New Brunswick.[23] Of course, those sailing during this period had to endure the risks of travelling in wartime. The *Ploughman's* passengers bound for Halifax or Pictou in 1813 were assured that she was "fast-sailing and armed" and "she sails to join the convoy," while in 1814 the *Cambria* sailed with two guns.[24]

There was a surge in passenger numbers when hostilities ceased, but this was short-lived. Large-scale and sustained emigration from Aberdeen would have to await the rise in popularity of Upper Canada which only gathered pace from 1830. Meanwhile, Aberdeen shipowners like Peter Ritchie were seeking their passengers further afield. Fares could be found from the increasing numbers in the Highlands and Islands who wanted Atlantic crossings. Ritchie had spotted the sale details for the *Perseverance* in 1811 and purchased it. By 1814 he had sent her to Cromarty to collect passengers and soon after that, on three further occasions, this 112-ton galliot took Highlanders to British America. Probably a former bulk carrier for coal, it seems an odd choice. But as Aberdeen shipyards began producing new vessels, designed for the rapidly growing North American timber trade, Ritchie could offer emigrants the newest and best shipping available.

Table 1: Emigrant crossings from Aberdeen to British America 1806–55

★ denotes that a vessel was registered at the Port of Aberdeen

Year	Mth	Vessel	Master	Psgr Nos	Arr Port	Comments/Doc. Ref.
1806	04	*Emerald*	Anderson Alexander	7	Quebec	Cabin passengers: Joseph Lesly, Mr R. Blair, wife & family QM June 2
1810	06	*Fairfield*★	Morrice, James	4	Quebec	Carried passengers again in 1817 QG Aug 16
1811	03	*Ploughman*★	Yule, Alex'r	28	Pictou	E.504/1/24
1811	04	*Malvina*★	Smith, John	12	Quebec	No record in *Quebec Gazette* of passenger arrivals (may have disembarked at Nova Scotia) E.504/1/24
1811	04	*Mary*★	Morrison, James	30	Halifax	E.504/1/24
1811	06	*Spring*★	Grant, Peter	15	Quebec	Crew of 11 seamen & Capt. Robson E.504/1/24; QG Aug 29
1811	07	*Centurion*★	Morrison, James	18	Halifax	E.504/1/24
1812	03	*Barbara* of London	Epsom, William	4	Quebec	E.504/1/24
1812	03	*Ploughman*★	Main, James	12	Pictou	The shipping agents were: Saunders & Mellis "on the quay" at Aberdeen and John Forsyth of Keith. E.504/1/24
1812	04	*Alert*★	Johnston, Andrew	2	Quebec	QG May 30
1812	04	*Mary*★	Morrison, James	20	Halifax	E.504/1/24; *AJ* Jan 29
1812	04	*Patriot*★	Anderson, Alexander	2	Quebec	Advertised as "a fine new brig." QG May 30; *AJ* Feb 26

Year	Mth	Vessel	Master	Psgr Nos	Arr Port	Comments/Doc. Ref.
1812	05	Cambria★	Pirie, James	33	Halifax & Quebec	E.504/1/24; *AJ* Jan 29
1813	03	Cambria★	Oswald, James	25	Halifax	E.504/1/24
1813	03	Ploughman★	Main, James	7	Halifax	E.504/1/24
1813	04	Venus★	Begg, Alexander	3	Quebec	E.504/1/24
1814	03	Mary★	Oswald, James	30	Halifax	E.504/1/25
1814	08	Cambria★	Clayton, James	35	Halifax	E.504/1/25
1814	08	Halifax Packet★	Hogg, John	7	Halifax	E.504/1/25
1815	03	Amethyst★	Gray, Alexander	29	Halifax	E.504/1/25
1815	03	Fame★	Masson, George	4	Halifax	E.504/1/25
1815	03	Mary★	Oswald, James	35	Halifax	E.504/1/25
1815	04	Carolina★	Duncan, Alexander	24	Quebec	E.504/1/25
1815	04	Halifax Packet★	Hogg, John	3	Halifax	E.504/1/25
1815	04	Seven Sisters★	Brown, A.	19	Halifax	E.504/1/25
1815	05	Phesdo★	Pennan, Andrew	16	St. Andrews & Saint John	E.504/1/25; *NBRG.* Jul 27; *IJ* May 5
1815	06	Wellington★	Stephens, Alexander	6	Miramichi	E.504/1/25
1815	07	Ruby★	Love, Thomas	2	Halifax	E.504/1/25

Year	Mth	Vessel	Master	Psgr Nos	Arr Port	Comments/Doc. Ref.
1815	08	*Glentanner*★	Laird, James	17	Halifax & Pictou	E.504/1/25
1815	08	*Helen*	Moore, James	4	Halifax	E.504/1/25
1816	03	*Amethyst*★	Greig, H.	36	Halifax	E.504/1/26
1816	03	*Carolina*★	Duncan, Alexander	25	Quebec	E.504/1/26
1816	03	*Granite*★	Scorgie, Alexander	6	Miramichi	E.504/1/26
1816	03	*Louisa*★	Oswald, James	36	Halifax, Pictou & Mir.	55 packages passengers' wearing apparel and belongings E.504/1/26; *AJ* Feb 14
1816	03	*Ythan*★	Craigie, Alexander	17	Halifax & Mir.	E.504/1/26
1816	04	*Ann and Elizabeth*	Gray, John	3	Quebec	3 settlers *QM* June 7
1816	04	*Flora*	Work, James	2	Quebec	Cabin passengers: Miss Patterson and Mr. Leys *QM* June 25; *AJ* Jan 3
1816	04	*Mary*★	Clayton, James	21	Quebec	7 men, 4 women, &10 children settlers E.504/1/26; *QM* July 23
1816	04	*Phesdo*★	Pennan, Andrew	37	Halifax & Saint John	90 packages passengers' wearing apparel and bedding E.504/1/26; *AJ* Jan 3; *NBRG* June 29
1816	04	*Ploughman*★	Duncan, Alexander	7	Halifax & Pictou	20 packages passengers' wearing apparel and bedding. E.504/1/26; *IJ* Mar 15
1816	04	*William*★	Laird, James	6	Halifax	20 packages passengers' wearing apparel and belongings. E.504/1/26; Martell, *Immigration Nova Scotia* 40. Hereafter referred to as *Immig. N S.*

Year	Mth	Vessel	Master	Psgr Nos	Arr Port	Comments/Doc. Ref.
1816	05	*Cambria*★	Lawrence, Alexander	12	Pictou & Mir.	25 packages passengers' wearing apparel and bedding. E .504/1/26
1816	06	*Helen*★	Legatwood, George	11	Quebec	11 men, women and children. 16 packages passengers' wearing apparel and bedding. E.504/1/26; *QM* Sept 26
1816	06	*Sprightly* of Dundee	Philip, Alexander	20	Halifax, Pictou & Mir.	E.504/1/26; E.504/11/18; *DC* Jan 17, 1817
1816	07	*Jessie*★	Thomson, James	8	Quebec	Cabin passengers were: Mr. Thom and servants, Mr. Gordon and Miss Hossack; 16 trunks passengers' luggage E.504/1/26; *QM* Sept 13
1816	09	*Louisa*★	Oswald, James	13	Halifax	25 packages passengers' wearing apparel and luggage E.504/1/26
1817	03	*Aimwell*★	Morrison, John	32	Halifax	100 packages passengers' wearing apparel and belongings. E.504/1/26; *AJ* May 8
1817	03	*Fairfield*★	Morrice, James	13	Quebec	50 packages passengers' wearing apparel and belongings. E.504/1/26; *QM* June 3
1817	03	*Good Intent*★	Rodgers, Alexander	30	Pictou	120 packages passengers' wearing apparel and belongings. E.504/1/26
1817	03	*Louisa*★	Oswald, James	65	Halifax	90 packages passengers' wearing apparel and belongings. E.504/1/26
1817	03	*Mary*★	Clayton, James	6	Miramichi	30 packages passengers' wearing apparel and belongings. E.504/1/26

Year	Mth	Vessel	Master	Psgr Nos	Arr Port	Comments/Doc. Ref.
1817	03	*Patriot*★	Anderson, Alexander	14	Quebec	50 packages passengers' wearing apparel and belongings. E.504/1/26
1817	03	*Phesdo*★	Pennan, Andrew	8	Halifax	25 packages passengers' wearing apparel and bedding. E.504/1/26
1817	03	*Ythan*★	Craigie, Alexander	6	Miramichi	12 packages passengers' wearing apparel and belongings. E.504/1/26
1817	04	*Douglas*★	Morrison, John	7	Halifax	Journey of 63 days. E.504/1/27; *Immig. NS*, p. 43
1817	04	*Highlander*★	Donald, Archibald	32	Saint John	E.504/1/27
1817	04	*Hunter*★	Logan, James	5	Halifax	E.504/1/27
1817	05	*Jessie*★	Thomson, James	21	Quebec	E.504/1/27; *QM* Aug 1
1817	07	*Cambria*★	Wilson, John	15	Quebec	E504/1/27; *QM* Sept 9
1817	07	*Earl of Dalhousie*★	Levie, John	24	Halifax	E.504/1/27
1817	08	*Louisa*★	Oswald, James	19	Halifax	E.504/1/27
1817	09	*Ganges*★	Martin, Alexander	4	Saint John	E.504/1/27
1818	03	*Earl of Dalhousie* ★	Levie, John	44	Quebec	30 packages of passengers' wearing apparel and belongings. E.504/1/27; *QM* May 15
1818	03	*Star*★	Blackett, Alexander	n/k	Saint John	25 packages of passengers' wearing apparel and belongings. E.504/1/27

Year	Mth	Vessel	Master	Psgr Nos	Arr Port	Comments/Doc. Ref.
1818	03	Aimwell★	n/k	33	Halifax	*Immig. NS*, 45
1818	03 & 07	Louisa★	n/k	40	Halifax	25 left Aberdeen in March and 15 in July. *Immig. NS*, 45–6
1818	05	Union	Ord, J.	7	Quebec	*QM* June 19
1818	07	Norval★	Walker	3	Quebec	*QM* Aug 23
1819	03	Louisa★	n/k	n/k	Halifax	*Immig. NS*, p. 47
1819	04	Patriot★	Anderson, Alexander	7	Quebec	7 cabin passengers *QM* May 4
1819	04	Earl of Dalhousie★	Levie, John	19	Quebec	7 cabin passengers & 12 settlers *QM* May 14
1819	04	Rob Roy★	Nairn, W.	7	Quebec	*QM* May 14
1820	04	Monarch	Martin, A.	n/k	Saint John	6 chests and 7 bundles containing passengers' wearing apparel and belongings. E.504/1/28
1820	04	Traveller★	Goldie, James	20	Quebec	20 settlers *QM* May 12
1821	03	Louisa★	n/k	9	Halifax	Immig NS, p. 52
1821	04	Venus★	Begg, Alexander	10	Quebec	10 settlers *QM* May 15
1821	04	Juno	Henderson, J.	6	Quebec	6 settlers *QM* May 15
1821	04	Earl of Dalhousie★	Levie, John	15	Quebec	15 settlers *QM* May 15
1821	04	Mary Ann	Moore, Joseph	6	Quebec	6 settlers *QM* May 15
1821	04	Norval★	Leslie	7	Quebec	7 settlers *QM* May 17

Year	Mth	Vessel	Master	Psgr Nos	Arr Port	Comments/Doc. Ref.
1822	04	*Quebec Packet*★	Anderson, Alexander	10	Quebec	10 settlers *QM* June 4
1822	05	*Pilot* of Newburgh	Law, John	7	Miramichi & Saint John	*NBRG* June 18
1822	05	*Nestor*★	Thorn, George	5	Quebec	5 settlers *QM* July 9
1823	04	*Quebec Packet*★	Anderson, Alexander	4	Quebec	4 settlers *QM* May 16
1823	07	*Quebec Packet*★	Anderson, Alexander	16	Quebec	10 cabin and 6 steerage *QM* Sept 23
1824	05	*Good Intent*★	Thomson, Hugh	1	Quebec	1 settler *QM* June 16
1825	04 & 07	*Quebec Packet*★	Anderson, Alexander	10	Quebec	4 cabin on the April crossing and 4 cabin & 2 settlers left in July. *QM* May 14
1826	04	*Quebec Packet*★	Anderson, Alexander	19	Quebec	10 steerage and 9 cabin (4 female, 2 children and 3 male) *QM* May 13
1826	04 & 07	*City of Aberdeen*★	Duthie, Alexander	11	Quebec	8 left in April and 3 in July *QM* May 15, Sept. 16
1826	07	*Quebec Packet*★	Anderson, Alexander	4	Quebec	4 cabin (1 female, 3 children) *QM* Sept 16
1826	08	*Atlantic*★	Lawson, Alexander	2	Quebec	Cabin passengers: Messrs Parker and Plympton *QM* Sept 26
1827	03	*Aberdeenshire*★	Oswald, James	23	Halifax	*Immig. NS*, 58
1827	04	*City of Aberdeen*★	Duthie, Alexander	3	Quebec	3 settlers *QM* May 5
1827	04	*Margaret*★	Troup, James	10	Quebec	10 settlers *QM* May 12

Year	Mth	Vessel	Master	Psgr Nos	Arr Port	Comments/Doc. Ref.
1828	08	*Aberdeenshire*★	Oswald, James	8	Halifax	*Immig. NS*, 61
1829	03	*Albion*★	Leslie, Alexander	18	Halifax	Receipt for £35 for 5 people who travelled as cabin passengers. SRO GD316/15; *Immig. NS*, 62
1829	08	*Aberdeenshire*★	Oswald, James	27	Halifax	*Immig. NS*, 62
1830	03	*Albion*★	Leslie, Alexander	7	Halifax	*Immig. NS*, 64
1830	04	*Aberdeenshire*★	Oswald, James	6	Halifax, Pictou & Mir.	Ship crossing advertised in Inverness and Elgin newspapers. *Immig. NS*, 64; *IJ* Feb 12; *EC* Feb 5
1830	04	*Quebec Packet*★	Anderson, Alexander	14	Quebec	3 cabin & 11 settlers *QM* May 20
1830	04	*Brilliant*★	Barclay, Alexander	20	Quebec	20 settlers *QM* May 24
1831	03	*Albion*★	Leslie, Alexander	17	Halifax	*Immig NS*, 68
1831	04	*Brilliant*★	Barclay, Alexander	75	Quebec	Thomas Fowler, a cabin passenger, describes the crossing in his journal. There were 18 cabin and 57 steerage passengers. The ship was described as having six feet between decks. Fowler, *Tour Through British North America*, 5–42
1831	04	*Hercules*★	Walker, Duncan	63	Quebec	*QM* June 18
1831	05	*Pilgrim*★	Allan, George	n/k	Richibucto	The *Elgin Courier* stated that "if sufficient numbers offer, the vessel will land them at Three Rivers in PEI and in Pictou." *EC* May 6

Year	Mth	Vessel	Master	Psgr Nos	Arr Port	Comments/Doc. Ref.
1831	07	*Aberdeenshire*★	Oswald, James	20	Halifax	*Immig. NS*, 68.
1831	07	*Brilliant*★	Barclay, Alexander	68	Quebec	*QM* Sept 8
1831	07	*Annandale*★	Anderson, Alexander	23	Quebec	*QM* Sept 8; *AJ* July 13
1832	03	*Albion*★	Leslie, Alexander	31	Halifax	*Immig. NS*, 71
1832	03	*Brilliant*★	Barclay, Alexander	175	Quebec	175 settlers *QM* May 17
1832	03 & 08	*Aberdeenshire*★	Oswald, James	79	Halifax	40 left in March and 39 in August *Immig NS*, 71
1832	04	*Aimwell*★	Morrison, John	24	Quebec	24 settlers *QM* May 19
1832	04	*Annandale*★	Anderson, Alexander	61	Quebec	61 settlers *QM* May 19
1832	04	*Helen*★	Anderson	18	Quebec	18 settlers *QM* May 23
1832	05	*Lady of the Lake*★	Grant	13	Quebec	13 settlers *QM* June 2
1832	09	*Emma Zeller*	n/k	9	Quebec	9 settlers *QM* Oct 6
1833	03 & 08	*Aberdeenshire*★	Oswald, James	34	Halifax	13 left in March and 21 in August *Immig. NS*, 74–5
1833	03 & 08	*Albion*★	Leslie, Alexander	57	Halifax	26 left in March and 31 in August *Immig NS*, 74–5
1833	04	*Brilliant*★	Duthie, Alexander	64	Quebec	64 settlers *QM* May 17
1833	04	*Sir William Wallace*★	Anderson, Daniel	28	Quebec	28 settlers *QM* May 18

Year	Mth	Vessel	Master	Psgr Nos	Arr Port	Comments/Doc. Ref.
1834	03 & 08	*Aberdeenshire*★	Oswald, James	35	Halifax	24 left Aberdeen in March and 11 in August *Immig. NS*, 78
1834	04	*Hercules*★	Walker, Duncan	75	Quebec	*QM* May 15
1834	04	*Brilliant*★	Duthie, Alexander	137	Quebec	*QM* May 13
1834	04 & 07	*Quebec Packet*★	Anderson, Alexander	6	Quebec	3 on each crossing *QM* May 17, Sept 2
1834	07	*Albion*★	Leslie, Alexander	31	Halifax	*Immig. NS*, 78
1834	07	*Hercules*★	Walker, Duncan	133	Quebec	*QM* Sept 20
1834	08	*Brilliant*★	Duthie, Alexander	169	Quebec	*QM* Oct 7
1835	03	*Albion*★	Leslie, Alexander	25	Halifax	*Immig. NS*, 80; *AJ* Jan 21
1835	03 & 08	*Aberdeenshire*★	Oswald, James	14	Halifax	7 left in March and 7 in August *Immig. NS*, 80
1835	04	*Bolivar*★	Ganson, Herman	7	Quebec	*QM* June 4
1835	04	*Carleton*★	Anderson, Alexander	64	Quebec	*QM* June 6
1835	04	*Hercules*★	Walker, Duncan	70	Quebec	*AH* Apr 11
1835	04	*Nautilus*★	English, William	7	Cape Breton	*AH* Apr 25
1835	04 & 07	*Robert McWilliam*★	Williamson	31	Quebec	6 on the April crossing and 25 on the July crossing *QM* Apr 11, Sept 19

Year	Mth	Vessel	Master	Psgr Nos	Arr Port	Comments/Doc. Ref.
1835	04 & 08	*Amity★*	Rae, David	51	Quebec	A total of 39 came in the first crossing and 12 in the second. The June arrivals were described as "respectable farmers" who came with considerable capital—some intended to view the townships at Craig's Road (in Lower Canada) to consider their settlement potential. *PP* w/e June 6; *QM* June 6, Oct 29
1835	05	*Pacific★*	Morrison, John	24	Quebec	*QM* June 17
1835	06	*Pilgrim★*	Allan, George	49	Quebec	*QM* Aug 4
1835	08	*Quebec Packet★*	Stephens	3	Quebec	*QM* Sept 29
1835	08	*Brilliant★*	Duthie, Alexander	70	Quebec	*QM* Oct 13
1836	04	*Albion★*	Leslie, Alexander	49	Halifax	The *Albion* returned in July with timber from Miramichi which was due to be sold by public auction "on the Links adjoining the Works of the Aberdeen Rope and Sail Company." *Immig. NS*, 82; *AH* July 23; *AJ* June 29
1836	04	*Amity★*	Rae, David	13	Quebec	13 settlers *QM* June 4
1836	04	*Brilliant★*	Duthie, Alexander	80	Quebec	The *Quebec Mercury* names the 13 cabin passengers who disembarked at Quebec but makes no mention of the 67 steerage passengers who left Aberdeen. The Cabin passengers were: Mr., Mrs., and Miss Guthrie, Mr., Mrs. Webster and 2 children, Messrs Berg, Urquhart, Beatty, Taylor, Mrs. Farquhar, Miss Leslie. *QM* June 4; *AH* April 16

Year	Mth	Vessel	Master	Psgr Nos	Arr Port	Comments/Doc. Ref.
1836	04	*Pacific*★	Morrison, John	122	Quebec	*AH* April 23
1836	04	*Sir William Wallace*★	Anderson, Daniel	17	Quebec	13 settlers and 4 cabin passengers: Mr., Mrs. and Miss Beatty, Mr. Rose *QM* May 28; *AH* April 23
1836	04	*Annandale*★	Craig	7	Quebec	4 settlers & 3 cabin passengers: Mrs. Edwards & 2 children *QM* May 28; *AH* April 23
1836	05	*Augusta*★	Rae, William	46	Quebec	44 settlers and 2 cabin passengers: Dr. Stewart, Mrs. Alex Perry *QM* June 22
1836	05	*Shakespeare*★	Rosie	84	Quebec	84 settlers *QM* July 19
1836	06	*Hercules*★	Walker, Duncan	158	Quebec	153 steerage and 5 cabin *QM* Aug. 27; *AH* June 18
1836	07	*Circassian*★	Ritchie, Thomas	117	Quebec	117 settlers *QM* Sept. 3
1836	08	*Albion*★	Leslie, Alexander	42	Halifax	*Immig. NS*, 82; *AH* Aug. 6
1836	08	*Sir William Wallace*★	Anderson, Daniel	18	Quebec	17 steerage and 1 cabin *QM* Sept. 27
1836	08	*Brilliant*★	Elliot, James	28	Quebec	24 steerage and 4 cabin *QM* Oct. 6
1837	03 & 08	*Albion*★	Leslie, Alexander	41	Halifax	15 left in March and 26 in August *Immig. NS*, 85
1837	04	*Sir William Wallace*★	Anderson, Daniel	7	Quebec	*QM* May 23
1837	04 & 08	*Brilliant*★	Elliot, James	52	Quebec	40 left Aberdeen in April and 12 in August *QM* May 23, Sept. 14

Year	Mth	Vessel	Master	Psgr Nos	Arr Port	Comments/Doc. Ref.
1837	05	*Pacific*★	Thompson	50	Quebec	48 steerage and 2 cabin QM May 30
1837	06	*Quebec Packet*★	Stephens	35	Quebec	QM July 22
1838	04	*Brilliant*★	Elliot, James	24	Quebec	24 steerage QM May 12
1838	04	*Carleton*★	Anderson, Alexander	32	Quebec	32 steerage QM May 22
1838	06	*Pilgrim*★	Allan, George	81	Quebec	4 cabin and 77 steerage QM Aug. 19
1838	08	*Albion*★	Leslie, Alexander	21	Halifax	*Immig. NS*, 88
1839	04 & 08	*Albion*★	Leslie, Alexander	59	Halifax	29 left in April and 30 in August Morse, "Immigration to Nova Scotia," 104.
1839	06	*Kincardine-shire*★	Goven	55	Quebec	*Montreal Transcript* Sept 3; QG Aug 31
1839	06	*Sir William Wallace*★	Tulloch, James	19	Quebec	QM Aug 24
1839	08	*Sarah*★	Allan, George		Quebec	The Immigration Agent noted that the passengers possess "considerable capital" PP w/e 21Sept
1840	04	*Brilliant*★	Elliot, James	n/k	Quebec	The Immigration Agent noted that all who arrived on the *Brilliant* were in "easy circumstances" PP w/e May 16
1840	04	*Caroline*★	Marsh, James	16	Quebec	Most were farmers PP w/e May 23
1840	04	*Heroine*★	Walker, Duncan	11	Quebec	Most were farm labourers. PP w/e May 23

Year	Mth	Vessel	Master	Psgr Nos	Arr Port	Comments/Doc. Ref.
1840	04	Sarah★	Allan, George	29	Quebec	Farmers and farm labourers. Some were going to Kingston and Toronto, some were joining friends in the United States and several labourers were to be employed in Quebec. PP w/e May 23
1840	04 & 08	Albion★	Leslie, Alexander	31	Halifax	22 left in April and 9 in August (4 cabin and 5 steerage) Morse, "Immigration to Nova Scotia," 104–5
1840	05	Hercules★	Davidson	42	Quebec	They were described by the Immigration Agent as a "very respectable body of passengers" who were all "in good circumstances." They were "amply provided" with the means to get to their destinations. All were proceeding to Upper Canada except for 2 families who were returning to Illinois. They were mainly farmers.
1840	05	Sisters★	Hull	41	Quebec	They were farmers, labourers and tradesmen. They were described as "all have plenty of means." A few were going on to the United States. PP w/e July 18
1840	07	Brilliant★	Elliot, James	23	Quebec	Mainly farmers. PP w/e Sept 12
1840	07	Sarah★	Allan, George	22	Quebec	Described as "respectable farmers and tradesmen" PP w/e Sept 19
1841	04	Brilliant★	Elliot, James	82	Quebec	PP1842(301)xxxi
1841	06	Bon Accord★	Sim, James	70	Quebec	Described as all being in "good circumstances." They landed in good health and were well supplied. The ship's departure from Aberdeen and space for passengers was advertised in the *Moray, Nairn and Banff Courant.* PP w/e Sept 4; *MC* June 11

Year	Mth	Vessel	Master	Psgr Nos	Arr Port	Comments/Doc. Ref.
1841	06	*Taurus*★	Martin, John	134	Quebec	Described as "intelligent Scotch," most having friends in London and Western districts of Upper Canada. PP w/e July 17; PP1842(301)xxxi
1841	08	*Albion*★	Leslie, Alexander	28	Halifax	28 steerage Morse, *Immig. to NS*, 107
1842	04	*Brilliant*★	Elliot, James	52	Quebec	Mainly farmers and tradesmen. PP w/e May 28; *AH* Mar. 19, Apr. 23
1842	04	*Sarah*★	Allan, George	28	Quebec	Mainly farmers and labourers PP w/e May 28; *AH* April 23
1842	04	*St. Lawrence*★	Tulloch, James	25	Quebec	Mainly farmers PP w/e May 28; *AH* March 5
1842	06	*William Glen Anderson*	Gillespie	152	Quebec	Farmers, labourers, mechanics and servants PP w/e Aug 13; *AH* June 18
1842	08	*Brilliant*★	Elliot, James	32	Quebec	Mainly farmers and mechanics PP w/e Oct 15
1842	08	*Heroine*★	Walker, Duncan	14	Quebec	Mainly farmers PP w/e Oct 15
1842	08	*Sarah*★	Allan, George	25	Quebec	Mainly farmers and labourers PP w/e Oct 15
1843	03 & 07	*Albion*★	Leslie, Alexander	29	Quebec	13 departed in March and 16 in July PP1844(181)xxxv
1843	04	*Brilliant*★	Barr, Robert	37	Quebec	PP1844(181)xxxv
1843	04	*Heroine*★	Walker, Duncan	48	Quebec	PP 1844(181)xxxv
1843	04	*Sarah*★	n/k	33	Quebec	PP1844(181)xxxv
1843	04	*Sedulous*★	Levie, George	8	Quebec	PP1844(181)xxxv

Year	Mth	Vessel	Master	Psgr Nos	Arr Port	Comments/Doc. Ref.
1843	04	St. Lawrence★	Tulloch, James	32	Quebec	PP1844(181)xxxv
1843	06	Rose★	n/k	94	Quebec	PP1844(181)xxxv
1843	08	Brilliant★	Elliot, James	36	Quebec	Described as "highly respectable farmers" who were "bringing out considerable capital" PP1844(181)xxxv; PP w/e Sept 23
1843	08	Sir William Wallace★	n/k	8	Quebec	PP1844(181)xxxv
1844	04	Albion★	Leslie Alexander	13	Halifax	AH Apr. 27, Jul. 20
1844	04	St. Lawrence★	Tulloch, James	139	Quebec	AH April 27
1844	08	Albion★	Leslie, Alexander	13	Halifax	30 packages of passengers luggage AH Aug. 17
1845	04	Albion★	Leslie, Alexander	13	Halifax	AH March 29
1845	05	Brilliant★	Elliot, James	35	Quebec	AH May 10
1845	05	Heroine★	Walker, Duncan	70	Quebec	AH May 24, 31
1845	05	St. Lawrence★	Tulloch, James	98	Quebec	AH May 10
1846	04	St. Lawrence★	Tulloch, James	97	Quebec	Arrivals described as "respectable" and "generally in good circumstances" QM May 19; PP w/e May 23
1846	06	Heroine★	Walker, Duncan	132	Quebec	QM Aug 25
1847	04	St. Lawrence★	Tulloch, James	55	Quebec	PP1847–48(964)xlvii

Early Atlantic Crossings, 1774–1815

Year	Mth	Vessel	Master	Psgr Nos	Arr Port	Comments/Doc. Ref.
1847	06	*Heroine*★	n/k	81	Quebec	6 cabin, 75 steerage. PP1847–48(964)xlvii
1847	08	*Lord Metcalfe*★	n/k	51	Quebec	15 cabin, 36 steerage. PP1847–48(964)xlvii
1847	08	*St. Lawrence*★	Tulloch, James	26	Quebec	3 cabin, 23 steerage. PP1847–48(964)xlvii
1848	04	*Berbice*★	Elliot, James	33	Quebec	All travelled as steerage passengers who were described as "respectable settlers with good means." PP1847–48(971)xlvii
1848	04	*Lord Metcalfe*★	Bain	31	Quebec	Farmers. PP1847–48(971)xlvii
1848	04	*St. Lawrence*★	Tulloch, James	120	Quebec	1 cabin passenger. The ship was fined for having "two passengers more than her list certified." PP1847–48(971)xlvii
1849	04	*Berbice*★	Elliot, James	28	Quebec	5 cabin and 23 steerage QM May 29
1849	04 & 07	*St. Lawrence*★	Tulloch, James	53	Quebec	36 came on the first crossing and 17 on the second QM May 29, Sept 11
1849	07	*Berbice*★	Elliot, James	56	Quebec	13 cabin and 43 steerage QM Sept. 11
1850	04	*Berbice*★	Elliot, James	45	Quebec	AH April 13
1850	04	*St. Lawrence*★	Tulloch, James	95	Quebec	AH April 20
1850	04 & 08	*Albion*★	Leslie, Alexander	21	Halifax	13 left in April and 8 in August AH Apr. 6, Aug. 17
1850	08	*Berbice*★	Elliot, James	60	Quebec	AH Aug. 3

Year	Mth	Vessel	Master	Psgr Nos	Arr Port	Comments/Doc. Ref.
1850	08	St. Lawrence★	Tulloch, James	69	Quebec	AH Aug. 3
1851	04	St. Lawrence★	Tulloch, James	139	Quebec	QM May 26
1851	04 & 07	Berbice★	Elliot, James	178	Quebec	98 on April crossing and 80 on June crossing QM May 26; AJ Aug. 20
1851	04 & 07	Sarah★	Sim, James	172	Quebec	85 came on April crossing and 87 on July crossing. The Sarah was due to call at Cromarty and Findhorn for passengers in mid-July. Fares were advertised as very low. The agents were: William Watson in Cromarty, John Watt in Thurso and John Bruce in Kirkwall. AJ Apr 23, Aug. 20; IC July 10; JJ June 20, July 18
1851	06	Albion★	Leslie, Alexander	12	Quebec	AJ Aug. 20
1851	07	St. Lawrence★	Tulloch, James	102	Quebec	An advertisement in the John O'Groat Journal stated that Mr. Merrylees of Lerwick, John Bruce of Kirkwall and John Watt of Thurso were local agents and that the Aberdeen agent was Donaldson Rose. JJ June 20; AJ Aug. 20
1852	04	Berbice★	Elliot, James	115	Quebec	QM May 23; AH Feb. 21, July 31
1852	04	Sarah★	Sim, James	81	Quebec	The ship's departure was advertised in the John O'Groat Journal. QM June 21; AH April 24; JJ March 12, April 16
1852	04	St. Lawrence★	Tulloch, James	184	Quebec	The Aberdeen Herald records 184 departing passengers while the Quebec Mercury records 136 arrivals. The ship's departure was advertised in the John O'Groat Journal. QM May 25; AH Feb 21, Apr 24; JJ Mar 12, Apr 16

Year	Mth	Vessel	Master	Psgr Nos	Arr Port	Comments/Doc. Ref.
1852	06	*Albion*★	Leslie, Alexander	13	Quebec	*AJ* Aug. 18
1852	08	*Berbice*★	Elliot, James	133	Quebec	*AJ* Aug. 18; *QM* Sept. 24
1852	08	*St. Lawrence*★	Tulloch, James	59	Quebec	1 cabin , 58 steerage *QM* Sept. 28
1853	04	*Jane Boyd*★	Ganson, Herman	n/k	Quebec	Adult fares were £3.10s; children under 14 travelled at half price. The *Inverness Courier* stated that passengers from Morayshire, Inverness-shire, Ross-shire & Sutherland were to be taken free of charge by steamer to Aberdeen. If the response from the area was sufficiently great, the ship might call at Cromarty and Scrabster (Thurso) to collect passengers. The Aberdeen agent was George Thompson and the Cromarty agent was J.W. Forsyth, the Harbourmaster. *IC* March 24
1853	04	*Albion*★	Leslie, Alexander	11	Halifax	*AH* Apr 16
1854	04	*Alexander Hall*★	Findlay	n/k	Quebec	The *Alexander Hall* and *St Lawrence* together took 300 passengers. *AH* March 4
1854	04	*Aurora*★	Morison, Alexander	277	Quebec	*AH* Feb 4, June 7
1854	04	*Berbice*★	Elliot, James	126	Quebec	*AH* Jan 28
1854	04	*Caroline*★	Marsh, James	9	Quebec	*AH* Feb. 25
1854	04	*Jane Boyd*★	Ganson, Herman	119	Quebec	*AH* Jan. 14
1854	04	*Renown*★	Walker, William	115	Quebec	*AH* March 11

Year	Mth	Vessel	Master	Psgr Nos	Arr Port	Comments/Doc. Ref.
1854	04	*St. Lawrence*★	Tulloch, James	300	Quebec	The *St. Lawrence* and *Alexander Hall* together took 300 passengers. *AH* Jan.21
1854	07	*Berbice*★	Elliot, James	59	Quebec	AH June 17
1854	07	*Jane Boyd*★	n/k	126	Quebec	*AH* June 10
1854	07	*St. Lawrence*★	Tulloch, James	118	Quebec	*AH* June 17
1855	04	*Berbice*★	Scott	124	Quebec	8 cabin & 116 steerage *QM* May 16
1855	04	*Renown*★	Walker, William	55	Quebec	55 settlers *QM* June 3
1855	05	*Sir William Wallace*★	Andrews, A.	95	Quebec	*QM* June 10
1855	05	*Aurora*★	Morison, Alexander	340	Quebec	29 cabin & 311 steerage *QM* June 19
1855	06	*St. Lawrence*★	n/k	n/k	Quebec	There were three deaths on the crossing caused by the spread of disease. PP w/e Sept. 19
1855	07	*Berbice*★	Scott	134	Quebec	10 cabin & 124 steerage *QM* Sept 25
1855	07	*Jane Boyd*★	Munn	n/k	Quebec	*QM* Sept 25
1855	08	*Aurora*★	Morison, Alexander	93	Quebec	2 cabin & 91 steerage *QM* Oct 16

III. The Timber Trade Grows and Emigrants Follow, 1816–30

"First Spring ship for America—Halifax, Pictou & Miramichi: That fine new copper-fastened vessel, about 205 tons register, building in Mr. Adamson's yard, James Oswald Master, well known in that trade for the last three years…. She will have excellent accommodation for passengers. As the greater part of her cargo is engaged the time of her sailing may be depended upon. For freight or passage apply to P. Ritchie, Queen Street, [Aberdeen] January, 1816."[1]

Peter Ritchie was wasting no time in announcing that he had a new brig departing for the Maritimes, doing so even before she had been completely built and given a name.[2] Soon to be known to the outside world as the *Louisa*, she would become one of Ritchie's regular emigrant carriers from Aberdeen to the Maritimes. She would make four of the 109 vessel crossings from Scotland to British America in 1816, helping to bring Aberdeen's share of the total up to 25 per cent and reducing what had been previously the Clyde's near monopoly over Atlantic trade.[3]

Although only given a second class rating for her quality of construction by Lloyd's, the *Louisa* was more spacious than average. Measuring 85' 3" long-by-24' 2" wide-by-15' 9" deep, she was one of the new generation of brigs which could cope with the demands of the Atlantic trade. This was a great step forward in carrying capacity when compared with Peter Ritchie's other vessel, the *Perseverance*, measuring only 65' 4" long-by-20' 10" wide and 11' 6" deep.[4] But the *Louisa's* key selling point was her captain, James Oswald. These were the very early days of passenger crossings to the Maritimes from Aberdeen and few could match his experience. Oswald had captained the *Cambria* in 1813, the *Mary* in 1814 and again in 1815, each vessel taking about 30 passengers from Aberdeen to Halifax.[5] The *Louisa,* captained by Oswald, left Aberdeen for Halifax in March 1816 with 36 passengers, made another journey in September with 13 passengers, and on both occasions returned to Aberdeen with a cargo of timber from the Miramichi region of New Brunswick.[6] The *Louisa* and Peter Ritchie's other vessels, which included the *Cambria* and *Mary,* were to repeat this sequence of two-way Atlantic crossings with timber and emigrants over the next few years.

Ritchie secured fares from a large proportion of the people who left Aberdeen between 1815 and 1818, a time when the severe economic depression, which followed the Napoleonic Wars, stimulated emigration from all parts of Scotland. His success is hardly surprising since he usually offered emigrants a choice of new or nearly new, mostly "A1" (first-class) vessels, under a captain who had previously sailed the Atlantic. Ritchie's *Cambria,* an "A1" brig, built in 1808, carried 58 of the 100 or so emigrants who sailed from Aberdeen to the Maritimes in 1812–1813.[7] During the peak years of 1815 to 1818, he secured just under half of the total passenger trade to British America from Aberdeen and dominated the field until 1821. In 1817, 150 people, or fifty per cent of those who sailed from Aberdeen to Halifax or Quebec that year, travelled on one of five Ritchie brigs: the *Cambria, Earl of Dalhousie, Jessie, Louisa* and *Mary.* (see Table 1).[8] With James Oswald as captain, the *Louisa* proved the most popular, taking 84 people.

While Ritchie's vessels dominated the field, there were other merchant shipowners, men like Alexander Duthie, Donaldson Rose and John Catto, who had also established themselves by this time in the transatlantic passenger trade. And like Ritchie, they achieved success by offering good, spacious vessels run by experienced captains. Alexander Duthie's operation was focussed on the *Phesdo,* captained by Andrew Penan, whose "care and attention was seldom to be met with." An "A1" brig, she sailed with emigrants to St. Andrews and Saint John, New Brunswick, in 1815, the year she was built, and repeated the crossing in the two subsequent years, taking a total of 61 passengers to Halifax and Saint John.[9] Donaldson Rose provided the *Aimwell,* an "A1" brig, built in 1816, which, in the next two years, took 65 emigrants from Aberdeen to Halifax.[10] In charge was John Morrison, who was "perfectly acquainted in the American trade for many years past."[11] John Catto had the least success, getting fares from only 20 passengers for the *Sprightly,* captained by Alexander Philip who, we are told, was "well acquainted with the trade." Captured in wartime, and given an "E2" rating by Lloyd's, she was not up to the standard of Catto's other vessels or indeed, those of his competitors. But a good Lloyd's rating clearly was not always the deciding factor. In 1817, when he had offered the *Patriot,* an "A1" brig, she attracted even fewer passengers than the *Sprightly* had in 1816.[12] The *Sprightly* was fairly broad for her length, and it may be that this or other aspects of her hull design gave her added stability and made her better equipped to withstand gales and heavy seas.[13]

The *Aberdeen Journal* regularly published shipping advertisements at this time announcing the availability of passenger accommodation on vessels preparing to sail for British America. Understandably, former troop transports like the *Ganges* and *Nestor,* used by the government during wartime, attracted little interest but new, "A1" brigs like the *Earl of Dalhousie* did little better (see Table 1).[14] The *Fancy* of Aberdeen, ranked as an "A1" brig, only ever attracted emigrants once and that was from Greenock.[15] Even in 1816, when emigrant numbers generally were far higher than normal, only two hundred and sixty people sailed to British America from Aberdeen. Although sixteen vessels were involved, only the *Louisa* and *Phesdo* carried more than 30 people.[16] In that same year just over 1,900 Scots are known to have left Scotland for British America, with most originating from the Highlands.[17] Thus, the exodus from the northeast of Scotland, even in the peak years from 1815 to 1818, was a mere fraction of the total. Throughout the 1820s, emigrant numbers from Aberdeen rarely exceeded fifty per year.[18] The region's economic prospects were good in spite of the postwar industrial depression which had engulfed much of the country and there was, therefore, less reason to be dissatisfied. It was a time when Aberdeen's shipping had nearly double the tonnage of Leith's and when Aberdeen had more vessels than Greenock.

So emigrants had to be found elsewhere. Aberdeen shipowners sent their vessels to Fort William, Tobermory, Stornoway, Cromarty and Thurso to collect emigrants, and having taken them across the Atlantic, they returned to Aberdeen with a timber cargo.[19] The vessels were not making a special trip but were incorporating passenger collections by making diversions from their regular routes across the Atlantic. The arrangement gave emigrants affordable transport while shippers got extra revenue on their vessels' outward journeys. Crucial to the smooth functioning of this operation were the emigration agencies which undertook to match passenger demand with shipping supply. Intricate networks of agents and sub-agents would have relayed information on the volume and location of potential emigrants to shippers back in Aberdeen, who in turn would have provided schedules together with the selling features of the vessels on offer.

Only 260 of the 625 or so emigrants who crossed the Atlantic on Aberdeen vessels in 1816 actually left from Aberdeen (Table 1). Nearly 200 had sailed from Stornoway, while around 140 left from Cromarty and Thurso (Table 2).[20] Another 70 had sailed on the *Good Intent* from Fort William, while the *Amity* of Peterhead took a further 126 emigrants that year from Thurso to Halifax.[21] By 1819, nearly all of Aberdeen's passenger trade was based in the Western Isles. While a mere handful of emigrants left Aberdeen that year, just over 800, all collected at Tobermory, sailed on one of four Aberdeen-registered vessels to either Pictou, Charlottetown or Quebec.[22]

Peter Ritchie's network of sub-agents had clearly been hard at work in the Highlands and Islands. Between 1816 and 1819 his agency got fares for just under 800 emigrants, representing about 60 per cent of the total Highland and Island passenger trade. Ritchie's *Morningfield* and *Perseverance* collected emigrants from Stornoway in 1816, the *Perseverance* doing so again in 1818, and in 1819 the *Morningfield, Louisa* and *Traveller* took emigrants from Tobermory to Pictou, Quebec and Charlottetown (Table 2). It seems strange that Ritchie continued to use the *Perseverance* after 1816. A galliot of uncertain age, refurbished in 1811 but not recorded in the *Lloyd's Shipping Register,* she may have been of dubious quality.[23] Why, when he could offer his newly-built *Morningfield, Louisa, Earl of Dalhousie*

MIRAMICHI TIMBER.

There will be sold by public roup, upon an early day, to be afterwards fixed,

THE Entire CARGO of the Brig ALBION, Capt. LESLIE, just arrived from Miramichi consisting of
320 Loads YELLOW PINE.
12 Do. BIRCH.
1400 Superficial Feet FIR PLANK; and
2550 ASH BILLET STAVES.

The above Cargo is of excellent quality, and of very large scantling. It may be seen on the piece of ground belonging to Messrs Duffus & Co. adjoining Footdee Church Yard; and farther particulars can be known, on applying to ROBERT DUTHIE
Quay, Nov. 7, 1826.

FOR HALIFAX, PICTOU, AND MIRAMICHI.

THE FINE NEW AND FAST SAILING
BRIG ALBION,
266 Tons per Register,
ALEX. LESLIE, Commander,

Will be ready to receive Goods on board for the above ports in the course of a few days, and will positively be dispatched on first March. The accommodation for Cabin and Steerage Passengers is superior, having good height between decks.

For Freight and Passage, apply to Captain Leslie or to ROBT. DUTHIE.

Who has for Sale, 15,000 feet Miramichi TIMBER of fine quality, imported in November last, per the Albion. Also, for Sale, 100 Barrels Belfast Prime MESS PORK, newly cured.
(One concern.)
Quay, Jan. 15, 1828.

Advertisements in the *Aberdeen Journal* for the sale of the *Albion*'s timber cargo in Nov. 1826 and her Spring departure in 1828 for the Maritimes (Nov. 8, 1826; Feb. 6, 1828). *Courtesy* Aberdeen Journal, *Nov. 8, 1826 and Feb. 6, 1828.*

and *Traveller*, which all had good Lloyd's ratings, did Ritchie continue to use the *Perseverance*? Unusual in being a galliot, it is likely that she was strongly built and relatively wide for her length, giving her added ability to cope with heavy seas.[24] Perhaps it was her design features which made her an attractive choice, particularly if they enabled her to better accommodate passengers or to be manoeuvered into smaller Highland ports.[25]

The devastation in the Western Isles caused by the decline in kelp production contributed greatly to the influx of its people to Cape Breton during the 1820s. And as before, many emigrants sailed on Aberdeen vessels. In 1820 and 1823, the *Glentanner* and *Emperor Alexander* between them, took about 300 emigrants from Tobermory to Cape Breton.[26] In 1828, the 281-ton *Universe* took 484 souls from Stornoway to Cape Breton while in the following year the *Louisa* took a further 170 people from Stornoway.[27] This was also a period of growing unrest in the northeast Highlands. The disruption caused by the advancing clearances for sheep farms on the Sutherland estate, led increasing numbers to move to Pictou.[28] The exodus from the Sutherland estate would generate a great deal of business for Aberdeen shippers over the years which followed.

In 1821–1822, three hundred and sixty tenants from the Sutherland estate sailed off to Pictou in the *Ossian* of Leith, the *Harmony* of Aberdeen and the *Ruby* of Aberdeen.[29] They had been helped by Thomas Dudgeon, a Ross-shire farmer, who tried to assist them in raising the funds for their fares through the formation of a Sutherland and Transatlantic Friendly Association. However he and the association were stopped in their tracks by outraged estate managers who greatly resented what they considered to be Dudgeon's interference in their affairs.[30] With the financial backing of an unnamed "association at Edinburgh" and unknown sources in Bengal, they found money for saws, spades, nails, Bibles and yards of tartan. They had a struggle on their hands to raise their fares and basic supplies but, even so, they sailed on reasonable quality vessels and, in the case of the *Harmony*, had the benefit of George Murray, a well-respected and experienced captain.[31]

Between 1820 and 1830 only about 300 passengers left on Aberdeen vessels for British America, with just over 60 per cent landing at Quebec and most of the remainder at Halifax. But change was in the air. From the year after she was built in 1822, Robert Catto's *Quebec Packet*, with her highly experienced captain, Alexander Anderson, was taking passengers regularly on twice yearly crossings between Aberdeen and Quebec. Soon after she was built in 1826, the *Aberdeenshire,* another of Catto's vessels began repeat crossings with emigrants for a period of ten years. With her steerage "of a great height and heated by a stove" and captain, James Oswald, known for his "uniform kindness" and being "long experienced in the trade," having captained the *Louisa* from 1816 to 1821, she provided a regular passenger service from Aberdeen to Halifax.[32] But the longest running service of all, was the one offered by Robert Duthie's *Albion*. She did regular crossings with emigrants from Aberdeen to Halifax from 1829 to 1853, often twice yearly, and the captain was always Alexander Leslie (Table 1).[33]

From 1830, Aberdeen began to develop an Atlantic passenger trade of its own. By then Upper Canada's wide-ranging economic and farming opportunities were glaringly obvious. On top of this, improvements in transportation, inland from Quebec made access to its fertile, western frontiers far easier and less costly. Thus, instead of mainly taking High-landers to the Maritimes, as had been the case before, Aberdeen shippers now had local people, in the northeast of Scotland, who wanted passages to Quebec.

Combining the roles of shipbuilder, shipowner and timber merchant, William Duthie was particularly well-placed to benefit from Aberdeen's bur-geoning Atlantic passenger trade. He dominated the trade most years from 1830. He knew from his technical knowledge of ship construction which vessels would be most suitable for carrying passengers. They needed to be well-built, be in good condition, have plenty of steerage space and be able to ride out gales and heavy seas. That was why he made three very astute purchases. First, he bought the *Brilliant* in 1830, then the *Hercules* in 1834, and the *Heroine* sometime after that. Although the *Hercules* was a staggering 52 years old when he bought it, Duthie knew what he was doing. The *Her-cules, Brilliant* and *Heroine* were all former whaling ships.[34]

Table 2: Emigrant crossings in Aberdeen-registered vessels to British America from Fort William, Stornoway and Tobermory, 1801–1840

Year	Mth	Vessel	Master	Psgr. Nos.	Departure Port	Arrival Port
1801	n/k	*Good Intent*	n/k	n/k	Fort William	Pictou

Roman Catholic Highlanders who originated from Glen Moriston (Inverness-shire). The *Good Intent* was incorrectly recorded as the *Golden Text* of Aberdeen. MacDonald, "Early Highland Emigration," 44.

Year	Mth	Vessel	Master	Psgr. Nos.	Departure Port	Arrival Port
1801	06	*Dove*	Crane	219	Fort William	Pictou

Mainly Roman Catholic Highlanders from west Inverness-shire (especially Moidart, Knoydart and Morar). The disreputable Hugh Dunoon was the shipping agent. His ships were notorious at the time for subjecting passengers to severe overcrowding and ill treatment. SRO RH2/4/87; NLS MS9646.

Year	Mth	Vessel	Master	Psgr. Nos.	Departure Port	Arrival Port
1806	07	*Isle of Skye*	Thom, John	37	Tobermory	Prince Edward Island

Passsenger baggage consisted of: 22 chests, 5 trunks, 7 parcels and 13 casks containing used wearing apparel and bed clothes. PAPEI 2702; E.504/35/1.

Year	Mth	Vessel	Master	Psgr. Nos.	Departure Port	Arrival Port
1816	08	*Good Intent*	Beverly, R.	69	Fort William	Pictou

69 men, women and children. The journey time was 2 to 3 months. The *Good Intent* arrived back in Aberdeen from Pictou in December with a timber cargo. E.504/12/6; Martell, *Immigration. Nova Scotia*, 41. Hereafter referred to as *Immig., NS; LL.*

Year	Mth	Vessel	Master	Psgr. Nos.	Departure Port	Arrival Port
1816	08	*Hibernia*	Lamb, R.	42	Stornoway	Quebec

The *Hibernia* arrived back in Aberdeen from Quebec in December with a timber cargo. E.504/33/3; *LL.*

Year	Mth	Vessel	Master	Psgr. Nos.	Departure Port	Arrival Port
1816	08	*Morningfield*	Perie, J.	63	Stornoway	Quebec

The *Quebec Mercury* noted the arrival of 60 men, women & children settlers. The Aberdeen agent was Peter Ritchie. The *Morningfield* arrived back in Aberdeen from Quebec in December with a timber cargo. E.504/33/3; *QM* Sept 20; *LL.*

Year	Mth	Vessel	Master	Psgr. Nos.	Departure Port	Arrival Port
1816	08	*Perseverence*	Philip, J.	52	Stornoway	Quebec

E.504/33/3.

Year	Mth	Vessel	Master	Psgr. Nos.	Departure Port	Arrival Port
1817	06	*Minerva*	Strachan, W	26	Fort William	Halifax & Quebec

26 men, women & children. The *Minerva* arrived back in Aberdeen from Quebec in November with a timber cargo. E.504/33/3.

Year	Mth	Vessel	Master	Psgr. Nos.	Departure Port	Arrival Port
1818		*Perseverence*	n/k	150	Tobermory	Pictou

MacLaren, *The Pictou Book*, 119.

Year	Mth	Vessel	Master	Psgr. Nos.	Departure Port	Arrival Port
1819	07	*Louisa*	Oswald, James	120	Tobermory	Pictou

E.504/35/2; *Immig. NS*, 49.

| 1819 | 07 | *Morningfield* | Laing | 264 | Tobermory | Pictou & Charlottetown |

64 people arrived at Pictou and 200 at Charlottetown . E.504/35/2; *PEIG* Sept 3.

| 1819 | 07 | *Traveller* | Goldie, James | 143 | Tobermory | Quebec |

Arrived late E.504/35/2; *QM* Sept 14.

| 1819 | 08 | *Economy* | Frazer, James | 285 | Tobermory | Pictou |

The *Acadian Reporter* published a commendation to the Captain from the passengers "for the kind treatment they received from him for a passage which consisted of 5 weeks." It also reported that the passengers "were landed in good health and spirits" and that 4 children "were born upon the passage." E.504/35/2; *Immig. NS*, 49.

| 1820 | 07 | *Glentanner* | Murray, George | 141 | Tobermory | Cape Breton & Quebec |

123 arrivals at Cape Breton and 18 at Quebec. The *Inverness Journal* printed a commendation to Captain Murray for his humane treatment and to the owners for the good quality of the provisions from 4 people who had made the crossing, one of whom was John MacRa, a surgeon from Plockton. E.504/35/2; *QM* Aug 25; *IJ* Nov 23.

| 1821 | 08 | *Thistle* | Allan, Robert | 96 | Tobermory | Pictou & Quebec |

53 arrived at Pictou & 43 at Quebec. *QM* Oct 19; *IJ* June 22.

| 1823 | 07 | *Emperor Alexander* | Watt, Alexander | 160 | Tobermory | Sydney, Cape Breton & Quebec |

Many of the passengers originated from South Uist. In the following year, the *Inverness Journal* printed a list of 30 heads of families giving parish origins. The humanity of the Captain was praised and John McEachern was named as the "steward on board." The Agent was Archibald McNiven. The *Quebec Mercury* recorded the arrival of 49 settlers at Quebec. *QM* Oct 7; *IJ* Jan 30, 1824.

| 1828 | 05 | *Universe* | n/k | 464 | Stornoway | Sydney, Cape Breton |

Immig. NS, 61.

| 1829 | 04 | *Louisa* | n/k | 170 | Stornoway | Sydney, Cape Breton |

Seventy of the 170 passengers went on to Prince Edward Island.
Immig. NS, 63.

Year	Mth	Vessel	Master	Psgr. Nos.	Departure Port	Arrival Port
1837	06	*Hercules*	Walker, Duncan	112	Stornoway	Pictou & Quebec

42 passengers arrived at Quebec & 70 at Pictou. *Immig. NS*, 86; *QM* July 27.

Year	Mth	Vessel	Master	Psgr. Nos.	Departure Port	Arrival Port
1840	08	*Heroine*	n/k	281	Stornoway	Prince Edward Island

The passengers originated from Skye. Orlo, "Those Elusive Immigrants" (Part 3) *Island Magazine,* No. 18 (1985) 34.

IV. UPPER CANADA BECKONS, 1831–55

"Sale on Saturday, 13th February [1836]. Canada Oak, Ash, Elm and Red and Yellow Pine Timber, just now landed from the ship *Brilliant*, Alexander Duthie [Captain] from Quebec: 6,500 feet Yellow Pine, 4,000 feet Red Pine, 2,250 feet Oak, 3,000 feet Elm, 500 feet Ash, 4 large mast pieces from 70 to 80 feet in length, by 20 to 20 inches.

All of the best quality and will be exposed to sale by Public Roup on the ground where it lies, adjoining the Works of the Aberdeen Rope and Sail Company, Footdee. The sale will commence at 11 o'clock forenoon and credit will be given. Apply to William Duthie, Footdee."[1]

When this advertisement appeared in the *Aberdeen Herald* in 1836, Aberdeen's timber trade with British America was in full swing. In two months time advertisements would announce that passengers wanting places on the *Brilliant*, the first ship that year for Quebec, should apply to her owner, William Duthie or his brother Alexander, the ship's captain. She often was the first to sail and in some years her passengers were amongst the first arrivals at Quebec.[2] Ice and storms posed a considerable threat in early Spring, but Alexander Duthie may have been less nervous about crossing the Atlantic than most ship masters. The *Brilliant*, a former whaler, had exceptional strength and was well-protected against the hazards of sailing through ice. After all, she was built to withstand the extremes of climate to be found in the Arctic.[3] And, with "her height between decks being six feet," she could offer more

William Duthie founded a shipbuilding firm in Aberdeen in 1816 which
was eventually taken over by his brothers Alexander and John. Many of
the ships which took emigrants from Aberdeen to Canada were owned
by the Duthies. *City of Aberdeen, Art Gallery and Museums Collections.*

spacious accommodation in the steerage than would be available on many
other vessels. She also had a first class rating from Lloyd's.[4]

Duthie's timing had been perfect. Purchasing the *Brilliant* in 1830, just
when an economic depression was starting to take its toll and the south-
western regions of Upper Canada were being opened up, he launched
into the passenger trade when enthusiasm for emigration was on the rise
(Figure 1). Although she was not a new ship, being built at Alexander Hall's
shipyard in 1814, the *Brilliant* dominated the passenger trade from the time
Duthie bought her. Carrying a total of 1,343 emigrants from Aberdeen

MIRAMICHI TIMBER.

There will be sold by public roup, upon an early day, to be afterwards fixed,

THE Entire CARGO of the Brig ALBION, Capt. LESLIE, just arrived from Miramichi consisting of
320 Loads YELLOW PINE.
12 Do. BIRCH.
1400 Superficial Feet FIR PLANK ; and
2550 ASH BILLET STAVES.

The above Cargo is of excellent quality, and of very large scantling. It may be seen on the piece of ground belonging to Messrs Duffus & Co. adjoining Footdee Church Yard ; and farther particulars can be known, on applying to ROBERT DUTHIE
Quay, Nov. 7, 1826.

FOR HALIFAX, PICTOU, AND MIRAMICHI.

THE FINE NEW AND FAST SAILING
Brig ALBION,
266 Tons per Register,
ALEX. LESLIE, Commander,

Will be ready to receive Goods on board for the above ports in the course of a few days, and will positively be dispatched on first March. The accommodation for Cabin and Steerage Passengers is superior, having good height between decks.

For Freight and Passage, apply to Captain Leslie or to ROBT. DUTHIE.

Who has for Sale, 15,000 feet Miramichi TIMBER of fine quality, imported in November last, per the Albion. Also, for Sale, 100 Barrels Belfast Prime MESS PORK, newly cured.
(One concern.)
Quay, Jan. 15, 1828.

The *Brilliant's* timber cargo offered for sale followed by an announcement of its return crossing to Quebec (*Aberdeen Herald*, March 5, 1836).

to Quebec over a fifteen year period, the *Brilliant's* passenger numbers jumped dramatically from twenty in 1830 to one hundred and seventy five in 1832, rising to just over 300 in 1834.[5]

The *Brilliant* had long been used in Atlantic trade even under her previous owner. Alexander Barclay had been kept on as captain by Duthie possibly because of his experience in selecting suitable timber loads from St. Lawrence suppliers.[6] Barclay went on to captain the *Brilliant* on voyages from Aberdeen to Quebec with passengers until 1833. He was replaced by Alexander Duthie, William's brother, who had been captain of the *City of Aberdeen,* when she made Atlantic crossings during the late 1820s.[7] James Elliot took over in 1836, having previously captained the *Molson* of Dundee, when she carried emigrants to Quebec from Dundee in 1833.[8]

William Duthie made another key purchase in 1834. He bought the *Hercules,* another former whaler. Although over 50 years old, she had a reasonable, although not top-class, Lloyd's rating and promised steerage passengers the relative comfort of a 6 feet 3 inches distance between decks.[9] She carried 208 emigrants from Aberdeen to Quebec in 1834, 70 in 1835 and 158 in 1836, always under the same captain, Duncan Walker.[10] Yet when Duthie built the *Circassian* in 1835, which apparently offered 7 feet between decks, he ran it as an emigrant carrier for only one year. She took 117 emigrants to Quebec from Aberdeen in 1836, but never repeated the crossing. Although brand new and with a first-class, "A1" rating, the *Circassisian's* overall dimensions were smaller than the *Hercules*, and considerably smaller than the *Brilliant,* Duthie's other former whaling ship. Thus, Duthie's greater reliance on the *Brilliant* and *Hercules* may reflect a higher priority being given to sturdiness and strength than to quality of construction or newness.

Of course, William Duthie was not alone in providing a passenger service to Quebec. One competitor was Donaldson Rose. In 1836, he attracted fares from 119 passengers who had sailed on his *Shakespeare* and *Sir William Wallace*[11] That same year the Aberdeen merchant, Alexander Cooper, provided the *Pacific,* which took 122 emigrants to Quebec in a single crossing. Robert Duthie had bought her in 1835 from Samuel Cunard, a merchant from Halifax and immediately transferred ownership to a group headed by Alexander Cooper and Captain John Morrison. Built in Nova Scotia in 1826, the *Pacific* was a top class barque of generous proportions having 6 feet 9 inches between decks and a captain, John Morrison, who was "well known in the trade for many years past."[12] In fact, Morrison's experience dated back to 1816 when he first captained another of Donaldson Rose's vessels, the *Aimwell*. But neither Donaldson Rose nor Alexander Cooper could match Duthie's success. In 1836, Duthie had fares from 400 people while the two of them taken together had only just over half that amount.

There were two other merchants who had a significant, although minor, share of the Atlantic passenger trade throughout the 1830s—Robert Duthie and Robert Catto. Robert Duthie's principal vessel was the "A1" rated *Albion*, which from 1829 to 1853, always under her long-

George Thompson Jr., principal partner of Walter Hood & Co. and the Aberdeen White Star Line. *City of Aberdeen, Art Gallery and Museums Collections.*

serving Captain Alexander Leslie, took a total of 582 people from Aberdeen to Halifax, averaging about 20 passengers per crossing (Table 1).[13] Duthie's *Highlander* also carried 150 emigrants from Cromarty to Quebec in 1836.[14] Ninety-six emigrants sailed to Quebec, in 1835 and 1838, on Robert Catto's *Carleton*, an unusually large vessel with a top class rating and a very experienced captain, Alexander Anderson.[15] During this period Anderson also captained another of Catto's vessels, the *Annandale*. "Lofty between decks," and with an "A1" rating, she took 91 emigrants to Quebec in three crossings.[16] In fact, Anderson's associations with Robert Catto date back to 1822 when he captained yet another of his vessels, the newly-built *Quebec Packet,* which, until 1837, made regular crossings to Quebec, usually with a small number of passengers. She too had an "A1" rating.

By now the merchant shipowner George Thompson was running vessels from Aberdeen to Quebec but few of them took passengers. Launching his shipping business in 1825, he proclaimed:

"I have commenced business as a Commission Agent, Ship and Insurance Broker, and having been bred in the mercantile line with a general acquaintance of people in business, I flatter myself I shall be able to afford satisfaction to those who may employ me."[17]

And he clearly did "afford satisfaction." Thompson was the founder of the famous Aberdeen Line, a shipping business which would, from 1840, extend to most corners of the world.[18] The Line came to be associated with its fast-sailing "clippers," which especially catered for trade in South Africa and Australia.[19] Thompson's passenger trade to Quebec was but a sideline and slow to develop. The *Helen* and *Lady of the Lake* took a combined total of 31 people from Aberdeen to Quebec in 1832, while the *Amity's* total for 1835–1836 was just 64.[20] Thompson's poor showing is significant since he was the only owner/agent at this time to be consistently offering second class ('E1') rather than first class vessels to Quebec-bound passengers. Even after the *Amity* had been "newly doubled from the keel to the main wales and completely repaired in every respect," she was still only rated by Lloyd's as an "E1" brig.[21] In 1836, the number of emigrants leaving the port of Aberdeen for Quebec reached an all time peak of 700. This was the one year when Aberdeen actually out-ranked the Clyde, which dealt with only 551 emigrants.[22] The zeal to emigrate had cooled from 1837, following the rebellions which broke out in parts of Upper Canada. Although the skirmishes were quickly suppressed, the unrest which had been unleashed reflected widespread discontent with the government and its management of the economy. These concerns were to deter many from emigrating.[23] But by the early 1840s the numbers leaving Aberdeen for Quebec were on the increase again.

A severe economic depression had hit the northeast of Scotland and, unlike the manufacturing areas further south which were expanding their iron and coal production, Aberdeenshire had few opportunities for industrial growth. Because it lacked minerals and metals, it was excluded from

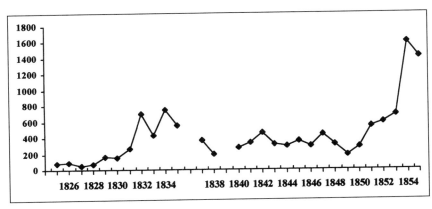

Figure 1: Emigration to British America from Aberdeen 1825–55
Source: British Parliamentary Papers, Emigration Returns 1830–40; Colonial Land and Emigration Commissioners Annual Reports 1841–54.

this new era of expansion. Rising unemployment in the area, particularly amongst factory workers led many to opt for a new life in Upper Canada.[24] Thus, Aberdeen shippers like Donaldson Rose once again found growing numbers of emigrants wishing to buy fares on their Atlantic bound vessels.

Rose's purchase of the *St. Lawrence* in 1841, soon put him top of the field. Rivalling the *Brilliant* in overall size, having an "A1" rating, seven feet between decks and Captain James Tulloch, who had taken passengers on the *Sir William Wallace*, another of Rose's vessels, the *St. Lawrence* was bound to succeed.[25] Between 1842 and 1855 she took 1,750 emigrants to Quebec, beating the *Brilliant*'s record and giving Rose the largest share of the Atlantic passenger trade. He used the much smaller *Sarah* to take emigrants to Quebec in the years from 1839 to 1843 and again in 1851–1852. Having purchased the *Sarah* in 1839, he had clearly anticipated these extra demands. By providing yet another "A1" vessel and a long-serving captain in George Allan, he was able to get fares from around 400 emigrants to add to those accommodated on the *St. Lawrence*.[26] Rose's other two vessels, the *Sisters*, used in 1841, and the *Rose* in 1843, appear to have been his last line of defence in these peak years. Taking a combined total of 135 emigrants, they did no repeat business.[27]

William Duthie's response to the rising demand from emigrants at this time was to phase out his former whaling ship, the *Hercules* and replace it by another former whaler, the *Heroine*. He duly transferred the *Hercules'* captain, Duncan Walker to her. Sailing from 1840 to 1847 on the Aberdeen to Quebec route, she carried a total of 356 passengers.[28] By the late 1840s, when the *Brilliant* had ceased her regular crossings with passengers to Quebec, and Alexander Duthie, his brother had taken over the family business, the *Berbice* was in place. In just eight years her total passenger count reached 1091—not far off the *Brilliant*'s overall total after 15 years. Longer, but slimmer than the *Brilliant*, she offered greater speed of sailing and the security of an experienced captain in James Elliot, who had previously been in charge of the *Brilliant*.

George Thompson also responded to the heightened interest in emigration coming from the city of Aberdeen by writing to the Colonial Office in 1848. Having served as an elected Councillor, and by now Lord Provost, he described the severity of the depression being experienced by Aberdeen's manufacturing industries.[29] Arguing that the distressed condition of the many unemployed workers would be alleviated through emigration, he put forward a case for public funds to be made available to help fund their travel costs. Claiming that there were two to three hundred who could travel to Quebec on "merchant vessels from this port," he requested funding for general provisions and for exemption from the emigrant head tax. The Colonial. Office generally resisted calls for subsidies and like most requests of this nature, his was turned down.[30] However, in spite of this setback, the exodus to Quebec gained ground, and two of Thompson's vessels were on hand to provide transport. The *Lord Metcalfe* sailed with 82 emigrants in 1847–1848, while the *Jane Boyd* took 245 in 1854.[31]

The *Lord Metcalfe* was one of the new generation of very large ocean-going vessels brought into use at this time. But at just over 500 tons she was no match for Alexander Cooper's 709-ton *Aurora,* which took 710 emigrants from Aberdeen to Quebec in just two crossings, in 1854–1855.[32] Passenger travel across the Atlantic was now entering into a completely new era. Specialist steamships, capable of taking ever greater numbers of passengers, were available and as technology gathered pace, greatly improved services were on offer. Sea transport was also becoming more centralized, with passenger services being increasingly concentrated at

A general view of Fergus, Upper Canada, in 1835 drawn by Janet Dingwall-Fordyce and lithographed by Forrester and Nichol, Edinburgh. Fergus was only a short distance from Bon Accord. Both settlements attracted Aberdeenshire emigrants from the mid-1830s. *Metropolitan Toronto Reference Library J. Ross Robertson Collection.*

major ports like Glasgow and Liverpool. Aberdeen's role as a departure port, for emigrants wishing to get to British America, declined after the boom years of 1854–1855 and by 1861 it had ceased.[33]

Meanwhile, Aberdeen shipowners continued to look to the Highlands to extend their Atlantic passenger trade, but by the 1830s its focus had moved from west to east. Whereas before 1830 most of the emigrants taken on Aberdeen vessels had originated from the Western Isles or along the northwest coast, after 1830 they came mainly from the northeast Highlands. In fact, the emigrant departures from Stornoway on William Duthie's two former whalers, the *Hercules* and *Heroine,* in 1837 and 1840 respectively, were the few known occasions when Aberdeen vessels became involved in the post–1830 exodus from the northwest (Table 2). Large numbers continued to leave from the crofting districts in the northwest Highlands, particularly during the Highland Famine years from 1846 to 1856, but it seems that only these two groups were taken in Aberdeen vessels.

The economic depression of the early 1830s and rising popularity of Upper Canada had stimulated emigration from the northeast Highlands just as it had done in many other regions of Scotland. Now there was no need for Aberdeen shippers to send their vessels all the way to Tobermory or Stornoway to collect emigrants, since they had a passenger trade in the northeast Highlands which could be accessed at minimum disruption to their shipping routes. However, these people were scattered over huge distances. To minimize delay it was necessary to have a single collecting point which could draw people from a large catchment area. Cromarty, situated midway between the Dornoch and Moray firths was the perfect choice. Emigrants from East Sutherland down to the Morayshire coastline could get to Cromarty relatively easily by coastal steamers, and Cromarty had the added advantage of having a particularly good harbour. Thus, with only a minor deviation to their routes, vessels from Aberdeen could call at Cromarty for passengers. And later Thurso would perform the same function in the far north.

V. CROMARTY AND THURSO: HIGHLAND GATEWAYS TO BRITISH AMERICA

"Such is the high level of poverty, multitudes are emigrating to the Canadas.... There are three vessels just now in the Bay of Cromarty, within three or four miles of this house, taking away at an average 250 passengers of all ages each vessel, and a fourth sailed three weeks ago with about 300. The passage money for each adult to Quebec is 2 guineas and three children under seven will be carried for the same amount; the people provide their own victuals—the shipowners do not furnish them with anything but fuel and water. The emigrants in general are of the poorest class although some can be found in comfortably affluent circumstances."[1]

On observing the vessels arriving in Cromarty Harbour in June 1831 to take on board passengers bound for either Pictou or Quebec, Lewis Rose's thoughts were with the many who he knew desperately wanted to emigrate but lacked the funds to pay their fares.[2] Living at the manse of Nigg, located on the side of a hill overlooking the Harbour, he would have had a perfect view of the *Baronet, Corsair, Rover, Lord Brougham, Industry* and *Cleopatra* as they called to collect emigrants that summer. The two-guinea fare to Quebec seems amazingly low, but it was the going rate for the cheapest and most basic transport service available at the time.[3] Hundreds of people were now leaving the northeast Highlands spurred on by low fares, the worsening economic situation at home and the prospects of a better life abroad. The influx from Britain that year had been so large that immigration taxes were introduced the following year at Quebec and other British American ports in an attempt to contain numbers and raise money to assist needy emigrants. The taxes were strongly opposed by shipowners, who feared they would be a serious cost deterrent to emigration. However, although they had little impact in reducing the numbers wishing to emigrate, the taxes were a lifeline for the many poor emigrants who got funds from the sums collected to finance their onward journeys.[4]

At least four of the six vessels which called at Cromarty in the summer of 1831 had originated from Leith.[5] Leith's role as a supplier of emigrant vessels to the northeast Highlands was very much in the ascendancy largely through the efforts of William Allan, a Leith shipping broker. Having well-established contacts with the Sutherland estate managers from as early as 1817, Allan had been well placed to secure fares from the large numbers of tenants who eventually moved to British America.[6] But in 1817, when he first began to look for business on the Sutherland estate Allan faced stiff competition from Aberdeen. When he got his first major contract in 1821, Allan got fares for just one of the three vessels which took Sutherland tenants from Cromarty to Pictou that year. He supplied the *Ossian* of Leith, but Aberdeen shippers provided the *Harmony* of Aberdeen and the *Ruby* of Aberdeen.[7]

Aberdeen shipowners had become quite accustomed to sending their vessels to Cromarty to collect passengers *en route* to crossing the Atlantic. In fact, Cromarty first started being used as an emigrant port by Aberdeen shippers from at least as early as 1784. Fares were high and the service was irregular, but it marked the beginning of a trade which was to blossom into a major industry and last for some sixty years.[8] With only a minor deviation to their routes, vessels could collect emigrants on their way north to the Pentland Firth, thus helping to offset the added distance of crossing the Atlantic from the east coast of Scotland. But, by the 1820s, with the continuing growth of the timber trade and increased volume of Atlantic shipping, Aberdeen's near monopoly came to an end. Leith along with other east coast ports became engaged in the lucrative passenger trade which was fast developing in the northeast Highlands.

Between 1814 and 1822 most of the vessels calling for passengers at Cromarty were registered in Aberdeen. Initially, shipowners simply advertised details of their vessels and departure dates for Atlantic crossings in local newspapers and relied on local contacts to uncover emigrant locations across wide stretches of the Highlands. Cromarty's good harbour and central location made it an ideal collecting point and, by employing postmasters, shoremasters, innkeepers, tradesmen and others whose work brought them into contact with people, shippers could hope to reach their potential customers. Shipowners also used men like George Logan "from America," who could offer first-hand reports of pioneer life in Nova Scotia. Active in Cromarty and Thurso from 1815 to 1817, he was the agent for emigrant crossings on the *Perseverance* of Aberdeen, the *Aimwell* of Aberdeen, the *Vine* of Peterhead and *Amity* of Peterhead.[9] But men like Logan were few and far between.

James Campbell, innkeeper of the Star Inn at Inverness, was more typical. Owning several small fishing and coastal vessels, and having an occupation which gave him ready access to people in the Cromarty Firth region, Campbell was an ideal recruit. He was an agent from 1815 to 1822, working first for Peter Ritchie, then for various other Aberdeen shipowners.[10] Joined by other agents residing in small settlements along the Great Glen and others further to the west at Arisaig and Lochalsh, Campbell was part of an intricate network. Its task was to relay information on emigrants to shippers, and to tell emigrants about schedules and features of the vessels being offered. And as embarkation day approached, it organized pick-up services for the scattered clientele.

So a long time before William Allan came on the scene, individual Aberdeen shipowners had set up schemes to co-ordinate passenger collections from Cromarty. Allan very cleverly centralized the operation by placing himself as the middleman between the vessels on offer and the emigrants seeking crossings. He took over the existing agencies, greatly extended his coverage throughout Easter Ross and Sutherland and invited east coast shippers to compete with each other for the Atlantic passenger trade. Not surprisingly, being based in Leith, many of the vessels which he offered originated from Leith. He had what looked like a purpose-built shipping fleet, but of course the vessels had no common owner and rarely did the

NOTICE TO EMIGRANTS
FOR
BRITISH AMERICA.

DUNCAN MACLENNAN, who ac companied his Passengers, (per the CANADA) to PICTOU and QUEBEC begs leave to inform the Public, that he will have a succession of first class Ships to Sail from CROMARTY this season. The Vessels w'l' be fitted up in a very superior manner; and Passengers may rely that nothing shall be wanting which his exertions can suggest for their comfort and convenience whilst at sea. The first Vessel will be cleared out for Pictou and Quebec early in April.

It is indispensibly necessary that Passengers make early application.

D. M'L., while in America, made it his study to be put in possession of every information on the leading points connected with Emigration, and will be glad to communicate with intending settlers.

LANDS FOR SALE,
IN
UPPER CANADA.

D. M'L. has the Sale of about Eighteen Thousand Acres of LANDS in the WESTERN, LONDON, HOME, and NIAGARA Districts, partially cultivated. The soil is fertile, and easily brought into cultivation. and well adapted far the various crops that are common in this country. The terms are liberal, and will be disposed of in Lots of from Fifty to Five Hundred Acres, payable in yearly instalments.

The Proprietor leaves this country early in Spring, to superintend the arrangements necessary for the conveyance of the Lards. Should a sufficient number of Passengers offer for a Vessel to Sail early in June, D. M'L. will accompany them and proceed to Upper Canada with those who intend to locate on the above Lards.

44, High Street,
Inverness, 12th Feb. 1833. }

Advertisement in the *Inverness Journal*, Feb. 15, 1833, put out by Duncan MacLennan of Inverness, an emigration agent who organized Atlantic ship crossings from Cromarty.

same journey more than once. In a way, Allan ran the equivalent of a modern-day shuttle service from Cromarty to British America.

William Allan achieved his dominant position by 1831, a time of heightened demand from emigrants for Atlantic crossings and when the large volume of Atlantic shipping created a huge amount of spare capacity on westward bound vessels. His business remained very brisk in 1832 and

1833, when he provided a total of six vessels, and peaked again in 1836 when large numbers from the Duke of Sutherland's estate left for Pictou, St. Anns, Cape Breton and Quebec (Table 3). Visiting Tongue in the northern part of the county to oversee the collection of passengers at Thurso and Loch Eriboll, Allan provided the *Albion* of Scarborough and the *Mariner* of Sunderland as well as two other vessels which sailed with emigrants from Cromarty.[11] But by this time, Allan's commanding position was coming to an end. An Inverness lawyer, Duncan MacLennan had been hot on his heels from 1832.[12] A cryptic announcement in the *Inverness Journal* that "D. MacLennan late of the Glasgow Warehouse, Inverness, has entered into an arrangement with a major shipping establishment of Liverpool for the transport of passengers to Quebec, Pictou and New York" marked the beginning of an emigration agency which was to dominate emigrant travel from the Highlands.[13]

It was pretty clear that the "Duncan MacLennan who accompanies his passengers" and had 18,000 acres of partially cultivated land in western Upper Canada to sell on to emigrants, was going to attract much business.[14] But it was when he formed a partnership in 1839 with John Sutherland, a man who, having been born in Wick, had just returned from Nova Scotia after spending 20 years there, that the agency achieved its really dominant position. With Sutherland managing Sutherland and Caithness, the partners covered the whole of the Highlands and controlled most of the passenger services made available to emigrants from the Orkneys in the north, down to Fort William (Figure 2). And with the rising levels of emigration from Caithness and northwest Sutherland and the establishment of John Sutherland's emigration agency at Wick, Thurso came into its own as a major emigrant embarkation port after 1840.[15]

The partners always made great play of Sutherland's Nova Scotia connections and the fact that he could be consulted personally at Wick or anywhere in Caithness and Sutherland by prior arrangement. Although their newspaper articles and advertisements always gave highly optimistic accounts of the agricultural and economic opportunities on offer in British America to emigrants, Sutherland was always on hand to be challenged. Many of those who emigrated at this time settled in or near the Huron Tract, a vast area in western Upper Canada being administered by the Canada Company.[16]

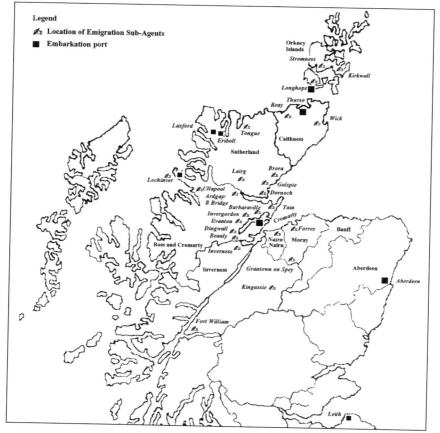

Figure 2. Location of the Emigration sub-agents, in the north of Scotland employed by MacLennan and Sutherland, 1832–51.

Founded in 1826 to encourage settlement by those able to fund their own emigration costs, the Canada Company established Sutherland and MacLennan as its principal Highland agents.[17] We must therefore conclude that the prospect of getting land or employment in Canada Company townships was a decisive factor for many emigrants. The partners provided details of the terms being offered and were assiduous in taking their information to prospective clients in all parts of the Highlands.[18]

When large numbers of emigrants left Caithness and Sutherland in 1840, MacLennan and Sutherland supplied the *Osprey* of Leith, the *British*

King of Dundee and *Quebec Packet* of Aberdeen—the three vessels which took them to Pictou and Quebec.[19] And even though they arrived during an economic depression, not all were poor. According to the Quebec Immigration Agent, those who sailed on the *Quebec Packet* "brought £800 to £1000 in gold among them" while those who came on the *British King* of Dundee "brought capital of £7,000 to £8,000."[20] But the many who left the Reay parish in Caithness for Upper Canada in the years which immediately followed were far less fortunate, having to rely on the financial help they got from their landlord, Mr. James of Sandside.[21]

The Duke of Sutherland also helped his Assynt, Eddrachilles, Farr and Tongue tenants who left in large numbers during 1841–1842 and from 1847 to 1851.[22] MacLennan and Sutherland did brisk trade at this time providing the *Pacific* of Aberdeen, *Fairy* of Dundee, *Lady Grey* of North Shields, *Universe* of Aberdeen, *Margaret Bogle* of Leith, *Saphiras* of Whitby, *Superior* of Peterhead, *Joseph Green* of Peterhead, *Lady Emily* of Sunderland, the *George* of Dundee and the *Lord Seaton* of Aberdeen (Table 3). Between 1840 and 1845 they had arranged transport for nearly 3,000 emigrants in 19 vessels.[23]

The progress of the various vessels was monitored by newspapers on both sides of the Atlantic giving the partners both good and bad publicity. The *Pictou Observer* noted that "the healthy appearance" of the *Lady Emily's* passengers "indicated that the praise bestowed by them on Captain Stove and Mr. Sutherland had been well merited" while the *John O'Groat Journal,* commenting on the same crossing, praised Sutherland's "uprightness and integrity. His conduct to the poorer classes of emigrants has been very praiseworthy—he very frequently granting free passages to many members of a family where the head of it could not command sufficient means to carry them all out."[24] But the partners were also responsible for the disastrous crossings of the *Lady Grey* in 1841 and the *George* in 1843 when overcrowding and disease caused great suffering and, in the case of the *Lady Grey's* crossing, the loss of six people.[25] These were very much the exception with most voyages being free of mishap or wrong doing. But the most poignant account of all was the report in the *John O'Groat Journal,* picked up later by the *Pictou Observer,* that a bottle had been washed up on the shore at Thurso Bay just two miles

NOTICE TO INTENDING EMIGRANTS
TO THE
British Settlements of North America.

TO SUCCEED THE " OSPRAY,"

THE First Class British built Brig, BRITISH KING, Register 243 Tons, 400 Tons Burthen, A. BROWN, Commander, is on the Berth at Cromarty, and to Sail about 5th JUNE direct for QUEBEC.

The Subscribers pledge themselves to have this vessel fitted up in a manner that will give satisfaction to intending Emigrants, and as a great proportion of the Passengers are already engaged, they would earnestly request that those who have the intention of availing themselves of this conveyance, make immediate application to the Agents in their locality.

Messrs M'L. and S. having made arrangements to keep up a regular succession of first-rate Ships for the conveyance of Emigrants to these Colonies, beg leave to state that nothing shall be wanting on their part to make Passengers as comfortable as circumstances will admit ; and from the experience D. M'L. has had in the trade, and the universal satisfaction his arrangements have always given, they have no doubt of being able to meet the wishes of all parties ; and that they will continue to afford every facility and information to those who may require it.

DUNCAN MACLENNAN,
Emigrant Agent, Inverness ;
JOHN SUTHERLAND,
of Nova Scotia, Wick.

AGENTS.—Messrs T. Clark, Woollen Factory, 40, High Street, Inverness ; W. Munro, clothier and grocer, Cromarty ; A. Ross, ironmonger, Dingwall ; D. Macgregor, schoolmaster, Evanton ; R. Douglas, bookseller, Tain ; J. Mackenzie, merchant, Nairn ; J. Hamilton, Glasgow Warehouse, Forres ; L. Macbean, merchant tailor, Kingussie ; W. Kinloch, Fort-William ; William Innes, innkeeper, Reay ; William Munro, merchant, Dornoch ; John Ross, innkeeper, Bonar Bridge ; Thomas Mackay, innkeeper, Lairg ; Wm. Sutherland, post-master, Brora ; Peter Reid, bookseller, Wick.

N.B. Intending Passengers from Caithness for the British King, will have a Boat in waiting on the morning of the 4th June next, at Wick, to convey them and their luggage to the Ship's side at Cromarty.

Advertisement in the *Inverness Journal*, May 29, 1840, for the *British King* of Dundee which took 157 emigrants from Cromarty to Pictou and Quebec.

from where the *Superior* had called to collect emigrants. A note in the bottle read:

"May 13, 1842, on board the barque *Superior*. This morning a male child was born; mother and infant are in a fair way. Passengers all in a healthy state. We have experienced some heavy weather. Our latitude at this time is 53 48 north, longitude 24 west. On a voyage from Thurso to Quebec and Pictou, Donald Manson Commander."[26]

From the late 1840s, the mounting scale of poverty and the increasing pressures faced by many to emigrate brought a decline in MacLennan and Sutherland's share of the Atlantic passenger trade. More emigrants were now being assisted by their landlords. With the passing of the 1845 Poor Law Amendment Act, Scottish lairds were, for the first time, legally responsible for the destitute on their estates and most chose to resolve this new situation by promoting and funding large-scale emigration. The potato famine (1846 to 1856), which greatly exacerbated an already dire situation, contributed further to the rising levels of emigration. Self-funded emigrants had relied on MacLennan and Sutherland but when the landlord paid, cost was the decisive factor. Shippers based in the very large west coast ports usually offered the lowest rates. Thus, the 1,000 or so tenants in northwest Sutherland, who emigrated to Pictou and Quebec with landlord assistance in 1847–1848, sailed on vessels like the *Ellen* of Liverpool and the *Greenock* of Glasgow.[27] Although MacLennan and Sutherland continued to arrange for east coast vessels to call at Cromarty and Thurso to collect emigrants, their business declined sharply from 1849.

Looking at the overall standard of shipping offered to northeast Highland emigrants, it must be concluded that it was of a high standard. Most of the vessels had a first class rating and many had better than average space in the steerage and in cabins (Table 3). There is evidence to suggest that John Sutherland placed particularly high demands on shippers when specifying passenger accommodation. A journalist watching the arrival of the *Prince Albert* at Cromarty noted that even though she had obtained official certificates after being cleared from Leith, Sutherland refused to accept the state of the berths and "to secure greater comfort to the passengers he

Silver snuff box presented to John Sutherland of Wick in 1849 in recognition of his work as an emigration agent in the north of Scotland. *Copyright The Trustees of the National Museums of Scotland.*

caused several improvements to be made....The owner thereupon...complained that Mr. Sutherland was much more particular as to the fitting out of vessels than was customary with others in his line."[28]

John Sutherland was no ordinary businessman. He claimed that he had been so moved by the "wretched state of the poor tenantry" when he visited the Highlands in 1839 that he decided to move back to Scotland.[29] His decision to work as the Wick agent for the British Fisheries Society, a body promoting employment opportunities in fishing, and his many letters to the press requesting financial help for poor people wishing to emigrate, certainly suggest altruistic tendencies.[30] His appointment in 1849 as Agent to Her Majesty's Colonial Land and Emigration Commissioners was clearly a high point in his life. He had lobbied hard for this position, winning support from his local M.P. and from James Loch, the senior administrator of the Duke of Sutherland's estate.[31] A "sincere friend" marked the occasion by presenting him with a silver snuff box and its survival as a museum piece in Edinburgh suggests that it remained his and his descendants' prized possession over the years which followed.[32]

Sutherland resigned his position three years later. Angry that his sphere of influence as an Emigration Commissioner was being confined to Sutherland and Caithness, he withdrew his services.[33] But the motivation was probably financial since by this time the MacLennan and Sutherland agency was rapidly losing business to the far bigger shipping operations in Glasgow and Liverpool.

John Sutherland had appreciated that repeat business would only come if emigrants were treated well. He and MacLennan maintained high standards throughout the 1830s and 1840s and brought a human dimension to the world of shipping. In the days before enforceable passenger legislation such men were often all that stood between unscrupulous operators and vulnerable emigrants. Aberdeen shipowners like William Duthie also had a considerable impact on the smooth running of emigrant shipping services. A shipbuilder as well, he used his knowledge of ship design to good effect in the choice of vessels which he offered to emigrants.

From 1811, as the North American timber trade began its steep rise, Aberdeen's shipbuilders produced new brigs and snows to meet the growing demand for ocean-going vessels. William Duthie only entered the field as an emigration agent in the 1830s when the demand from local people for Atlantic crossings reached its high point. He consistently offered refurbished whaling ships while his competitors offered more conventional designs. At this time, vessels were selected primarily for their timber carrying capabilities and passenger requirements had little bearing on the choices made. Whatever the choice, the physical characteristics of a vessel greatly affected sailing performance as well as passenger comfort and safety. Next the changing pattern of shipping made available to emigrants will be considered as the exodus from the northeast of Scotland during the first half of the nineteenth century is followed.

Table 3: Emigrant crossings in East Coast Vessels to British America from Cromarty and Thurso, 1814–1851

Year	Mth	Vessel	Master	Psgr. Nos.	Departure Port	Arr Port	Vessel Type	Lloyd's Code
1814	07	*Perseverence* of Aberdeen	Moncur	n/k	Cromarty	Pictou	bg	n/k

Agents were: Peter Ritchie, Aberdeen; Alex McKenzie, Cromarty; James Lyon, Inverness. *IJ* May 27.

Year	Mth	Vessel	Master	Psgr. Nos.	Departure Port	Arr Port	Vessel Type	Lloyd's Code
1815		*Prince William*	n/k	95	Cromarty or Thurso	Pictou	bg	n/k

Nineteen families from Sutherland who petitioned for land in West Pictou. Some of the petitioners had served in the Local Militia of Scotland, probably the Reay Fencibles. PANS MG 100 Vol. 226 #30.

Year	Mth	Vessel	Master	Psgr. Nos.	Departure Port	Arr Port	Vessel Type	Lloyd's Code
1815	04	*Perseverence* of Aberdeen	n/k	n/k	Cromarty	Halifax	bg	n/k

Agents were: George Logan from America at Dornoch and James Campbell, Star Inn Inverness. *IJ* Apr 7.

Year	Mth	Vessel	Master	Psgr. Nos.	Departure Port	Arr Port	Vessel Type	Lloyd's Code
1816	06	*Vine.* of Peterhead	Pirie, Alexr.	81	Cromarty & Thurso	Pictou	bg	E1

A muster list is noted but does not survive. Engaged by Mr. George Logan, a settler in Canada; vessel will call at Thurso for passengers. A medical person in attendance . E504/7/5; *IC* 28 June, *IJ* Apr 26.

Year	Mth	Vessel	Master	Psgr. Nos.	Departure Port	Arr Port	Vessel Type	Lloyd's Code
1816	07	*Aimwell* of Aberdeen	Morrison, John	139	Thurso from Aberdeen	Halifax	sw	A1

Martell states "139 passengers mostly farmers and mechanics," arrived from Aberdeen on the *Aimwell* in Sept. The Scottish Customs Records show that there were "74 passengers as particularly specified in a list signed by the captain" who left from Thurso. They had 65 chests, 18 boxes and 6 trusses of wearing apparel and passenger luggage. The Scottish Customs Records also show that 27 people left from Aberdeen who had 45 packages of wearing apparel and luggage. E 504/1/26, 7/5; Martell, *Immigration Nova Scotia*, 40. Hereafter referred to as *Immig. NS.*

Year	Mth	Vessel	Master	Psgr. Nos.	Departure Port	Arr Port	Vessel Type	Lloyd's Code
1817	05	*Amity* of Peterhead	Anderson, Alexander	126	Thurso	Halifax	bg	A1

E504/7/5; *Immig. NS*, 43.

Year	Mth	Vessel	Master	Psgr. Nos.	Departure Port	Arr Port	Vessel Type	Lloyd's Code
1818	07	*Ann*	n/k	n/k	Cromarty	Pictou	n/k	n/k

Agent was James Campbell, Star Inn Inverness. *IJ* June 19.

Year	Mth	Vessel	Master	Psgr. Nos.	Departure Port	Arr Port	Vessel Type	Lloyd's Code
1819	09	*Ann* of Banff	n/k	60	Cromarty	Pictou	sr	A1

The master was charged with having inadequate provisions for the passengers; court case held in Stromness; schooner owned by Captain. *Immig. NS*, 49; [SRO] GD 263/63/2/54.

Year	Mth	Vessel	Master	Psgr. Nos.	Departure Port	Arr Port	Vessel Type	Lloyd's Code
1820	06	*Diligence*	Kirk, R.	130	Cromarty from Leith	Quebec	bg	E1

Ten settlers arrived at Quebec, others disembarked at Pictou; vessel owned by captain. HA D207; *QM* Aug 13.

1821	06	*Ossian* of Leith	Hill	108	Cromarty	Pictou	bg	A1

Twenty-two families in all. Fares were 4 1/2 guineas per adult and 1 1/2 guineas for passengers under 14 years of age. Agent: William Allan of Leith; *IJ* June 29.

1822	06	*Harmony* of Aberdeen	Murray, George	125	Cromarty	Pictou	sw	E1

Tenants from the Sutherland estate. Together the *Harmony* and *Ruby* took 250 passengers. E504/17/9; *IJ* July 12.

1822	06	*Ruby* of Aberdeen	Bodie, J.	125	Cromarty	Pictou	bg	A1 in 1816 E1 in 1822

See comments for *Harmony* of Aberdeen.

1823	04	*Eliza* of Thurso	n/k	8	Thurso	PEI	n/k	n/k

The *Eliza* arrived at Thurso from the Miramichi, New Brunswick, in January. She set sail again in early Spring and arrived at Charlottetown in May. Orlo and Fraser "Elusive Immigrants," *Island Magazine* No. 16, 39; E504/7/6.

1830	06	*Canada*	Potts	244	Cromarty from Leith	Quebec	n/k	n/k

Emigrants mainly from Sutherland who were influenced by favourable reports from friends already settled; many possessed property and were young and eager for adventure. *IC* June 23, Oct 6, *IJ* Nov 6, *QM* Aug 19.

1830	06	*John*	Mann	120	Cromarty	Quebec	n/k	n/k

QM Aug 10.

1831	06	*Baronet*	Rankin	187	Cromarty	Quebec	n/k	n/k

Seventy-five day journey. *QM* Sept. 8.

1831	06	*Corsair*	Scott	218	Cromarty from Leith	Pictou and Quebec	bg	AE1

Fifty-seven left at Quebec. The 161 who landed in Pictou were in good health. The agent was William Allan of Leith. *Immig. NS*, 70; *IJ.* May 27, *QM* Aug. 30.

Year	Mth	Vessel	Master	Psgr. Nos.	Departure Port	Arr Port	Vessel Type	Lloyd's Code
1831	06	*Rover*	Briggs, Allan	116	Cromarty, Thurso from Leith	Pictou	bg repaired 1823, 1824 & 1829	E1

Agent, William Allan of Leith. *Immig. NS*, 70; *IJ* May 27.

| 1831 | 07 | *Cleopatra* | Morris | 246 | Cromarty | Quebec | n/k | n/k |

Agent: William Allan of Leith; *QM* Sept. 8.

| 1831 | 07 | *Industry* | Carr | 57 | Cromarty | Pictou and Quebec | n/k | n/k |

Agent: William Allan of Leith. *Immig. NS*, 70; *IJ*. June 24, *QM* Sept. 29.

| 1831 | 07 | *Lord Brougham* | Watt, James | n/k | Cromarty | Pictou and Quebec | n/k | n/k |

Vessel collected passengers at Invergordon; *Immig. NS*, 70; *IJ* June 24.

| 1832 | 04 | *Hedleys* of Newcastle | n/k | 209 | Cromarty | Quebec | bk | E1 |

Agent: William Allan of Leith. *QM* June 3.

| 1832 | 05 | *Sylvanus* of North Shields | Lawson | 237 | Cromarty | Pictou & Quebec | sw | A1 in 1831 E1 in 1841 |

Agent: William Allan of Leith. 41 settlers left at Quebec and 196 left at Pictou. *Immig. NS*, 73; *IJ* April 20, *QM* July 26.

| 1832 | 06 | *Blagdon* | Thomson | 132 | Cromarty | Pictou & Quebec | bg | A1 repairs 1831 |

132 settlers left at Quebec. Agent: William Allan of Leith. *Immig. NS*, 73; *IJ* May 18, *QM* Aug 20.

| 1832 | 06 | *Canada* | Hunter | 241 | Cromarty | Pictou & Quebec | s | E1 |

Landed 130 passengers at Pictou and 111 passengers at Quebec; Agent: Duncan MacLennan of Inverness. *Immig. NS*, 73; *QM* Aug. 22.

| 1832 | 06 | *Sharp* | Almond | 206 | Cromarty | Quebec | sw | A1 |

Agent: William Allan of Leith. *QM* Aug. 13, *IJ June 15.*

| 1833 | 04 | *Hedleys* of Newcastle | Morris, John | 138 | Cromarty | Quebec | bk | E1 |

Agent: Duncan MacLennan. The *IJ* advertisement states that "Captain Morris intends fitting up a second cabin should that meet the wishes of a sufficient number of passengers—say from 20 to 30." *QM* June 4. *IJ* Feb 22, Mar 8.

Year	Mth	Vessel	Master	Psgr. Nos.	Departure Port	Arr Port	Vessel Type	Lloyd's Code
1833	04	*Triton*	McClean	71	Cromarty	Quebec	s	E1

Agents: William Allan, Leith; Campbell Rose, Inverness; William Watson, Cromarty. The *IJ* advertisement states "she is 100 ft long in the twixt decks, 30 ft broad and 7 feet high." *QM* June 1, *PC* Feb. 21, *IJ* Feb. 22.

Year	Mth	Vessel	Master	Psgr. Nos.	Departure Port	Arr Port	Vessel Type	Lloyd's Code
1833	05	*Poland*	Ridley, John	n/k	Cromarty	Pictou & Quebec	s	n/k

Due to call at Cromarty in early May to pick up passengers. Agent: Duncan MacLennan. *IJ* 26 Apr.

Year	Mth	Vessel	Master	Psgr. Nos.	Departure Port	Arr Port	Vessel Type	Lloyd's Code
1833	06	*AMI* of Sunderland	Miller, Matthew	n/k	Cromarty	Quebec	bk	n/k

Agents: J. Newton, ship owner Invergordon, K. MacKenzie, shoremaster, Inverness. *IJ* advertisement states the captain "will limit the number of steerage to 150." *IJ* 29 Mar, 3 May.

Year	Mth	Vessel	Master	Psgr. Nos.	Departure Port	Arr Port	Vessel Type	Lloyd's Code
1833	06	*Diligence*	n/k	n/k	Thurso	Quebec	bg	E1

At Thurso on 10th June. Agents: David Robeson, Thurso; John Broadfoot, Leith. *IJ* 31 May.

Year	Mth	Vessel	Master	Psgr. Nos.	Departure Port	Arr Port	Vessel Type	Lloyd's Code
1833	06	*Economist* of Newport	Stokeham	89	Cromarty from Leith	Pictou & Quebec	bk	A in 1833 AE1 in 1841

Vessel registered at Newport on Tay near Dundee. Agents: William Allan of Leith. 47 settlers left at Quebec & 42 at Pictou. *Immig. NS*, 76; *IJ* May 17, *QM* Aug. 25.

Year	Mth	Vessel	Master	Psgr. Nos.	Departure Port	Arr Port	Vessel Type	Lloyd's Code
1833	06	*Jane Kay*	Toft, Daniel	170	Cromarty & Thurso	Pictou & Quebec	sw	A1

Agent: D. MacLennan, Inverness. 106 for Pictou; 66 settlers left at Quebec; all reported to be in good health at Pictou. *Immig. NS*, 75; *IJ* May 17, *QM* Aug. 12.

Year	Mth	Vessel	Master	Psgr. Nos.	Departure Port	Arr Port	Vessel Type	Lloyd's Code
1833	06	*Marjory*	Stocks, James	24	Thurso from Leith	Quebec	bg	AE1

"She will be comfortably fitted up for a limited number of passengers; will be at Thurso on 26 June and remain a few days"; Agents: David Robeson, Thurso; John Broadfoot, Leith. *IJ* June 7,14,21, *QM* Aug. 29.

Year	Mth	Vessel	Master	Psgr. Nos.	Departure Port	Arr Port	Vessel Type	Lloyd's Code
1833	6	*Zephyr*	Tucker	150	Cromarty	Pictou & Quebec	n/k	n/k

"William Allan (shipping agent) is now at Cromarty superintending the fitting up; upwards of 7 ft. between decks, second cabin to be fitted up if passengers wish it. The *Staffa* steam boat will leave the Sea Loch at Clachnaharry with passengers for the *Zephyr*, returning home the same day." 99 settlers left at Quebec and 51 at Pictou. *Immig. NS*,76; *IJ* May 31, *QM* Aug. 21.

Year	Mth	Vessel	Master	Psgr. Nos.	Departure Port	Arr Port	Vessel Type	Lloyd's Code
1833	07	*Robert & Margaret*	n/k	66	Cromarty	Pictou & Quebec	s	n/k

"A most desirable conveyance being upwards of 6 feet between decks"; Agent: D MacLennan of Inverness "who accompanies the passengers; also a surgeon." *Immig. NS*, 76; *IJ* May 14, June 21.

Year	Mth	Vessel	Master	Psgr. Nos.	Departure Port	Arr Port	Vessel Type	Lloyd's Code
1834	06	*Chieftain* of Kirkaldy	n/k	119	Cromarty	Pictou	bk	A1

Immig. NS, 79.

Year	Mth	Vessel	Master	Psgr. Nos.	Departure Port	Arr Port	Vessel Type	Lloyd's Code
1834	06	*William Henry*	n/k	102	Cromarty	Pictou	n/k	n/k

Immig. NS, 79.

Year	Mth	Vessel	Master	Psgr. Nos.	Departure Port	Arr Port	Vessel Type	Lloyd's Code
1834	07	*Bowes*	Faulkner	172	Cromarty	Quebec	n/k	n/k

QM Aug. 14.

Year	Mth	Vessel	Master	Psgr. Nos.	Departure Port	Arr Port	Vessel Type	Lloyd's Code
1835	06	*Maria*	Davieson	111	Inverness & Cromarty	Quebec	n/k	n/k

On arrival, vessel remained at quarantine with smallpox aboard. *PP* w/e Aug. 22, *QM* Aug. 1.

Year	Mth	Vessel	Master	Psgr. Nos.	Departure Port	Arr Port	Vessel Type	Lloyd's Code
1835	07	*Chieftain* of Kirkaldy	Spark	85	Cromarty	Quebec	bk	A1

QM Aug 4.

Year	Mth	Vessel	Master	Psgr. Nos.	Departure Port	Arr Port	Vessel Type	Lloyd's Code
1835	09	*Paragon*	Goodchild	100	Cromarty	Pictou & Quebec	n/k	n/k

QM states 46 arrived at Quebec. Some settlers left at Pictou. MacLaren, *The Pictou Book*, 121; *QM* Oct. 27.

Year	Mth	Vessel	Master	Psgr. Nos.	Departure Port	Arr Port	Vessel Type	Lloyd's Code
1836	06	*Albion* of Scarborough	Hicks, Michael	103	Cromarty & Loch Eriboll from Leith	St. Ann's Cape Breton & Quebec	sw	A1

Agent: William Allan of Leith. "Who is now at Tongue. Vessel will lay by for eight days at Loch Eribol to embark passengers." Customs officer at Sydney reported 75 passengers landed on 6 Dec. 1836. Martell reports arrival of 104 Highlanders at St. Ann's, Cape Breton, in the autumn of that year. Twenty-eight passengers left at Quebec. *Immig.NS*, 84; *IJ* 10 June, 1 July, *QM* Sept. 16.

Year	Mth	Vessel	Master	Psgr. Nos.	Departure Port	Arr Port	Vessel Type	Lloyd's Code
1836	06	*Tweed*	Slocombe	245	Cromarty	Quebec	bk	A1

Agent: William Allan of Leith. *QM* July 19, *IJ* Feb/Mar, *MC* May 20.

Year	Mth	Vessel	Master	Psgr. Nos.	Departure Port	Arr Port	Vessel Type	Lloyd's Code
1836	06	*Viewforth*	Elden	150	Cromarty	Quebec	bk	n/k

Agent: William Allan of Leith. *QM* July 19, *IJ* May, *MC* May 20.

Year	Mth	Vessel	Master	Psgr. Nos.	Departure Port	Arr Port	Vessel Type	Lloyd's Code
1836	07	*Mariner* of Sunderland	Collins	145	Thurso & Loch Eriboll	Quebec	n/k	n/k

Agent: William Allan of Leith. One hundred and forty-five steerage passengers disembarked at Quebec but 67 had intended to leave at Pictou. *PP* w/e 10 Sept.; *QM* Sept 6, *IJ* July 1, *IJ* July 1.

Year	Mth	Vessel	Master	Psgr. Nos.	Departure Port	Arr Port	Vessel Type	Lloyd's Code
1836	07	*Highlander* of Aberdeen	Fluckark	150	Cromarty	Quebec	bg	E1

150 settlers. *QM* Aug. 19.

1837	06	*Swift* of Sunderland	Beveridge	215	Cromarty	Quebec	sw	A1

Second cabin apartments restricted to a limited no of passengers. Fares were: steerage 52 s., children under 14, 26 s., children below 7, 17s. 4d; Second cabin fares were 60 s., under 14, 30 s., under 7, 20 s.; First cabin fares were 80 s., under 14, 40 s., under 7, 26 s. 8d; Agent D MacLennan, Inverness. *QM* July 27, *MC* Apr. 28.

1840	04	*Osprey* of Leith	Kirk	150	Cromarty & Thurso	Pictou & Quebec	s	AE1

One of three vessels (*British King, Quebec Packet*) chartered by Sutherland & MacLennan. A total of 403 people sailed on the three vessels of whom 248 were from Caithness. 60 landed at Pictou and the rest went on to Quebec. *IC* Aug. 5, *JJ* Apr. 10, *MC* Apr. 3.

1840	07	*British King* of Dundee	Brown, A.	157	Cromarty	Pictou & Quebec	bg	AE1 some repairs 1835 & 1838

All landed in good health and brought capital of £7000-£8000; with the exception of 20 all going to Upper Canada to settle in London district; 10 to PEI. Also see comments for the *Osprey* of Leith (1840). *PP* w/e Aug. 22; *IC* Aug. 5, *JJ* May 29.

1840	07	*Quebec Packet* of Aberdeen	Stephens	60	Cromarty	Quebec	bg	A1 in 1841 repairs 1838 & 1840

Quebec Packet carried farmers, farm labourers and tradesmen; they brought £800 to £1000 in gold with them; most to settle in Gore District; also see comments on *Osprey* of Leith (1840). *PP* w/e Sept. 12; *IC* Aug. 5, *JJ* June 26.

1841	04	*Fairy* of Dundee	Peters, George	123	Cromarty & Thurso	Quebec	s	E1

Agents: McLennan & Sutherland. The *Fairy* was a former whaling ship, built in 1801. *PP* 1842(301)XXXI; *JJ* March 12.

1841	04	*Pacific* of Aberdeen	Morrison, John	193	Thurso	Pictou & Quebec	bk	AE1

Most passengers were former tenants of the Duke of Sutherland, twenty-two of whom left at Pictou. Advertisement states that "George McKay merchant in Reay will be every Friday at McKay's Hotel to enrol names." Agent: Alexander Cooper, shipowner, Aberdeen. *PP* 1842(301)XXXI; *JJ* Feb. 5.

Year	Mth	Vessel	Master	Psgr. Nos.	Departure Port	Arr Port	Vessel Type	Lloyd's Code
1841	06	*Lady Grey* of North Shields	Grey, William	240	Cromarty & Thurso	Pictou & Quebec	sw	A1

Seventy-five passengers destined for Pictou and the rest for Quebec but 135 stayed in Pictou. Typhus broke out causing six deaths on crossing. A partial passenger list records people protesting at the captain's ill-treatment. Principal Agents: MacLennan & Sutherland. MacLaren *The Pictou Book*, 104–5; *PP* w/e Aug. 28, *PP* 1842(301)XXXI; [SRO] RH 1/2/908; *IJ* June 25.

Year	Mth	Vessel	Master	Psgr. Nos.	Departure Port	Arr Port	Vessel Type	Lloyd's Code
1841	06	*Margaret Bogle* of Leith	Smith, Walter	117	Thurso & Loch Laxford	Pictou & Quebec	s	E1

Quebec Immigration Agent found emigrants "respectable and except for 1 family all in good circumstances." Agents: MacLennan & Sutherland. *PP* w/e July 24, *PP* 1842(301)XXXI; *IJ* June 4, *JJ* April 30.

Year	Mth	Vessel	Master	Psgr. Nos.	Departure Port	Arr Port	Vessel Type	Lloyd's Code
1841	05	*Saphiras* of Whitby	Brown, Richard	202	Loch Laxford	Quebec	sn	A1

Agents: MacLennan & Sutherland; *PP* 1842(301)XXXI; *IJ* June 4.

Year	Mth	Vessel	Master	Psgr. Nos.	Departure Port	Arr Port	Vessel Type	Lloyd's Code
1841	09	*Universe* of Aberdeen	n/k	124	Thurso	Pictou & Quebec	bk	AE1 in 1841

Most were former tenants of the Duke of Sutherland. 105 passengers left the vessel at Pictou; the remainder disembarked at Quebec to join relatives in vicinity of Kingston & Toronto. Agent: William Allan, shipowner, Aberdeen. *PP* w/e Oct 9; MacLaren *Pictou Book*, 122.

Year	Mth	Vessel	Master	Psgr. Nos.	Departure Port	Arr Port	Vessel Type	Lloyd's Code
1842	04	*Pacific* of Aberdeen	Morrison, John	89	Cromarty, Thurso & Longhope	Quebec	bk	AE1

Pacific to call at Longhope (Orkneys) and Scrabster to collect emigrants. Agent: Alexander Cooper, shipowner, Aberdeen. *PP* w/e June 4; *IJ* Mar. 11 (advert), *AH* Mar. 19, *JJ* Feb. 11.

Year	Mth	Vessel	Master	Psgr. Nos.	Departure Port	Arr Port	Vessel Type	Lloyd's Code
1842	05	*Superior* of Peterhead	Manson, Donald	191	Cromarty & Thurso	Pictou & Quebec	bk	AE1

Fifty-two left at Pictou; 139 left at Quebec. Captain Manson, a native of Cromarty was experienced and "known to possess that manner of urbanity that will secure to him the good will and respect of all the passengers." Agents: MacLennan & Sutherland. *PP* w/e July 9; MacLaren *Pictou Book*, 122; *IJ* Mar. 18, 25, July 29.

Year	Mth	Vessel	Master	Psgr. Nos.	Departure Port	Arr Port	Vessel Type	Lloyd's Code
1842	06	*Joseph Green* of Peterhead	Volum, James	239	Cromarty, Thurso & Lochinver	Quebec	s	AE1

Advert states "Intending emigrants from Loch Broom, Gairloch and Torridon would do well to avail themselves of this conveyance." Vessel will have second cabin restricted to a limited number. 38 received financial help; arrived in good health. Agents: MacLennan & Sutherland. *PP* w/e July 23; *IJ* March 25.

Year	Mth	Vessel	Master	Psgr. Nos.	Departure Port	Arr Port	Vessel Type	Lloyd's Code
1842	07	*Sir William Wallace* of Aberdeen	Anderson, Robert	78	Thurso from Aberdeen	Quebec	bg	n/k

Agents: James Gordon, Aberdeen and George Allan, Wick. *PP* w/e Aug. 20; *IJ* June 3, *AH* June 4, *IJ* June 10.

| 1842 | 08 | *Lady Emily* of Sunderland | Smith, James | 150 | Cromarty, Thurso & Loch Laxford | Pictou & Quebec | sw | A1 |

Eighty-six left at Pictou and 64 at Quebec. Agents: MacLennan & Sutherland. *PP* w/e Oct. 1; *MacLaren Pictou Book*, 122, *IJ* June 10, Sept. 30.

| 1843 | 04 | *Pacific* of Aberdeen | n/k | 39 | Thurso | Quebec | bk | AE1 |

Agent: Alexander Cooper, shipowner, Aberdeen. *PP* 1844(181)xxxv.

| 1843 | 04 | *Symmetry* | n/k | 128 | Thurso | Quebec, Charlottetown & Pictou | n/k | E1 |

The Quebec arrivals were described as being in good circumstances. Around 18 had disembarked at PEI and Pictou. *PP* 1844(181)XXXV; *PP* w/e July 1.

| 1843 | 06 | *George* of Dundee | Hanley, Francis | 215 | Cromarty, Thurso & Loch Laxford from Dundee | Pictou & Quebec | s | n/k |

Ninety-five left at Pictou; long delays caused by many port calls; disease broke out before arrival in Pictou and emigrants taken to temporary accommodation on beaches. Poster for crossing states "vessel has her cabins on deck, the whole space between decks nearly 8 ft in height and 26 ft in length. Is fitted expressly for intermediate and steerage passengers." Agents: MacLennan and Sutherland. *PP* 1844(181)XXXV, *PP* w/e Sept. 16; *DC* Apr. 28.

| 1843 | 07 | *Jean Hastie* of Grangemouth | Robertson, James | 44 | Thurso from Dundee | Quebec | s | E1 |

Eighteen passengers boarded at Dundee and 26 at Thurso. *PP* 1844(181)XXXV; *DC* June 2.

| 1844 | 04 | *Pacific* of Aberdeen | Morrison, John | n/k | Cromarty & Thurso | Quebec | bk | AE1 |

Agents: MacLennan and Sutherland. *IJ* April 5.

| 1844 | 06 | *Harriet* | Chambers, W. | n/k | Cromarty & Thurso | Quebec | n/k | n/k |

Advert states that because of "unprecedented scarcity of suitable vessels for passengers" the owners will not allow the *Harriet* to call at Pictou—if a suitable place cannot be found to land passengers in Nova Scotia a "safe & cheap conveyance will be procured for them in Quebec." Agents: MacLennan & Sutherland. *IJ* June 21.

Year	Mth	Vessel	Master	Psgr. Nos.	Departure Port	Arr Port	Vessel Type	Lloyd's Code
1845	04	*Lord Seaton* of Aberdeen	Talbot, William	71	Cromarty & Thurso from Aberdeen	Quebec	s	A1

Agents: MacLennan and Sutherland. *IC* March 26.

| 1845 | 07 | *Joseph Harrison* | Hutchison, John | n/k | Cromarty & Thurso | Quebec | n/k | n/k |

New ship and great height between decks. Agents: MacLennan and Sutherland. Advert states steamers go regularly between Quebec and Pictou—fare only 8d. *IC* June 18, 25.

| 1846 | 04 | *Lord Seaton* of Aberdeen | Talbot, William | 18 | Cromarty & Thurso | Quebec | s | A1 |

Agents: MacLennan and Sutherland, 3 cabin & 15 steerage. *IC* April 2,, *QM* May 19.

| 1846 | 07 | *Kate* of Newcastle | Taylor, Thomas | 43 | Cromarty & Thurso | Quebec | bk | A1 |

Agents: MacLennan and Sutherland. Steamers to take people to Cromarty from Nairnshire, Morayshire and Clachnaharrry. *IC* June 17, *QM* Sept. 8.

| 1847 | n/k | *Serius* | n/k | 117 | Thurso | Pictou | n/k | n/k |

Duke of Sutherland's tenants. MacLaren, *Pictou Book,* 122.

| 1849 | 04 | *Lord Seaton* of Aberdeen | Talbot, William | 23 | Cromarty & Longhope (Orkney) | Quebec | s | A1 |

Agent: George Oswald, shipowner, Aberdeen. *IC* March 8, *QM* May 22.

| 1849 | 06 | *Prince Albert* of Arbroath | Rodgers, Alexander | 125 | Cromarty & Thurso from Leith | Quebec | sw | AE1 |

Agents: MacLennan and Sutherland. *QM* reports Master to be Clarke. *JJ* April 27, June 15, *IC* May 3, *QM* Aug. 14.

| 1850 | 06 | *Argo* | Breslace | 50 | Thurso from Leith | Quebec | n/k | n/k |

Agents: MacLennan and Sutherland. Duke of Sutherland's tenants. PP 1851(348)Xl; *IC* Apr. 18, May 30.

| 1851 | 04 | *Empress* of Banff | Leslie, A. | n/k | Thurso from Banff | Quebec | bk | AE1 |

Agents: MacLennan and Sutherland. Passengers from Inverness, Ross and Sutherland counties to be taken by steamer to Banff from Inverness, Cromarty & Invergordon. *IC* March 13.

Year	Mth	Vessel	Master	Psgr. Nos.	Departure Port	Arr Port	Vessel Type	Lloyd's Code
1851	06	*Vesper*	Bennett	52	Thurso	Quebec	n/k	n/k

Agents: MacLennan and Sutherland. Duke of Sutherland's tenants. *QM* reports 75 passengers landed at Quebec. *PP* 1852(1474)XXXIII; *IC* May 1, June 26, *QM* July 12.

VI. THE ABERDEEN SAILING SHIPS WHICH CARRIED EMIGRANTS

"We have this week to record, which we do with regret, the death of our townsman, Mr. William Duthie, late shipbuilder. Mr. Duthie was a native of Stonehaven and always evinced a peculiar attachment to the place of his birth. He commenced business as a shipbuilder here about 1815 and after carrying it on very successfully for about thirty years, retired in favour of his brothers and nephew, Messrs. Alex. Duthie and Co, which firm again has lately been succeeded by that of Messrs John Duthie and Son. Mr. Duthie was for a good many years a Police Commissioner, and for a very long period and up to the time of his death, he was a Harbour Commissioner. In politics he was a Conservative. Mr. Duthie, besides building ships, was an extensive shipowner. He was much respected as an employer and greatly esteemed both in public and private for his unobtrusive worth. Mr. Duthie had attained his 72nd year."[1]

William Duthie's obituary describes a man who was remembered as much for his public spiritedness as for his success in business. He provided vessels for emigrants over many years and all reached their destinations safely and without incident. Yet popular perception would have us believe that emigrant shipping services were usually run by wicked rogues out for a quick profit. The facts and circumstances in Aberdeen show quite the reverse. Duthie's success actually depended upon on his good reputation both in his personal and

The *Abergeldie* of Aberdeen was a clipper ship of 1,152 tons built in 1869 by John Duthie and Sons, Aberdeen. *City of Aberdeen, Art Gallery and Museums Collections.*

business dealings. He could only have continued to attract his customers by providing a good service. The fact is that any Aberdeen shipowner or agent wishing to remain in business as a supplier of Atlantic crossings to emigrants had to be like Duthie. Paying customers came from within local communities and news of just one bad crossing would have been enough to drive them away. There were few effective regulations to protect emigrants against unscrupulous operators, but the one weapon they did have was the certain knowledge that a shipowner's follow-on business depended on a record of good service and reliability.

Entrepreneurial flair and technical skills gave William Duthie his entree into Aberdeen's foreign trade markets. By 1815 he had built his first vessel in Alexander Hall's shipyard, where he initially worked as an apprentice. A year later Duthie had his own shipyard at Footdee and then quickly rose to prominence as a major shipbuilder. Purchasing as well as building vessels, he established himself as a large-scale timber merchant, trading with British America. William Duthie and his family soon acquired a major stake in Aberdeen's shipping and trade activities and they maintained their strong position over several decades. And this was very much a family business. Duthie handed over his business in 1837 to his two brothers, Alexander and John and to John's son, John Jr. Both brothers had actually captained family-owned vessels. In fact, Alexander had been in charge of the *City of Aberdeen* in 1826–1827 when she had taken 14 passengers from Aberdeen to Quebec, and the *Brilliant* from 1833 to 1836, when she carried a total of 548 emigrants to Quebec.[2] Following his death in 1861, most of the Duthie firm came under the ownership of John and his six sons.[3]

Aberdeen's clipper ship era was a high point in its maritime history. Produced from 1839, the clippers were famous throughout the world for their outstanding designs and record-breaking speeds.[4] The great clippers were designed to compete with American ships in the Chinese opium and tea trade and regularly made fast passages to Australia for wool and gold.[5] Alexander Hall and Sons led the way with new schooner designs which became the forerunner of the famous clippers. Soon other Aberdeen shipbuilders, notably Walter Hood and, William Duthie were producing clipper ships which ranked with the best in the world. But Aberdeen's dominance as a shipbuilding centre had been established long before the heady days of the clipper ship.

In 1801, Aberdeen's output of shipping and associated tonnage exceeded that of Glasgow, making it the top shipbuilding centre for the whole of Scotland.[6] While Aberdeen eventually lost prominence to the Clyde, its shipbuilding industry continued to expand. By the 1820s about a dozen firms, located at the east end of the harbour at Footdee, were in operation, with some of the earliest including William Stephen's yard, founded in 1788, Alexander Hall's yard founded in 1790, and Nicol and Reid's yard established sometime before 1790. James Anderson's yard was in operation from at least as early as 1811, while William Duthie had, by 1816, set up his own shipyard at York Place. Walter Hood's firm appeared much later, being established in 1839. Together these shipbuilders made the vessels which would form the backbone of Aberdeen's Atlantic passenger sailing services (Appendix).[7]

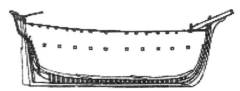

Mary 139 ton Snow built 1810 in Aberdeen
13' 1" x 21' 6" x 12' 5"

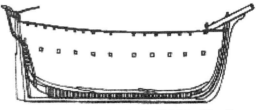

Brilliant 332 ton Ship built 1814 in Aberdeen
97' 2" x 28' 8" x 19' 3"

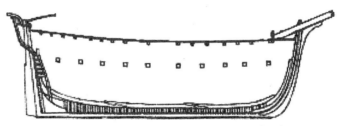

St. Lawrence 352 ton Barque built 1841 in Aberdeen
105' x 24' 6" x 18'

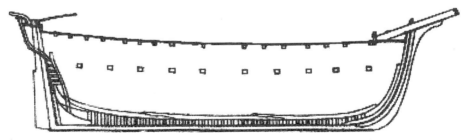

Aurora 709 ton Barque built 1843 in New Brunswick
144' 5" x 28' 9" x 21'

Figure 3. Hull length to depth ratios of selected vessels (dimensions shown are length, breadth and depth)

James Anderson's vessels, especially the *Louisa, Earl of Dalhousie, Glentanner* and *Traveller* were widely used to carry passengers during the first peak in emigration levels from 1816, while, from 1827, his *Aberdeenshire* provided a regular service between Aberdeen and Halifax for some ten years, carrying goods both ways and taking emigrants on westward crossings. But most prominent of all were Alexander Hall's vessels. His *Brilliant,* a whaling ship built in 1814, and the *Albion,* built in 1826, were two of the mainstays of Aberdeen's Atlantic passenger trade, while some of his other vessels, like the *Sir William Wallace* built in 1835 and the *Sarah* in 1839, also found regular use as emigrant carriers. The St. *Lawrence,* the other great workhorse of the Atlantic passenger trade, was the product of Walter Hood's yard, carrying just over 1,700 emigrants in a thirteen-year period from 1842. The *Jane Boyd,* built by Walter Hood and owned by George Thompson, founder of the Aberdeen Line and principal partner of Walter Hood's firm, also attracted substantial numbers of emigrants. Vessels built by William Duthie were not as a rule much used in the regular Atlantic passenger services from Aberdeen, but some of his vessels, like the *Thistle, Highlander* and *Universe,* took large numbers of emigrants from the Highlands and Islands to British America on an occasional basis. And there were many others, such as the *Quebec Packet,* built at Nicol and Reid's yard and the *Pilgrim,* built by William Rennie and the *Aimwell, Cambria, Phesdo, Harmony, Ruby* and *Morningfield,* built in Aberdeen but not traceable to a particular shipyard, all of which saw significant service as emigrant carriers.

While most emigrants crossed the Atlantic on Aberdeen built vessels there were some notable exceptions (Table 4). There was William Duthie's *Hercules* and *Heroine,* both ex-whaling ships, the former built in 1781 in Stockton and the latter in 1831 in Dundee, each of which carried over 600 emigrants. And increasingly, ships were being constructed in British America and used to take emigrants on Atlantic crossings. Alexander Cooper's *Pacific,* built in 1826 in Nova Scotia, took just over 500 emigrants; his *Aurora,* produced in 1843 in Miramichi, New Brunswick, transported just over 700; while Alexander Duthie's *Berbice,* constructed in 1847 in the Miramichi, carried just over 1,000 emigrants. Ships built in British America were often much larger than those constructed in Britain, where

84

much of the timber had to be imported, and were particularly well-suited to carrying timber cargoes on Atlantic runs.[8] But it was William Duthie's ownership of the *Hercules* and *Heroine*, together with another former whaler the *Brilliant,* built by Alexander Hall in Aberdeen, which was to have such significance for the Atlantic passenger trade.[9]

Duthie's impact on the Atlantic trade thus went far beyond his ship-building activities. As a major timber merchant and shipbuilder, Duthie needed plenty of timber. Rather than offering relatively small vessels, designed for mixed cargoes, he opted for vessels which were capable of carrying the largest possible timber loads from Quebec to Aberdeen. Having been comparatively successful as a whaling port in the first two decades of the nineteenth century, Aberdeen's whaling interests had gone into decline by 1830.[10] Duthie's use of redundant whaling ships at a time when Aberdeen's Atlantic cargo and passenger trade were on the increase was a particularly inspired piece of lateral thinking. His success was quite phenomenal. By offering emigrants more spacious accommodation as well as better safety features than his competitors, he was able to dominate Aberdeen's passenger trade throughout the 1830s, and he only lost ground when the sleeker hull designs of the 1840s became available.

The whalers used in the Arctic were not particularly large, varying from 200 to 300 tons, not usually built to any particular design, but they were very strongly built and had extra sheathing to offer protection against ice.[11] They also had to be highly manoeuvrable, able to quickly escape from encroaching ice packs. While whales were pursued and harpooned from small boats, the task of stripping down the whale carcasses into manageable sections was undertaken on board ship by a large crew. To accommodate them and to give adequate work and storage space, whaling ships were exceptionally deep, usually having a full length and capacious fixed lower deck area. Thus in the 1830s, when they were first used, refurbished ex-whalers could offer emigrants far more spacious accommodation than was available on other vessel types.

It seems odd that Duthie made no attempt to advertise his use of former whaling ships. By contrast, Duthie's counterpart in Dundee, James Soot, openly boasted that his ships the *Fairy* and *Ebor* had "great height between decks," having been "doubled and fortified for the whale fishing."[12] Soot, who was a member of a long-established whaling family business in Dundee, had made a determined effort to find emigrants for his ex-whalers in the early 1830s but with little success. However, unlike Duthie, he faced fierce competition from the very large ports at Leith and the Clyde, which were close enough to Dundee to penetrate his market.[13]

William Duthie was not alone in using ex-whaling ships to carry timber loads from Quebec to Aberdeen. Neil Smith, an Aberdeen merchant, paid Thomas Adam for the use of the *Neptune* in 1843 to sail to Quebec for timber and transport it to a safe port between Aberdeen and Newcastle-upon-Tyne. A 282-ton barque built in 1786, the *Neptune* had been destined for the whaling industry and, as late as 1841, was still owned by the Union Whale Fishing Company.[14] At the time of the request, the *Neptune* was in Bridgwater, in the Bristol Channel. The signal to cross the Atlantic came with the agreement of a "charter party" between Thomas Adam and Neil Smith and remarkably it still survives. Neil Smith would have to pay penalty charges of 5 guineas per day if the total loading and unloading times at Quebec and Aberdeen exceeded 35 days:[15]

"that the said ship being tight, staunch, strong and every way fitted for the voyage shall by all convenient speed sail for Quebec and thence load a full and complete cargo of pine timber of wood not exceeding two thirds to be red pine and to be furnished with the necessary deals or staves for broken storage and being so laden shall proceed…to a safe port betwixt Aberdeen and Newcastle…also to lay the space of 35 running days for all purposes…such days to be computed from the time the said vessel shall be arrived at the proper places of loading and discharging reported at the Customs House and the Master shall have given notice to the Agent…demurrage [penalty payment] over and above the said laying days at 5 guineas per day.'[16]

This charter party survives because Thomas Adam had appended it to a letter which he had sent to his colleague, William Penny, with a request that he ask a colleague in Dundee to check one of its Clauses. At the time William Penny was Captain of the *St. Andrew,* yet another whaler owned by the Union Whale Fishing Company. Penny would have

A rare painting of an emigrant vessel, the *Circassian* took 117 emigrants from Aberdeen to Quebec in 1836. This view of the *Circassian* of Aberdeen, a brig of 180 tons built by William Duthie and Sons in 1835, is by an unknown artist. She is shown entering the harbour at Malta. *City of Aberdeen, Art Gallery and Museums Collections*.

known something about the previous arrangements, since he had sailed the *St. Andrew*, only the previous year to Sydney, Cape Breton, to collect a cargo of timber and take it to Hull.[17]

Duthie became a dominant figure in the 1830s, but Aberdeen's Atlantic trade had been underway long before this. The mushrooming of North American timber imports to Aberdeen had actually commenced from 1811, following the imposition of added tariffs on Baltic timber. Aberdeen shippers would have suddenly come under pressure to supply suitable vessels for this new and rapidly expanding trade. Their problem was that although Aberdeen was a major Scottish port by this time, only a small part of its total foreign trade had actually been conducted directly with foreign countries. Most of its foreign imports and exports had in fact arrived as coastal trade, having been sent to and from the ports of London, Hull, Newcastle,

Leith and Glasgow.[18] Since Aberdeen's priority initially was the coastal trade, most of its shipping would thus have been inappropriate for overseas transport. Some merchants would have reassigned the vessels they formerly used to collect Baltic timber to Atlantic routes; but the distances and sailing conditions were hardly comparable.

Predictably, there was a major surge in shipbuilding from 1810 and over the next decade many new brigs and snows of around 200 tons, built in Aberdeen shipyards, made their maiden voyage from Aberdeen on an Atlantic crossing. They would have been specifically designed to carry timber cargoes and cope with the severe conditions to be found in the North Atlantic. Thus, when the northeast of Scotland experienced a rise in emigration from 1815, with the ending of the Napoleonic Wars, newly built sturdy vessels were available to take emigrants from Aberdeen to either the Maritimes or Quebec. And, it was on these new vessels that many emigrants sailed (Table 4).

While many vessels left Aberdeen to collect timber from British America, only a select few ever carried emigrants. The Atlantic passenger trade was to some extent a speciality service since it required convivial sea captains, experienced in handling people in often hazardous circumstances, and vessels which were both capable of carrying large timber loads and versatile enough in design to accommodate passengers in their holds. The brig or snow, having two masts and square-rigged on both masts, was the most common vessel to be used on Atlantic crossings during the late eighteenth and early nineteenth centuries. The sails, suspended at right angles to the line of the hull, allowed for maximum propulsion from the prevailing winds on long sea voyages. Until the late 1830s, the typical emigrant who crossed the Atlantic, travelled on brigs or snows averaging about 200 tons, which tended to be squat and broad-beamed, having been primarily selected for their good stowage capabilities. While they performed well in heavy seas, they did not achieve the speeds of later hull designs.[19] But, there was never going to be the perfect hull design since there was always the need to satisfy what were often contradictory objectives.

A full-bottom might enable a vessel to be well-laden in relation its size, but she would sail badly when having to tack against prevailing westerly winds.[20] Vessels designed to carry the maximum amount of cargo were slow and could be demanding on labour costs if they came with a large amount of sail. Long, sleek hulls might provide greater speed but could have less carrying capacity. While emigrants and shippers valued speed, they also wanted the best possible chance of survival in heavy seas. A full-bodied, strongly built vessel did not necessarily promise speed but was well placed to ride out gales. Thus, there were always trade-offs to be made between carrying-capacity, speed, labour costs and overall sailing performance.[21]

Given the great distances involved, speed was still a critical factor. The shorter the travel time, the more return journeys a vessel could make. More return journeys gave shippers more revenue from cargoes transported. And it was major changes in hull design, introduced from the 1820s, which were to bring improvements in sailing speeds. Hulls gradually lengthened in proportion to their breadth and, as this trend continued, speed and vessel productivity increased. The sharpness of the hull as it entered the water, the long hull hollow at the bow, and the sheer lines which helped to reduce wave-making resistance all contributed to greater speed. As a result, vessels could regularly make up to three round trips across the Atlantic in a year, although achieving this often put crews to considerable risk of being stuck in the ice during early Spring passages.

Most emigrants sailed on vessels that had been specifically designed for the British American timber trade, but there were some, particularly those who left just as the passenger trade was developing, who went in vessels which pre-dated this era. The *Perseverance,* a 116-ton galliot captured in wartime sometime before 1811, was undoubtedly in this category. Between 1814 and 1818 she sailed four times with emigrants from the Highlands and Islands, taking them to British America, with one crossing having 150 passengers. She was 65 feet 3 inches long, by 20 feet 10 inches wide, by eleven feet six inches deep.[22] Her unusually high breadth in relation to her length may account for her use on Atlantic runs. The 128-ton *Ruby,* built in 1805, and the 133-ton *Thistle,* both snows, between them taking over 300 Highlanders and Islanders to Pictou and Quebec in 1821–1822, almost exactly mirrored the *Perseverance*'s overall proportions.[23] Before the days of sawn lumber and mixed cargoes, a full-bodied shape and deep hull may have been well suited to coping with unwieldy lengths of timber. And an added bonus of a chubby shape was the capacity to ride out gales and keep steady in heavy winds and stormy weather.

The *Mary*, a 139-ton snow built in 1810, made regular crossings with emigrants over a six-year period, but only with small numbers—never more than 35 at a time. The *Mary* was slightly less chubby than the *Perseverance,* being a little longer and may have been designed to transport coal. If she had been built as a bulk carrier—say to carry coal, her construction and design would have given her good stowage capabilities and she may well have had some fixed but limited space for passengers in a cabin area towards the after end or stern of the vessel.[24] Huge by comparison, the 364-ton *Nestor,* built in 1802, which could boast of six feet six inches between decks, managed only one crossing with passengers and that was in 1822 and with just five people. Used by the government to transport troops during the Napoleonic Wars, she was designed to accommodate large numbers of soldiers in cramped conditions, but paying passengers were quite another matter.[25] Even a 95-ton schooner like the *Helen* did better than the *Nestor* as an emigrant carrier, taking some 11 passengers from Aberdeen to Quebec in 1816, the year after she was built.[26]

When the 150-ton *Sprightly* took twenty emigrants to the Maritimes in 1816, they may have travelled as cabin passengers. But when thirteen years later the *Sprightly's* owner offered to "fit up very comfortably for their accommodation" any passengers who wished to travel in the hold, we know definitely that he was seeking steerage passengers.[27] Similarly when the *Glentanner,* a 160-ton brig built in 1811 with similar proportions to the *Mary*, carried her seventeen passengers in 1817, they may have been accommodated in a cabin area; but when in 1840 she took 140 emigrants from Tobermory to Cape Breton and Quebec in a single crossing, they travelled as steerage passengers. This number could only have been accommodated by placing temporary decking on crossbeams along the full length of the hold. Thus, before leaving Aberdeen for Tobermory, planks would have been laid and the sides of her hold would have been lined with wooden berths (or bunks). Then having disembarked her passengers, she would have returned to Aberdeen with her hold brimmed full with timber. This was to be the pattern of emigrant travel for the next thirty years or so.

Brig

Ship

Barque

Square-rigged vessels. *The Nova Scotia Department of Education.*

Until the 1820s emigrant travel was primarily governed by the needs of the timber trade. Vessels were selected for their suitability as timber carriers with the needs of passengers being quite secondary. As vessels grew in size and crossings grew in frequency, regular services came to be introduced by one or two shipowners. With this trend came the advent of specialized vessels which were designed to give passengers more cabin space and better accommodation. Built with a slighter finer hull than average, they were designed for extra speed and were specifically equipped to accommodate passengers and handle a wide range of cargoes.[28] Passengers were definitely not an afterthought.

Robert Catto owned two of the three regular traders which Aberdeen offered by the 1820s. Ranging from 196 tons to 240 tons and built in the 1820s, Catto's *Quebec Packet* and *Aberdeenshire* plied the Atlantic twice yearly between Aberdeen and Halifax or Quebec. They took mail, goods and passengers westward and timber eastwards back to Aberdeen.[29] The third was the 266-ton *Albion,* built in 1826 and owned by Robert Duthie, which operated between Aberdeen and Halifax for an astounding 25 years. Built to give greater speed, their slimmer hulls reveal the new trend in design when compared with earlier vessels like the *Perseverance* and *Mary.* In fact, the *Quebec Packet* gained distinction in 1827 for being the first arrival in Quebec, having taken only 28 days to sail from Aberdeen.[30]

The arrival of the regular trader marked a new era in passenger travel. For those who could pay for the greater privacy, space and better food which cabins had to offer, the regular traders were a great step forward. At first only a maximum of around 25 cabin passengers could be accommodated, but by the 1830s some North Atlantic packets could take up to 50 or 60 people in a long cabin or poop in the stern end of the vessel.[31] However, the three regular traders which operated from Aberdeen appear always to have had an upper limit of 25 people in their cabin area. The *Aberdeenshire* made two crossings with 40 passengers in 1832 and the *Albion* sailed once with 49 passengers in 1836, but these were exceptional occurrences. On the one occasion, in 1840, when the *Quebec Packet* was diverted to Cromarty to collect 60 emigrants, they were accommodated in the hold as steerage passengers along with the other goods which Robert Catto was under contract to take.[32]

However, the biggest development in the Atlantic passenger trade, which was to benefit everyone, was the use of bigger vessels offering more space and shorter journey times. From the mid-1820s there had been a gradual shift from two-masted vessels rigged as brigs or snows to three-masted vessels, rigged as barques or ships.[33] Vessels became longer and slimmer and, with their increased hull size and sail area to catch the wind, were capable of greater speeds than the brigs and snows which had preceded them. The shallower hull designs achieved not only faster speeds, but also had tax advantages. Since the new method for calculating tonnage, introduced in 1836, for the first time included a vessel's depth, it was in a shipper's interest to look for shallow designs.[34] The search for ways of reducing the taxable tonnage assessment of a vessel had, in fact, been one of the factors which inspired Alexander Hall & Sons to create their new hull forms.

Their new hull designs began to appear from 1839. Their invention of the so-called Aberdeen Bow led to the development of the famous clipper bow which broke speed records and placed Aberdeen at the forefront of shipbuilding throughout the world.[35] Hall's design produced even slimmer lines than was possible with traditional designs and far greater speeds. And yet with the exception of the *Taurus* built by Walter Hood, no clippers were ever used in Aberdeen's Atlantic trade. The over-riding consideration was always going to be cargo capacity. Full-bodied conventional vessels best suited the timber trade and it was on these that emigrants sailed.[36]

Thus it was portly shapes like Alexander Hall's *Brilliant* and not his graceful and sleek clippers which would become the dependable workhorses of the North Atlantic passenger trade. With his astute purchase of former whalers in the early 1830s, William Duthie was well ahead of his time in recognizing the gains to be made from size. Although his 332-ton *Brilliant* was far wider and deeper for its length and thus likely to be slower than later designs, it could offer six feet between decks for passengers—an almost unheard of luxury for the time.[37] Even by as late as 1828, the legislation still only required shippers to give their passengers at least five-and-one-half feet between decks.[38] It was not until the passing of the 1842 Act that six feet became the minimum legal requirement.[39]

By the mid-1840s, with the arrival of the new sleeker vessels like the *St. Lawrence* and *Aurora* which offered fast journey times as well as a height between decks of up to seven feet, William Duthie's ex-whalers had lost their appeal (Figure 3). Conditions on board ship for emigrants were gradually improving as services became more streamlined and frequent. However, crossing the Atlantic in a sailing ship was more than just a question of the soundness of the vessel used. There was always the fear of disease spreading, particularly on overcrowded vessels, of running out of food and water on long journeys or of meeting stormy conditions at sea. So much depended on the captain's navigational skills and his attitude to his passengers. Many Aberdeen captains worked for years for the same ship owner and often on the same vessel. The role of the captain was critical to the overall standard of service which emigrants might have experienced.

Table 4: The Aberdeen-registered vessels which took 60 or more emigrants to British America 1801–1855

(Information on vessel types and Lloyd's Codes can be found on page 1 of the Appendix, which gives details of all of the vessels covered in this study. This table is restricted to vessels that carried 60 or more passengers. Dimensions give length x breadth x depth.)

Vessel	Type	Tonn-age	Year Built	Builder	Owner/ Agent	Dimensions	L/B	Lloyd's Code	Pass. Nos
St. Lawrence	bk	352	1841	Aberdeen, by Walter Hood	Donaldson Rose	105 x 24.6 x 18	4.29	A1	1750
Brilliant	s	332	1814	Aberdeen, by Alexander Hall	William Duthie	97.2 x 28.8 x 19.3	3.38	AE1	1343
Berbice	bk	340	1847	Miramichi, New Brunswick	Alexander Duthie	107.8 x 23.4 x 17.2	4.62	AE1	1091
Aurora	s	709	1843	Miramichi, New Brunswick	Alexander Cooper	144.5 x 28.9 x 21	5.04	AE1	710
Hercules	bk	250	1781	Stockton (possibly Stockton-on-Tees)	William Duthie	88.6 x 26.2 x 6.3	3.38 btw'n decks	E1	653
Heroine	s	387	1831	Dundee	William Duthie	n/k	n/k	AE1	637
Universe	bk	281	1826	Aberdeen, by William Duthie	William Allen	n/k	n/k	A1 in 1828; AE1 in 1841	588
Albion	bg	266	1826	Aberdeen, by Alexander Hall	Robert Duthie (1829–38); Alexander Stephen (1839–41); Alexander Cooper (1842–53)	94.2 x 25.6 x 17.2	3.69	A1	582

Vessel	Type	Tonn–age	Year Built	Builder	Owner/ Agent	Dimensions	L/B	Lloyd's Code	Pass. Nos
Pacific	bk	386	1826	Nova Scotia	Alexander Cooper	102 x 26.2 x 18.7	3.90	AEI	517
Louisa	sw	213	1816	Aberdeen, by James Adamson	Peter Ritchie	85.3 x 24.2 x 15.9	3.53	EI	472
Sarah	bg	232	1839	Aberdeen, by Alexander Hall	Donaldson Rose	87.0 x 21.1 x 15.0	4.13	n/k	390
Morning-field	bg	141	1816	Aberdeen	Peter Ritchie	n/k	n/k	AI	327
Economy	n/k	n/k	n/k	n/k	n/k	n/k	n/k	n/k	285
Aberdeen-shire	sw	240	1825	Aberdeen, by James Adamson	Robert Catto	89 x 25.2 x 17	3.53	AI	246
Jane Boyd	bk	387	1843	Aberdeen, by Walter Hood	George Thompson Jr.	109.6 x 23.8 18.1	4.63	n/k	245
Aimwell	sw	232	1816	Aberdeen	Donaldson Rose	85 x 25.10 x 16.9	3.29	AI	228
High-lander	sw	174	1817	Aberdeen, by William Duthie	Robert Duthie	79.1 x 22.11 x 14.11	3.45	EI	223
Dove	n/k	186	n/k	n/k	n/k	n/k	n/k	n/k	219
Persever-ance	bg	116	n/k	Foreign	Peter Ritchie	65.4 x 20.10 x 11.6	3.12	n/k	202
Quebec Packet	bg	196	1822	Aberdeen, by Nicol Reid & Co	Robert Catto	82.10 x 23.11 x 15.4	3.46	AI	181
Renown	bk	311	1842	Aberdeen, by Alexander Duthie	William Duthie	97.4 x 23 x 17	4.23	AEI	170

96

Vessel	Type	Tonn-age	Year Built	Builder	Owner/ Agent	Dimensions	L/B	Lloyd's Code	Pass. Nos
Sir William Wallace	bg	183	1835	Aberdeen, by Alexander Hall	Donaldson Rose	79.9 x 22.9 x 14.5	3.50	n/k	164
Traveller	bg	195	1819	Aberdeen, by James Adamson	Peter Ritchie	82.10 x 23.7 x 15.1	3.51	n/k	163
Emperor Alexander	sw	236	1814	Sunderland	Robert Catto	83.11 x 25.8 x 15.11	3.27	A1	160
Glen-tanner	bg	160	1811	Aberdeen, by James Adamson	Robert Duthie	77.10 x 22.2 x 13.6	3.51	A1	158
Mary	sw	139	1810	Aberdeen	Peter Ritchie	73.1 x 21.6 x 12.5	3.40	n/k	142
Taurus	sr	184	1841	Aberdeen by Walter Hood	James Nisbet & David Robertson	84.6 x 20.5 x 13.5	4.14	A1	134
Pilgrim	bg	170	1828	Aberdeen, by William Rennie	Donaldson Rose	75.6 x 22.10 x 14.3	3.31	A1	130
Ruby	sw	128	1805	Aberdeen	Alexander Gibbon	67.9 x 21.5 x 11.1	3.16	A1 in 1816; E1 in 1822	127
Harmony	sw	161	1801	Aberdeen	n/k	n/k	n/k	E1	125
Cambria	bg	120	1808	Aberdeen	Peter Ritchie	n/k	n/k	A1	120
Circassian	bg	180	1835	Aberdeen by William Duthie	William Duthie	82.9 x 22.6 x 15.4	3.68	A1	117
Earl of Dalhousie	bg	183	1817	Aberdeen, by James Adamson	Peter Ritchie	n/k	n/k	A1	102

Vessel	Type	Tonn-age	Year Built	Builder	Owner/ Agent	Dimensions	L/B	Lloyd's Code	Pass. Nos
Carleton	bk	404	1834	New Brunswick	Robert Catto	111 x 28.10 x 20.9	3.85	AE1	96
Thistle	sw	133	1818	Aberdeen, by William Duthie	Alexander Machie	67.8 x 21.10 x 11.7	3.10	A1	96
Rose	bk	253	1843	Aberdeen, by Walter Hood	Donaldson Rose	n/k	n/k	A1	94
Annan-dale	bg	254	1828	New Brunswick	Robert Catto	91.10 x 25.2 x 17.3	3.65	A1	91
Shakes-peare	sw	179	1825	Aberdeen, by Nicol Reid & Co	Donaldson Rose	78.9 x 22.11 x 15	3.44	AE1	84
Lord Metcalfe	bk	510	1845	Quebec	George Thompson Jr.	120.7 x 26.1 x 18.3	4.62	AE1	82
Bon Accord	bk	365	1812	Blythe★	Lewis Crombie	101.6 x 28.10 x 6.4 btw'n decks	3.52	AE1	70
Amethyst	sw	132	1812	Aberdeen	Greig & Co.	n/k	n/k	A1	65
Amity	bg	312	1825	New Brunswick	George Thompson Jr.	n/k	n/k	E1	64
Phesdo	bg	245	1815	Aberdeen	Alexander Duthie	87 x 26.1 x 16.9	3.34	A1	61

★ Probably Blyth, Northumberland

VII. EMIGRANT SEA VOYAGES: A GOOD OR BAD EXPERIENCE?

"A sea voyage is a dull tiresome concern. We found it so in spite of some very pleasant days. Our never failing topic of conversation was the weather—How was the wind? Any prospect of a change? The age of the moon? what progress the ship was making; and that was little enough for many a weary day.

I had almost forgot to mention the grandeur of the Atlantic Ocean in a storm. Although we did not experience what sailors would call a storm, yet for some days the wind blew very hard and the sea ran literally mountains high—every wave like the Broadhill; and then the colour—not the dull green hue of the German Ocean but the deepest clearest blue. On the ridge of every wave just before it breaks into foam the tint is peculiarly rich."[1]

Most studies of early emigrant crossings to British America concentrate on the miseries of sea travel; and there were plenty. Instances of overcrowding, poor ventilation, inadequate supplies of food and contaminated drinking water were frequently reported. But, in judging how well emigrants were served by the men who ran the Atlantic passenger trade, it is necessary to put these problems into a proper context. During the first half of the nineteenth century, travelling by sailing ship was a rough and ready business. In preparing for steerage passengers, shipowners just put down temporary decking in the hold of their vessels and ordered in the carpenters to build some berths along the sides. There were no portholes, nor any means of ventilation beyond the hatches. In stormy seas the hatches could be kept battened down for days:

> "We had one night on the north of Scotland a terrible storm so that the hatches had to be shut and covered with tar cloth like to suffocate us and our helms-man had to be tied to his seat and the most of the passengers fell to crying and praying so that I thought prayer was a new exercise to them. It was only by fear. However, the Lord spared us and gave us a cheerful morning, only the waves were incredibly high like mountains; and no man can understand the glory of this sight but them who saw the same and understand the 107th Psalm aright."[2]

It was not that anyone was being deliberately cruel or irresponsible. Sea travel at this time was primitive. Large numbers of people had to be accommodated in the hold. There was simply no other place to put them. There were other dangers as well:

> "Another curious sight we had, birds to be seen every day on the sea; and also we happened to come through a shoal of whales—perhaps a thousand, spouting out water the height of a tree in the air, and some of them seemed to be as long as our ship and also likely to turn our ship upside down. Came so near us that our captain and some of the men took out their guns to shoot them; and by and by they left us— or we left them without any reluctance.
>
> And we thought then all danger was over, but no, the worst was before us yet. When about the banks of Newfoundland we saw a ship coming from the south and driving towards us our captain said to us 'On deck; That ship must be astray.' Then he sent a boy to put up colours but the other ship gave no sign. Then he said 'It must be a Pirate. I wish I had my cannons.' Then he called all hands and gave all possible speed to our ship and sailed all night, but in the morning the ship was in sight and about the same distance and coming straight after us; and we were that way all day. But at night the captain put more canvas to our ship and we never saw them again and in a few days we were in Pictou; and imme-

diately our captain sent a message to Halifax and a man of war was sent to hunt for them and found them and brought them to their doom."[3]

While bad weather, whales and pirates were difficult to control, over-crowding and inadequate provisioning were quite another matter. Legislation had been in place from 1803 stipulating minimum space and food requirements for passengers on ocean-going vessels. However, in the absence of any regulatory body, the legislation was largely unenforceable and thus it was frequently ignored. Against this backdrop emigrants would be expected to have been at the mercy of unscrupulous shipowners and thuggish captains. But that was not the case. It was the desire for repeat business which kept the ones, who wished to stay in business, in check.

Thus, an emigrant's principal weapon against unsavoury practices was the report he gave others of his travels. A shipowner's desire for a good personal recommendation was far more effective in ensuring that good standards were maintained than legislation. During the first half of the nineteenth century the government tried many times to regulate overseas travel, but its attempts made little practical difference. In the end emigrant travel was transformed for the better, not by legislation, but through the arrival in the 1850s of specialist steamships. Technology combined with capital investment and competition then brought affordable, consumer-friendly services to the masses.

Crucial to an emigrant's assessment of his choice of vessel was the good name of the captain. The long stint of continuous service that many Aberdeen captains had with either the same shipowner and sometimes the same vessel made them highly experienced on Atlantic routes and thus highly prized by emigrants. These captains were like magnets and attracted the bulk of the Atlantic passenger trade. James Oswald is a typical example. Having captained Peter Ritchie's *Cambria, Louisa* and *Mary* on their crossings to Halifax with emigrants, between 1813 and 1821, he then captained John Catto's regular trader, the *Aberdeenshire,* from 1827 to 1835. Taking around 20 passengers from Aberdeen in the Spring and Summer of most years, the *Aberdeenshire* offered a steady and reliable service to Halifax.

Alexander Leslie had an incredibly long association with just one brig—the *Albion*. A regular trader, she operated between Aberdeen and

View of Aberdeen Harbour from the east taken circa 1870. *Copyright George Washington Wilson Collection, Aberdeen University.*

Halifax from 1829 to 1853, taking passengers most years. Leslie's long experience clearly gave him high standing and, on one occasion immediately after the Spring crossing of 1836, his grateful passengers left us this account of the importance of a captain's skill and humanity; it was published in both the *Halifax Journal* and *Aberdeen Journal*:

"We the Cabin passengers of the brig *Albion* of Aberdeen, Alexander Leslie, Master, avail ourselves of the earliest opportunity of expressing through the medium of your respectable paper our unanimous testimony to the unremitted assiduity with which Captain Leslie attended to our comfort during a tedious, stormy passage. While we do not presume that we can add to the character which Captain Leslie has long since earned, and fully established on both sides of the Atlantic; we deem it a debt of gratitude due to him thus publicly to express our approbation of his conduct and we would strongly recommend to emigrants and others crossing the Atlantic to do so by the *Albion*, as from experience we can assure them that under the command of Captain Leslie the greatest care will be paid to their comfort and safety"[4]

The Duthie family employed two very experienced captains in James Elliot who was in charge of the *Brilliant* and *Berbice* and Captain Duncan Walker, who had a long stint of service on the *Hercules* and *Heroine*.[5] A favourable description of Captain Walker's sobriety and other qualities, contained in a personal letter written by one of his passengers, would no doubt be communicated to others. William Shand, having crossed on the *Hercules* in 1834, made no mention of the vessel in his letter; what had really mattered was the captain:

"We had reason to be thankful for we could have been much worse and I believe on the whole it is but rare to be so well—and what contributed a good deal to that was the attention of our captain. It is but justice to Mr. Walker to say that in my opinion there is not a man better adapted for his business than he is—a very clever shrewd man with a good deal of experience and so completely sober that he tastes no drink of any kind no stronger than water and seems to have his thoughts on nothing but his business and the safety of his crew. He acted as surgeon to the whole of them when they were sick, visiting them each day, giving them medicine."[6]

Similarly, William Talbot, who captained the *Lord Seaton,* also won praise from his passengers in this glowing tribute, published in the *Quebec Gazette*. All of the passengers had signed the commendation and each had sent a copy of the letter to their friends and family back home:

"The whole passengers on board the *Lord Seaton* having experienced the greatest kindness and attention from Captain Talbot, during their passage from Aberdeen feel it their duty to make this public acknowledgement of the same, by recommending him to their friends and countrymen, who may be intending to emigrate to America, as a person of much kindness and every way qualified to render all on board comfortable. The *Lord Seaton* is a commodious, fast-sailing and sea-worthy barque, Quebec, 9th September, 1845."[7]

Donaldson Rose also had his favourites. Having several vessels to offer to emigrants, he had three particularly experienced captains. He used John Morrison to captain the *Aimwell* intermittently from 1816 to 1832 and then moved him to the *Pacific* from 1836 to 1844. George Allan captained the *Pilgrim* in the 1830s and from 1839 was moved to the *Sarah,* captaining her for some five years. And on his most successful vessel, the *St. Lawrence,* which took just over 1711 emigrants to Quebec, Rose assigned James Tulloch as captain on each of her yearly crossings from 1842 to 1855. The same captain remained in charge of the same vessel over many years and often owed shares in the vessel he sailed.[8]

Thus, a captain's reputation and expertise were crucial to a shipowner's success in attracting fares from emigrants. Captains had to keep a close eye on their crew and be mindful of their passengers problems and anxieties. The misery of sea sickness afflicted many and cabin passengers were as prone to it as those who travelled in the steerage:

"…Captain Barclay came into the cabin with a forward bustling air and said: 'Aye good folks, we have now got you out at sea and the first thing we are going to do is to starve you,' but continued he: 'I have had such a work to get things in order—the men are nearly all drunk.'…after this, he rang the bell for the cook as we had not the honour of a cabin-boy. He appeared: 'Well, cook, have you boiling water?' 'Yes Sir.' 'Well, good folks, would you chose tea or some fish with bread and butter?'"[9]

Life at sea was basic. A drunken crew had to be brought into line, sea sickness would afflict many and there was the added discomfort of coping with smelly and foul tasting drinking water. Because it was stored for the duration of a journey in crude wooden casks, it soon became contaminated. Emigrants did what they could to counter the water's offensive taste by adding vinegar but often this proved ineffective:

"With respect to myself, I had not one hour's seasickness all the way—but I was seized with a kind of laziness—that I hated to do anything—even to read or write, and a loathing to everything either of meat or drink for the first four weeks…to my perverted taste the sea water itself would have been much more pleasant…the water that we had the first four weeks, being in coarse molasses casks, became so bad in a short time that it was impossible to disguise the taste of it with anything whatever…."[10]

Although many emigrants shared this man's dilemma of not being able to face food, vessels needed to carry sufficient provisions. Most did, but in the face of heated controversy over what constituted appropriate and adequate provisioning. The 1803 Passenger Act, the first attempt at legislation, stipulated the daily requirements of beef, bread, biscuit or oatmeal molasses and water which was to be provided for each passenger.[11] This was done even though it would have widely recognised at the time that beef was of little interest to a great many emigrants. Archibald Buchanan, the Immigration Agent at Quebec spoke out against the ludicrous of policy of requiring shippers to provide food to emigrants, "which they are not in the habit of using." In any case, as he told the Emigration Select Committee of 1826: "Instead of the ship finding provisions, the emigrants prefer to find them themselves."[12]

Thus, minimum daily food limits had little relevance to the large numbers of steerage passengers who actually supplied their own food. Not only could they economise on their fares; they could eat food which they knew would agree with them. Those who had experienced a sea crossing before knew that "if they [emigrants] become a little squeamish they will find that salt beef and biscuit will no go down."[13] So some of the food was neither required nor palatable to most steerage passengers. Shippers like the Leith-based William Allan complained about his extra food costs and the wastefulness of stocking items which were not being eaten, but to no avail.[14] John MacRa, a shipowner from Lochalsh, asked whether emigrants could "substitute such provisions as constitute their food at home which no doubt would better agree with them at sea."[15] He too was turned down. However, by 1828, government policy had moved in the right direction. The 1828 Passenger Act dealt only with minimum quantities of bread, biscuit and oatmeal and by 1842 food requirements met with widespread acceptance.[16] But conditions remained far from perfect and regulations continued to be flouted.[17]

The most contentious issue of all was the space allocation given to steerage passengers. Again it was the Passenger Act of 1803 which first specified a minimum space requirement. The formula allowed one person for every two tons burthen, an allocation which far exceeded earlier limits.[18] Overcrowding had been particularly excessive during the great surges of emigration in the late eighteenth and early nineteenth centuries. Hugh Dunoon, a Scottish-born merchant residing in Pictou, had chartered three vessels in 1801 on behalf of emigrants in the northwest Highlands who wished to sail to Pictou. That year the tiny 72-ton sloop, the *Hope* of Lossie, took 100 people from Isle Martin while the much larger *Dove* of Aberdeen and *Sarah* of Liverpool, took some 570 souls from Fort William to Pictou.[19] The *Dove* had, in fact, been two and one half times over the legal limit defined in the 1803 Act.[20]

The immediate effect of the 1803 Act was to cause fares to go through the roof; the price of a passage more than doubled, rising to as much as £12.[21] It also curbed extreme cases of overcrowding, but because later legislation allowed a weakening of the rules, the effect was short-lived. With the increased interest in emigration, which followed in the wake of the Napoleonic Wars, the government succumbed to pressure from shipowners as well as emigrants to slacken the food and space requirements. So, from 1817, vessels could once again carry less food and more people. The new space limit was one person for every one and a half tons and fares were reduced accordingly.[22]

Predictably, the relaxation of the rules caused some shippers to revert back to the bad old days preceding the 1803 Act. With the deepening economic recession from 1816 and the major agricultural changes which were taking place, large numbers from the Highlands and Islands were seeking a new life overseas. Many were extremely poor and only able to pay for their crossings if they could get the cheapest possible fares. Once again there were instances of severe overcrowding. An example is the 116-ton *Perseverance* of Aberdeen, which travelled from Tobermory to Pictou in

1818 with 150 emigrants. According to the terms of the 1817 Act, she should have taken only 77 people. An even worse case occurred in 1819, when the *Morningfield* of Aberdeen sailed from Tobermory to Pictou and Charlottetown with 264 emigrants.[23] A 141-ton brig, she should only have carried 94 passengers. Peter Ritchie, the *Morningfield's* owner had crammed three times that number into the hold of his brig. Exceeding his vessel's legal space limits was probably the only way in which Ritchie could have attracted these emigrants. The very poor could get a crossing, but only if they were willing to endure cramped conditions. Desperate times and inadequate safeguards produced such results although, in spite of the obvious overcrowding, the emigrants arrived safely.

Most vessels at the time appeared to have travelled within their space restrictions. The 232-ton *Aimwell* of Aberdeen, sailing in 1816 from Aberdeen and Thurso to Halifax with 139 emigrants, the 133-ton *Thistle* of Aberdeen, sailing in 1821 from Tobermory to Pictou and Quebec with 96 emigrants, the 236-ton *Emperor Alexander* of Aberdeen, sailing in 1823 from Tobermory to Cape Breton and Quebec with 160 passengers were each within, or very close to, their legal limits for passenger space allocations.[24] The *Inverness Journal* even published a commendation to Captain Watt the following year for his "humanity" when in charge of the *Emperor Alexander,* together with a list of the heads of families amongst those who had sailed.[25] While suspicions might be raised about the *Economy* of Aberdeen, which sailed in 1819 from Tobermory to Pictou with 285 emigrants, lack of tonnage information makes it difficult to comment. However, the commendation from passengers, published in the *Acadian Reporter,* praising Captain Frazer's "kind treatment" during a five-week passage and the newspaper's observation that "passengers landed in good health and spirits," is very positive feedback and suggests that these emigrants had few complaints over their treatment.[26]

By the early 1820s steerage fares were as low as £3. 4s to £4 for passengers who provided their own food.[27] Regulations were tightened up in 1823, but they were repealed again in 1827 in response to continuing commercial pressures.[28] The passenger to tonnage ratio was set at three passengers for every four tons in 1828 and made slightly more generous in 1835 when it was increased to three passengers for every five tons.[29]

This view is from a painting entitled *Cromarty Bay from the East* by T. Allan and was published in *Scotland Illustrated* by William Beattie, Vol. II, London 1838 (ref.: DA870.B4 [SR] Volume 2). Emigrants from the northeast Highlands boarded ship at Cromarty for Pictou or Quebec from 1814 to 1851. *Photograph courtesy of St. Andrews University Library.*

The numbers of vessels offering passages to emigrants increased sharply during the 1830s, as the numbers wishing to emigrate soared. Some shippers sought to relieve obvious emigrant anxieties of overcrowding by advertising that they were restricting their passenger numbers. Emigrants who boarded the 400-ton *AMI* of Sunderland at Cromarty in 1833 were assured that the owner "will limit the number of steerage to 150" while that same year those leaving from Thurso had a similar guarantee that the 173-ton *Marjory*, a Leith-registered brig, would "be comfortably fitted up for a limited number of passengers." In the end, the *Marjory* only took 24 passengers.[30] And that year Captain Morris was going to be "fitting up a second cabin" in the *Hedleys* of Newcastle, "should that meet the wishes of a sufficient number of passengers, say from 20 to 30." A total of 138 emigrants sailed from Cromarty to Quebec on this 279-ton barque and some presumably travelled in the second cabin.[31]

The introduction of a second cabin gave emigrants access to an intermediate standard of accommodation. They travelled in the hold, along with the other steerage passengers but were allocated far more space and privacy.[32] The *Swift* of Sunderland's second cabin accommodation in 1837 cost 60 shillings compared with the 52 shillings, which an ordinary steerage fare would cost.[33] And by the early 1840s, vessels increasingly offered the choice of both intermediate and steerage accommodation. At this stage, fares from Aberdeen to Quebec ranged from £10 for cabin passengers to £2. 15s (food not provided) in the steerage. [34]

Emigrants, who travelled as steerage passengers, sometimes had to share the ship's hold with other general cargo. This was the case in the 1840 crossing of the *Quebec Packet* of Aberdeen which took 60 emigrants from the northeast Highlands to Quebec.[35] Normally the *Quebec Packet's* passengers would have travelled in a relatively large cabin area; but this was a special case. When her imminent arrival in Cromarty was announced by the *John O'Groat Journal*, the agents acting for John Catto, the brig's owner, were careful to state: "In consequence of her being principally laden with goods, the subscribers can only take a limited number of passengers."[36] Regulations governing the combined use of a hold by both people and goods were at best vague: "When the ship carries the full number of passengers allowed by law, no part of the cargo and no stores or provisions may be carried between decks: but if there be less than the complete number of passengers, goods may be stowed between decks in a proportion not exceeding three cubical feet for each passenger wanting of the highest number."[37] Thus, being just sixty in number in a 196-ton brig did not guarantee a generous allocation of space within the hold.

The mounting poverty in the Highlands throughout the 1840s had been a factor in the rising numbers who sought passages to Pictou and Quebec. Poverty could increase susceptibility to disease. Typhus struck during the 1841 crossing of the *Lady Grey* of North Shields in 1841. Having collected a total of 240 emigrants at Cromarty and Thurso, the 285-ton snow sailed into Pictou harbour as the disease was spreading. Of course epidemics advance more rampantly when people are crowded together in cramped conditions. There had clearly been serious overcrowding on the *Lady Grey's* crossing. The passenger to tonnage ratio was woefully over the limit, given that, at the time, the legal limit was five tons for every three passengers. There were six deaths and to the consternation of Pictou's residents a long period elapsed before the typhus epidemic was finally quelled.

A similar outbreak occurred in 1843 just before the *George* of Dundee's arrival in Pictou. Long delays caused by three port calls at Cromarty, Thurso and Loch Laxford to collect passengers had exacerbated an already difficult situation. Described on her arrival by a Pictou inhabitant as "a floating pest-house," the *George* anchored at the quarantine ground with "malignant fever and dysentery on board." Emigrants were immediately taken to beaches where they stayed until a temporary building was constructed to accommodate them. Again, it was a long time before the quarantine regulations could be relaxed and Pictou could be declared free of disease.[38] But while horrific instances of suffering through disease did occur, they were rare occurrences. There were only these two cases reported for crossings from the northeast Highlands, while there was one instance of disease in an 1855 crossing from Aberdeen to Quebec. In that crossing, which was on the *St. Lawrence*, disease took the lives of three passengers, one of whom travelled in the cabin. Thirty-nine people were admitted to a quarantine hospital while the master and four crew received their treatment separately in a Maritime Hospital.[39]

Another important factor which could influence levels of comfort on board ship was the floor-to-ceiling space allocated to passengers in the hold. Before 1842 the only stipulation was that "ships are not allowed to carry passengers to the Colonies unless they be of the height of five and a half between decks."[40] Emigrants had to wait until 1842 before the minimum legal limit was increased to six feet although many Aberdeen vessels provided this amount of space long before then.[41] William Duthie's two former whaling vessels, the *Hercules* built in 1781 offered six feet three inches while the *Brilliant*, built in 1814, had six feet between decks. The *Pacific*, built in 1826, with six feet nine inches, the *Augusta*, built in 1828, with five feet, eleven inches, the *Sir William Wallace*, built in 1835, with six feet, ten inches were all well ahead of their time as was the *Circassian*, built in 1835, which offered seven feet.[42]

The move to larger and speedier vessels during the 1840s was accompanied by general improvements in passenger accommodation. In came a new generation of ships and barques which normally offered at least six feet between decks. Emigrants leaving Aberdeen could choose between the *St. Lawrence*, a 352-ton barque built by Walter Hood, the *Renown*, a 311-ton barque built at Alexander Duthie's shipyard, the *Aurora*, a 709-ton ship built in Miramichi, New Brunswick, and the *Berbice*, a 340-ton barque also constructed at Miramichi. Each had the sleeker lines of the latest hull designs, thereby offering good journey times and a height between decks which was often as much as seven feet.[43]

The final observations concern the vessels themselves. Certainly it is known that emigrants sometimes travelled in cramped conditions and had to endure many discomforts. One obvious way in which shipowners could have cut their costs is by offering poor quality vessels. But had they done so, they would have had no repeat business. Because emigrants were in such demand, competition between shippers worked in the emigrants' favour. The evidence collected is conclusive. Without doubt, far from being offered the worst in shipping, they were offered the best.

Fortunately, details of the quality of construction and condition of the Aberdeen vessels used in the Atlantic passenger trade can be obtained from the *Lloyd's Shipping Register*.[44] As major insurers, Lloyd's needed reliable shipping intelligence, which it procured through the use of paid agents in the main ports in Britain and abroad. Whether they insured their ships with Lloyd's or not, shipowners wishing to attract cargoes offered their vessels for inspection to Lloyd's surveyors. After a thorough survey, a vessel was assigned a shipping classification which categorized it according to the quality of its construction and materials used, as well as its condition and age.[45]

The classifications had high commercial significance to both insurers and shipowners. An honest and open inspection was vital to the insurer's risk assessment, and the shipowner's ability to attract profitable trade hinged on the survey results. Shipowners actually criticized the system for being too stringent, particularly in the way a ship's age and place of construction could affect its classification.[46] The maritime community consisted of commercially minded people and ship classification codes are their legacy. They give unequivocal evidence that the vessels which carried emigrants to British America were at the top-to-better end of the available shipping market.[47]

Table 4 gives the Lloyd's shipping classifications for the forty-four Aberdeen vessels which featured in Aberdeen's Atlantic passenger trade from 1800 to 1855. While over one hundred vessels carried some emigrants from Aberdeen to British America, these forty-four were the ones which got the repeat business or had fairly large numbers of emigrants sailing in single crossings. Many of the remainder carried small numbers of people and often only made one or two Atlantic crossings with passengers. This select group of forty-four vessels included fifteen brigs, eleven snows, twelve barques, three ships and a single clipper.

Eight are without classifications.[48] Thirty of the remaining thirty-six vessels had a first class ranking, having "A" or "AE" classifications.[49] The "AE" vessels had no defects but their age at the time of sailing, or the fact that they had been built in British America, placed them at the lower end of the first class ranking. Six vessels had an "E," or second class ranking. Although perfectly seaworthy, they had minor defects. Thus, most of the Aberdeen vessels involved in the Atlantic passenger trade were of high quality. Emigrants had access to some of the best shipping available at the time and, when including all of the vessels covered in this study it can be documented that none was unsound or unsafe, and most had "A" or "AE" rankings (Appendix).

Emigrant Scots generally crossed the Atlantic in good ships under the helm of experienced captains. Most shipowners ran their passenger services on a long-term basis. The successful ones maintained repeat business over many years because they offered a sound and reliable service. It was no picnic being cooped up in a ship's hold for four to six weeks, particularly during long stormy periods when the hatches had to be kept shut. In time, greater speed, comfort and safety would come from the large specialist steamships which became available from the mid-1850s at large ports like Glasgow and Liverpool. Before then it was mainly a case of putting one's faith in the good Lord and the captain's navigational skills. But when the question is raised as to whether emigrants crossing the Atlantic from Scotland in the first half of the nineteenth century generally travelled on the best shipping available at the time, the answer is an overwhelming yes.

Attention is next to be given to the first Aberdeen ship arrivals at their destinations in New Brunswick and Nova Scotia and then to the second wave of emigrants as they travel much further westwards, deep into the inland regions of Upper Canada. Upper Canada attracted a good many settlers from 1830. This was the second time that a surge in emigration to British America had claimed people from the northeast of Scotland. It had happened once before, in the late eighteenth century, but on a much smaller scale, when the timber-producing areas of the eastern Maritimes first began to attract emigrants.

VIII. NEW BRUNSWICK AND NOVA SCOTIA SETTLEMENTS

"Miramichi was settled as early as 1784 by a number of people chiefly from Speyside and being desirous of a minister according to the principles of that Church in which they first learned to lisp their prayers and accordingly they obtained a Mr. Frazer who had been a chaplain in one of the Regiments during the American War but owing to some misconduct he soon left them.... About 1802 a Mr. Urquhart, who had settled in the States and was then in Prince Edward Island came to visit Miramichi and having received a call from them became their Minister. In Mr. Urquhart's time there were two places of worship, one in the body of the river and the other about 10 miles higher up just on the point where the river divides into two branches [close to Newcastle]. He preached at these places alternately and the largest Assembly was at the Point Church."[1]

The Point Church was deserted when Reverend Thomson made these observations in 1826, in spite of a threefold increase in the local population. The initial influx of settlers from Speyside to this part of New Brunswick had not attracted follow-on interest from friends and family back in the northeast of Scotland. By 1826 they were a minority and it was the Irish population which was rapidly expanding.

Scots had been some of the earliest settlers in the Maritimes. Arriving sooner than their English and Irish counterparts, they dominated the timber-producing areas of the eastern Maritimes from the late eighteenth century. The many Scottish communities which emerged in northeastern Nova Scotia and in Cape Breton and Prince Edward Island, reflect the efforts of these early colonizers during the region's formative years (Figure 4). The consolidation of Scottish timber trade interests can also be seen in the Miramichi region of New Brunswick, beginning from the late eighteenth century with the steady drift of ex-soldiers and civilians into the region. Scottish colonization also played a major role in the initial development of the Restigouche trade to the north of the Miramichi, which was underway from the 1830s.[2]

Reverend Thomson actually had been speaking from the very heart of the hugely important Miramichi timber industry. He was in Beaubears Island, a place settled first by the French and which could trace its Scottish roots back to 1765.[3] This was the year when two men from the northeast of Scotland first came to the region. With their acquisition of 100,000 acres of crown land on either side of the Miramichi River, the Morayshire-born William Davidson and the Aberdeen-born John Cort obtained sole rights to a fishery and vast reserves of timber. By 1785, two other Scots, James Fraser, from Dores (Inverness-shire) and James Thom had moved into the area, establishing a major sawmill and shipbuilding centre at Beaubears Island. Taking over some of William Davidson's timber ventures following his death in 1790, their business rapidly expanded and soon they controlled all trade on the Miramichi River from their headquarters at Beaubears Island.[4]

One of the conditions of William Davidson's grant of land from the government was that he should encourage settlement. He, in fact, initially brought out only craftsmen, employing them in his fishery, shipyard and sawmill until they were able to establish themselves on the land. Davidson's recruits would thus have contributed to the steady progression of settlement along the Miramichi River and its tributaries.[5] They may even have been included amongst the passengers who travelled on the *Mercury* that year, boarding ship when she called at Portsoy, near Banff on her way to Halifax and Port Roseway, Nova Scotia.[6] Thus, the early influx of Speysiders to the Miramichi area may have been due to William Davidson. After all, as a Morayshire man, it is reasonable to expect him to have looked for potential settlers in the northeast of Scotland.

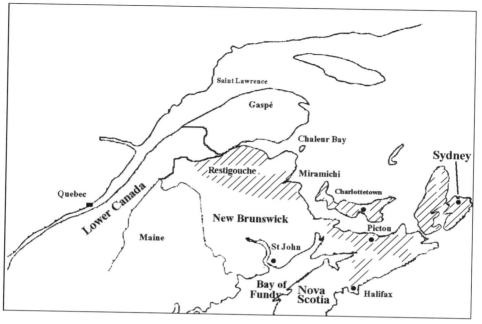

Figure 4. Concentration of Scottish Settlers in the Maritimes, 1851–71. (Based on census data.)

There are other possibilities. Following the ending of the American War of Independence in 1785, there was a huge influx of Loyalists into New Brunswick, with most settling in the Saint John River area around the Bay of Fundy. But a good many, who were of Scottish origin, did not stay but instead moved up river to the Miramichi settlements. Certainly, church ministers and shipping records tell us that people from Banffshire, Morayshire and Nairnshire had emigrated to North America a short time before the American War.[7] In May 1775, about two hundred people were reported to have gathered at Aviemore to march together to Greenock where they were to board ship for North America.[8] Most went to the southern colonies, with many ending up in New York or Philadelphia.[9] And, after the war, it might be that some of them re-established themselves as Loyalists in the Miramichi region.

After William Davidson and John Cort acquired their land in 1765, timber felling proceeded at a rapid pace. Scots were the first to colonize the shores of the Miramichi River. From 1785, as their numbers increased, Scots began a steady progression of settlements along the Miramichi and its tributaries and were joined later by Irish and English immigrants. The result was small pockets of scattered farms and timber-felling centres dotted throughout the inland and coastal areas of Northumberland County. By the early 1800s, a group of Ayrshire settlers, led by Robert Doak, established a substantial farming and lumbering centre at Doaktown, situated some 50 miles from the mouth of the Miramichi River. Blackville, just above it, was also founded by Scots and Loyalists who had moved up river from Saint John. James Fraser's company continued to thrive at Beaubears Island. In 1830, Peter Clyde, a Scottish-born surveyor, complained of being "bothered with so much timber and lumber of one kind and another that when we fairly embark into the business it is almost impossible to get away from it again."[10]

The neighbouring towns of Chatham and Newcastle, at the mouth of the Miramichi River, which were settled before 1785, principally by Scots, grew rapidly. They had large Loyalist populations, and initial settlers included disbanded members of the 42nd Highlanders who had moved from their previous holdings near Fredericton along the Nashwaak River. The Glasgow merchants, Pollock, Gilmour and Company opened up the Miramichi branch of their company in 1812. Situated on the north side of the river, halfway between Chatham and Newcastle, the firm, under Alexander Rankin's direction, soon controlled timber operations on the Miramichi River. The company rapidly became the major employer on the river's northern bank. By the 1820s both places acquired large Irish populations, while Chatham received a contingent of Annandale emigrants in 1822. A visiting Presbyterian minister found a thriving Church of Scotland congregation in Newcastle in 1833, but expressed concern at the absence of churches along the 70 mile stretch of the southwest branch of the Miramichi River.[11]

Highlanders also found their way to Northumberland County, forming a group of settlements along both sides of Miramichi Bay. Highland Catholics, who established a major foothold in Prince Edward Island in the 1770s, crossed the Northumberland Strait sometime before 1812 and formed the small settlement of Bartibog on the north side of Miramichi

Lumberers on the Miramichi, New Brunswick, c. 1855. A watercolour by James Fox Bland. *New Brunswick Museum, Saint John, N.B., Canada.*

Bay. They were led by Captain John MacDonald of Glenaladale, the same man who had led the 214 Catholic Highlanders and Islanders to Scotch-fort in 1772. Ex-servicemen from the 78th Highlanders settled Black River from 1790, while Tabusintac was established, from 1798, by Scottish and Irish settlers and Bay du Vin from 1786 by Loyalists. When the Presbyterian missionary visited the area in 1833, he found many Gaelic-speaking Scots, describing them as being "mostly settled for 60 years."[12]

But the Miramichi's attractions to people from the northeast of Scotland were short-lived. Angus Stewart's 1816 advertisement in the *Aberdeen Journal,* of his extensive lands on the northwest branch of the Miramichi River with "excellent salmon fishing," is a small reminder of the past but there is little else which survives.[13] Aberdeen ships did bring people to the area for a few years starting from 1815, just as the Napoleonic Wars were ending, but the numbers were never more than a trickle (Table 1). The settlers had come as individual families and small groups. They settled where the land and timber opportunities took them and were thus quickly dispersed.

It was similar story for the families of the Aberdeen fishermen who were first to settle at Campbellton in the Restigouche region of New Brunswick. Arriving in 1700, they established a salmon fishery on the Restigouche River and soon attracted others to join them. Purchasing the fishery in 1780, Henry Lee, an Aberdonian, brought out additional Aberdeen settlers, thus re-enforcing the links between Aberdeen and Campbellton.[14] They were joined by a few Loyalists and another wave of Scottish immigrants after 1796. But, however strong the original Aberdeen links may have been, they too were short-lived. Even with the rapid growth of the Restigouche timber industry from the mid-1820s, few Aberdeenshire settlers came to the region.[15]

The Reverend Christopher Atkinson had worked harder than most to convince his fellow Scots of New Brunswick's many attractions. He had left Scotland in 1838 to work as a minister at a salary of £100 per annum in Mascreen, a settlement near Saint John. Presiding over a thriving Presbyterian congregation established by settlers from Perthshire, Sutherland and Caithness, he returned home after three years as their minister. Blaming his departure on the area's inability to support a minister, he regretted having to leave his church before it had been fully completed. On his return, he wrote an extensive account of the prospects which he thought New Brunswick had to offer but to no avail.[16] Having lived for a time amongst fellow Scots, the Reverend Atkinson would be expected to be a highly credible advocate for New Brunswick. But Upper Canada's growing economic opportunities and better climate were drawing most emigrants and, by the time he had written his book, a steady migration of settlers from New Brunswick to Upper Canada was well underway.

However, Aberdeen's associations with New Brunswick did resume again in 1860–1861. Land schemes, offered by the provincial government in the still uncleared regions to the west, along the border with Maine, attracted large numbers from Aberdeen and the surrounding area. Some thirty families from Aberdeen colonized Glassville in Carleton County and, ten years later, large numbers from Kincardineshire, principally Stonehaven, established a "Scotch Colony" close by in Victoria County.[17] These settlements were the product of large-scale government-sponsored recruitment campaigns designed to turn thousands of acres of wilderness into farm-based communities. They were quite unlike the late eighteenth and early nineteenth century influx of individuals and small groups who following their entrepreneurial instincts to timber-producing areas in search of work and land. Their numbers were small and, in spite of early Scottish economic dominance, it would be the Irish, not Scottish settlers, who would come to dominate the regions first opened up by the timber trade.[18]

Nova Scotia's connections with the northeast of Scotland followed a similar pattern. While eastern Nova Scotia obtained a great deal of its early economic impetus and capital investment from men who had originated from the north of Scotland, particularly Banffshire, few of its settlers came from this region. The Keith-born Edward Mortimer had come to Halifax in the late 1780s, a time when Scottish businessmen were arriving in large numbers to take advantage its growing commercial opportunities. Mortimer acquired huge land holdings in Pictou, and through his continued association with William Liddell, a Glasgow merchant, he became the region's leading timber merchant.[19] With his many mercantile interests which extended into coal mining and fishing, Mortimer and his business partner, George Smith, from Banff, had considerable influence over the economic life of Pictou.[20] The Aberdeen-born John Black had also been particularly successful. Establishing a vast shipping and trading empire by 1804, he dominated the commercial life of Saint John and became one of Halifax's top merchants.[21] He even had a fine mansion built for himself in Halifax using granite brought out in his own ships directly from Aberdeen. Then there was James Dawson, from Banff, who had extensive interests in shipbuilding and traded with the West Indies.[22] And yet, in spite of their economic domination of the region's commercial life, these men enticed few of their countrymen to join them.

In fact, most of the early Scottish influx to Nova Scotia and Cape Breton had been from the Highlands and Islands. After a shambolic and at times distressing beginning, successive waves of emigrants turned the eastern mainland of Nova Scotia and most of Cape Breton into an enormous Scottish enclave.[23] A decade after the arrival of the *Hector* in 1773, Scots had penetrated the wilderness around Pictou Harbour and its river frontages and were moving east along the coast to Merigomish and Barney's River. They would be joined in 1784 by former members of the Royal Highland

Emigrant Regiment and the Hamilton Regiment, as well as by successive waves of emigrants from Sutherland, Ross-shire, Inverness-shire and Perthshire who began arriving in large numbers from 1791. By 1805 Scots had laid claim to vast swathes of Pictou County and much of Antigonish County to the east. They had moved westwards from Pictou into Colchester County and had moved beyond Colchester into Cumberland County with their major settlement at Wallace.[24] And by 1816, large numbers of Dumfries-shire emigrants were clearing land at New Annan, in Colchester County and at Dalhousie Mountain, in Pictou County.[25]

But it was Sutherland who was to develop the strongest and most enduring links with eastern Nova Scotia. The upheaval and uncertainties caused by the introduction of sheep farms, begun in the early 1800s, led many of the tenants on the Sutherland estate to seek their livelihood abroad.[26] In 1803, around 200 Sutherland emigrants settled *en masse* at New Lairg in Pictou County and were joined, a few years later, by others from the parishes of Lairg, Assynt and Rogart.[27] These were the tenants who had rejected their estate managers' plans to relocate them to new coastal communities. At this time there was no question of force being used to make them leave. Quite the contrary. If these Rogart tenants were typical, it seems that strenuous efforts were being made to convince the Sutherland tenantry to stay:

"I really cannot account for the emigration from Rogart—there is not a man has been dislocated but with a view to make him better and that in place of having his land in run ridge it may now be in a lot on a 19 year lease."[28]

But they left and did so "under favourable circumstances," paying the cost of their passages by selling their cattle "which then got extraordinary prices."[29] Once the Napoleonic Wars ended in 1815, other groups from Farr, Eddrachilles, Lairg, Rogart and Assynt arrived in Nova Scotia and they kept coming until the mid-1820s.[30] However, the 360 or so who emigrated in 1821–1822 were not so fortunate as those who left earlier, having to rely on "the liberal subscriptions made in foreign places" in order to finance their relocation costs.[31]

So this exodus from the Sutherland estate helps to explain the sudden increase in the numbers of Atlantic-bound vessels calling for passengers at Cromarty and Thurso (Table 3). Aberdeen and other east coast ships, on their way north to the Pentland Firth, had made only a slight diversion to collect them. And after taking emigrants to Pictou or Halifax, vessels like the *Perseverance,* the *Aimwell* and *Harmony* returned to Aberdeen with their timber cargoes.[32] Thus, the combination of unrest on the Sutherland estate together with the new transport facilities made possible by the burgeoning timber trade fuelled this sizeable and sustained influx of Sutherland emigrants to eastern Nova Scotia.

Successive waves of Sutherlanders settled at New Lairg and other sites in West Pictou. However, by 1820 new arrivals had to look further afield for land. Because all of the "land adjacent to towns and sea coasts" had been granted, emigrants had to take the uncleared land being offered for sale in outlying areas.[33] Consequently, by 1825 some sixty Sutherland families were living in "a remote place about 30 miles from Pictou" called Earltown in Colchester County.[34] In spite of its remoteness Earltown prospered, and by 1832 its 120 Sutherland families were petitioning the Glasgow Colonial Society for a Presbyterian Minister:

"To any person who knows the north of Scotland, Earlton with it some hundred and twenty families from Sutherland must be an interesting sight. They are settlers of about thirteen years standing—well versed in the prominent doctrines of the bible and require a Minister of no ordinary qualifications."[35]

Sutherland emigrants also founded another settlement at St. Anns, Cape Breton. Established in 1820, it was settled initially by Sutherlanders who, at the time, were living in Pictou. Led by Norman MacLeod, a charismatic Presbyterian minister from Assynt, the group had left Pictou after residing there for just two to three years. The pursuit of a newly available tract of land sparked this migration, and it also attracted a further wave of emigrants directly from Sutherland.[36] The 1836 arrivals on the *Albion* of Scarborough, described in Norman MacLeod's petition as "104 improvident emigrants from the Highlands of Scotland," re-enforced Sutherland's already strong

Tombstones for Alexander Sutherland and his wife Margaret McLeod, and for Hugh Sutherland, which lie in a cemetery near Widow Point close to Pictou, Nova Scotia. Both men are described as "natives of Sutherland" and both died in their 50s. Pictou and Colchester counties attracted particularly large numbers of emigrants from Sutherland during the late eighteenth and early nineteenth centuries. *Photograph by I.G. Campey.*

links with St. Anns. Judging from the eight-day period set aside to embark passengers at Loch Eriboll, we can conclude that most of them originated from scattered communities in Assynt and other areas of west Sutherland.[37]

But were they improvident or just very poor? Economic conditions in west Sutherland were dire and deteriorating. That had clearly been a factor in their decision to emigrate. But in choosing Cape Breton these Sutherland emigrants had gone against the trend. By this time Upper Canada, with its better climate, land quality and job prospects, had far more to offer and it was therefore the preferred choice of most Scots. But these emigrants were unusual in having a large number of their own people already settled in St. Anns. It was a home from home for Assynt emigrants and it promised cultural and lifestyle advantages which they could not get in Upper Canada. Eastern Nova Scotia attracted further Sutherland emigrants in the early 1840s. Originating from Assynt, Eddrachilles, Farr and Tongue, they received help in financing their travel costs from the Duke of Sutherland.[38] So did the tenantry from Eddrachilles and Assynt when these areas were partially cleared of their population during the Great Highland Famine of the late 1840s and early 1850s. Although most went to Upper Canada, 117 Eddrachilles tenants arrived in Pictou in 1847, and a further 154 tenants from Eddrachilles and Assynt arrived in 1848.[39]

When Highlanders from northeast Scotland emigrated to eastern Nova Scotia whole communities were relocated. This is in stark contrast to the short-lived influx of individuals and small groups from Aberdeenshire which occurred between 1811 and 1820 (Table 1).[40] Throughout this period a total of nine hundred or so emigrants left the port of Aberdeen for either Halifax or Pictou. But given that Aberdeenshire's maritime links were strongest in New Brunswick, the possibility that Halifax was simply a stepping stone to Saint John which was a relatively short distance to the west in the Bay of Fundy, cannot be ruled out.

Halifax attracted a little more interest in the 1830s, a time when the northeast of Scotland was losing people to emigration, although mainly to Upper Canada. But even then there is little knowledge of final destinations, nor can it be ascertained with certainty that all those who sailed to Halifax from Aberdeen actually remained in Nova Scotia. As the owners of the *Albion* were often keen to point out, Halifax offered good access to the United States—"there being regular conveyances thither from Halifax and the distance only about two days sailing."[41]

We can only speculate about final destinations. Some Aberdeenshire arrivals might have been drawn to Pictou County, the favoured choice of many Presbyterian Lowlanders.[42] Although much of Pictou's best land had been taken up by 1805, there was still plenty of good land left after 1815. Those who arrived at this stage may have joined the many Dumfriesshire settlers at the newly-formed Dalhousie Settlement, a short distance from Pictou harbour.[43] It was after all a large settlement, where the people "were principally Scotch, and as soon as they found themselves comfortably there, they added to their number by inducing their friends in Scotland to come out to them."[44] Perhaps the 84 people who travelled on the *Earl of Dalhousie* of Aberdeen and the *Louisa* of Aberdeen in 1818 were actually on their way to this settlement.[45] But this is just conjecture.

The fact is that the northeast of Scotland did not establish a home from home in the eastern Maritimes. Unlike so many of the early Highland colonizers who ultimately drew whole communities to their new locations, and effectively transplanted their culture and values, Aberdeenshire settlers dispersed and settled in mixed communities.

It was only when the economic and farming opportunities available in Upper Canada became known, that Aberdeenshire people decided to relocate themselves in Upper Nichol township. Then there was no mistaking their determination to move a part of Aberdeenshire to Upper Canada. Acquiring their land in 1833 and naming their site "Bon Accord," to commemorate their Aberdeenshire roots, they soon had a thriving community which, in just two years' time, was building its first Presbyterian Church.

IX. SETTLEMENTS IN WESTERN UPPER CANADA

"This part of the country is fast filling up, almost entirely with Scotch-men, many of whom are from Aberdeenshire. Within these two weeks, nearly a dozen families have settled beside us, all 'frae the North'.... You would be astonished as I was, if you saw the very respectable class of set-tlers between this and Fergus. There are of them who at home, would be moving into the first class of provincial society. I dined at Fergus lately with the St. Andrew Society and became a member. There were forty of us all Scotchmen, except one Englishman."[1]

It was Bon Accord and Fergus, in Upper Nichol township, Wellington County, which were "fast filling up," and with some very pre-eminent people. Located in western Upper Canada, both settlements offered excellent land and favourable business opportunities. These Aberdeenshire emigrants had chosen one of Upper Canada's prime locations. Centrally placed, their settlements were equidistant from Lake Ontario, Georgian Bay, Lake Huron and not much further from Lake Erie. And they were close to the growing population centres which were forming along the Grand River, a short distance to the west of Guelph. What was more, their location reminded them of home:

"Instead of that uniform flatness so common in Canada, and so for-eign to the eye of Scotsmen, you have here, now and then, a fine undu-lating country, intersected by numerous streams of the purest water."[2]

Hon. Adam Fergusson from Perthshire and James Webster
from Angus together purchased 7,367 acres in Nichol
township in 1833. The settlement of Fergus took shape
from 1834, attracting emigrants from Perthshire, the southern Lowlands and Aberdeenshire. This painting is by John
W. L. Foster. *Presented by the Grandsons, G. Tower Fergusson
and Robert G. B. Fergusson. University of Guelph Collection.*

In spite of its fertile land and good climate, western Upper Canada was
a late developer. Its vast tracts of fertile land to the west of Lake Ontario
only became readily accessible to colonizers after new roads and water-
ways were in place to provide inland routes from the St. Lawrence ports
of Quebec and Montreal. And as better water and road communications
became available from the 1820s, Upper Canada quickly overtook the
Maritimes as the preferred destination of most Scots. Another important

factor was the creation of the Canada Company in 1826. It encouraged the colonization of the so-called Huron Tract, just to the east of Lake Huron, through capital investment in roads, bridges and buildings, attracting those who otherwise would have balked at the prospect of chancing their luck in such a remote part of western Upper Canada.[3]

Lying to the east within the Huron Tract, Fergus and Bon Accord were not quite so far west, but getting to them was still a considerable undertaking. The seven-hundred-mile journey was both gruelling and expensive and, coming as it did after a long sea voyage, it gave emigrants the toughest of beginnings. They took steamers from Quebec to Montreal and, because stretches of the St. Lawrence River from Montreal were not navigable, they had to transfer to large Durham boats which were dragged upriver to Prescott; they then went from Prescott by steamer up the St. Lawrence to Lake Ontario, travelling westward on to Hamilton where they disembarked:

"The Durham Boats were a slow means of conveyance. It took a fortnight to make the trip from Montreal to Hamilton. At the various rapids all the passengers, except the infirm or sick had to get out and walk up the shore, the men carrying the smaller children. The [Durham] boats were then drawn by ropes or pushed with poles against the stream."[4]

Emigrants could have halved their journey time to Hamilton by taking road transport from Montreal to Prescott, but this would have cost nearly six times the amount payable when the entire journey was made by river.[5] Guelph lay ahead and it was approached by wagon:

"My next stage was to get to Guelph a rising city 30 miles further on in the woods....As good luck would have it I learned at breakfast that an open waggon was to start immediately for the city of the woods and that the driver was happy to take me there for a consideration....We started between eight and nine o'clock and got on about the usual Mail Coach rate of 3 miles an hour over roads that it was impossible for them to be worse....As bad luck would have it we had not proceeded above 2 to 3 miles when the driver (cautious man) miscalculating the height

Reverend Dr. Patrick Bell spent 1835–1837 in Fergus, Upper Canada, working as a tutor to the children of Adam Fergusson. Bell had already invented his reaping machine and took a version of it with him to Upper Canada. *Wellington County Museum and Archives, Fergus Ontario. Photo No 11375.*

of a stump by his eye, in endeavouring to avoid a perfect quagmire, drove so that the stump passed between the horses…caught the front axle—smash it went and down came we, wagon and all, in the middle of a forest without the least prospect of moving a foot further that night.

"In a short time the night became pitch dark and this road being full of stumps, we were every moment in bodily fear….With a determined stubbornness to get on we borrowed a lantern at the first house we came to and pursued our journey in the following order. My fellow traveller, not having paid full fare, was fixed upon to carry the

BELL'S IMPROVED REAPING MACHINE BY CROSSKILL
¼ of the full size
Blackie & Son, Glasgow, Edinburgh, & London.

It was the Reverend Dr. Patrick Bell who invented the world's first practical mechanized reaping machine. Living for about four years in Fergus, Upper Canada, he returned home to Forfarshire. He received no financial reward for his invention other than a £1000 prize from the Highland & Agricultural Society of Scotland, given to him in 1867, two years before his death. Engraving by J.W. Lowry. *Reproduced by permission of NMPFT/Science and Society Picture Library, Science Museum, London, U.K.*

lantern a few yards before the horses and when he came to a stump he called out and assisted us by his light to get past it. In this way we got on for a few miles like a snail at the gallop when bad luck again—a puff of wind put out the candle…our unfortunate lantern carrier therefore actually felt the road with his stick until we arrived at a house where we got our candle lighted—after which he took his advanced station as formerly and in this manner we reached Guelph between eleven and twelve o'clock without further incident."[6]

Thus did the Reverend Patrick Bell make his entrance to Guelph in April 1834, walking the final twenty mile distance to Fergus "without the trace of a man's foot" to guide him.[7] He had come to Fergus, in Upper

Nichol township, to take up his position as a tutor to the Hon. Adam Fergusson's children. At this time the Fergus settlement was barely a year old, having been founded in 1833, by the Perthshire-born Fergusson and James Webster from Angus, who together purchased the 7,367 acre site.[8] Bell was not best pleased with the conditions he had encountered and, although he wrote with great warmth of the people he encountered in his travels, he clearly did not approve of some aspects of pioneer life. He had little time for people who considered "themselves the first in the land" yet would only "be called middle class at home" and the "unmarried mechanics...[who] are to be seen hanging about the taverns and boarding houses."[9] Returning to his native Forfar in Angus, after three years in Fergus, he resumed his duties as a church minister.[10]

The initial spark behind the first influx to Fergus was the highly favourable account given by the influential Adam Fergusson. A prominent agriculturalist in Scotland, the publication of his *Practical Notes made during a tour in Canada...in 1831* struck a chord with many Scottish farmers who read of the many opportunities to be realized in western Upper Canada:

"And now comes the important question for individual considerations. Is emigration expedient? This must be decided by circumstances and every man must judge for himself. Of this however I think there can be no doubt that either the moderate capitalist or the frugal sober and industrious labourer or artisan cannot fail of success. Fortunes will not be rapidly or even readily acquired; but it must be the settlers' own fault if he does not enjoy in large abundance every solid comfort and enjoyment of life."[11]

Given that Fergusson's publication came out at a time of falling economic and agricultural prospects in Scotland, its impact was profound. Much of the initial response came from Perthshire, Fergusson's home county, and from Aberdeenshire, where his wife's had family connections.[12]

Meanwhile, groups of people in Aberdeenshire were rapidly coming round to the view that they should establish their own distinctive "Aberdeenshire Colony" in western Upper Canada. George Elmslie, an Aberdeen merchant, travelled to Fergus in the Autumn of 1834, on behalf of many others with the intention of purchasing a large tract of land from

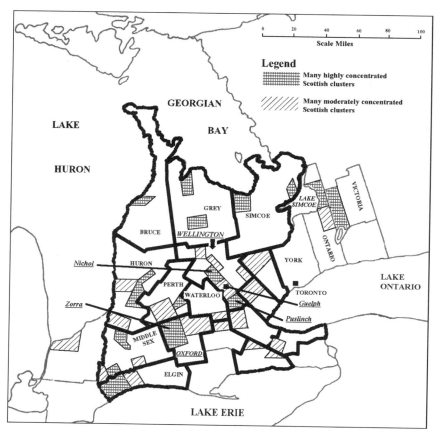

Figure 5. Concentration of Scottish-born settlers in Western Upper Canada, 1851.
Source: Brunger, A. G. The Distribution of Scots and Irish in Upper Canada 1851–71 in Can Geogr. Vol 34 (1990) pp. 250–58.

Adam Fergusson. But because so much of Fergusson's land had already been sold, he opted instead for a 1,200 acre site a short distance to the west of Fergus on the Irvine River.[13] Joining forces with his friend Alexander Watt, also from Aberdeenshire, Elmslie purchased the land and in less than a year the "Bon Accord" settlement had materialized. Very much an Aberdeenshire colony, it took its name from the motto on its native city's Coat of Arms.[14]

While Aberdeenshire emigrants stamped their identity very strongly on Bon Accord, they had also colonized other areas. Arriving in Upper Nichol township from 1831, even before Bon Accord had been founded, they settled in Elora, only a short distance to the southeast of it.[15] Possibly New Aberdeen, located to the south, near Berlin (Kitchener), provides evidence of a further influx of Aberdeenshire emigrants.[16] And, in 1835, some "respectable" Aberdeenshire farmers, "possessing considerable capital" considered and rejected the possibility of settling in the Eastern Townships.[17] But the main exodus was to Upper Nichol. Thus, in the mid-to-late 1830s, when passenger numbers from Scottish ports to British American ports were plummeting, the port of Aberdeen experienced an unprecedented growth in its numbers. While less than 100 people had left for Quebec between 1821 and 1830, nearly 1,700 sailed there in the period from 1831 to 1840 (Figure 1). Aberdeen's figures reached an all time peak of nearly 700 in 1836. However, numbers declined sharply the following year with the outbreak of Rebellions in Upper Canada. Although the Rebellions were a manifestation of widespread discontent, this dissent was quickly suppressed and emigration levels recovered their earlier fervour from 1841.[18]

The worsening economic conditions of the late 1840s brought even more emigrants and by 1848 Bon Accord had nearly doubled in size to 3,000 acres.[19] And by 1852 great numbers were reported to be leaving for Upper Canada "on timber-trading ships."[20] The Immigration Agent at Quebec often noted their "easy circumstances" as Aberdeenshire emigrants proceeded on their way to their settlements in Upper Canada.[21] He would comment on the "respectable body of passengers," who were "amply provided" with the means to get to their destinations or "the highly respectable farmers" with "considerable capital," and always they were heading west.[22] But some came too amply provided, taking out heavy equipment that eventually proved useless.[23]

Aberdeen ironmongers had certainly been keen to sell their goods to emigrants. Newspapers published long lists of kettles, basins, scythes, shovels, spades, camp ovens, percussion guns and fire irons which could be purchased. This was a new business opportunity for local ironmongers. Thomas Melville of 106 Gallowgate offered stocks of "his own manufacture which are well known in British America for their superiority." But as settler dissatisfaction with goods taken out filtered back to Aberdeen, firms like C. & R. McLeod, Ironmongers at 14 Union Street, had to promise "to guide purchasers to the

George Elmslie an Aberdeen merchant, who, along with
Alexander Watt, purchased 1,200 acres near Elora in Nichol
township in 1834. By the following year the settlement of
Bon Accord was taking shape. *Wellington County Museum and
Archives, Fergus Ontario. Photo No 8435.*

selection of those articles only which in reference to the destination of the
purchaser, may become positively advantageous." But few emigrants would
have been guided in such matters by their local ironmonger.[24]

Bon Accord thrived on its ability to attract "parties, relatives and friends,
following each other at intervals, and all from Aberdeenshire."[25] And even
though Bon Accord and Fergus were only three miles apart and shared
Scottish Lowland origins:

"There was a distinction broader than a concession road between the people of the Bon Accord settlement and those of the Fergus settlement. The former were very respectable, highly educated and intelligent but they could not boast of the Old Country connections that a number of the latter had. Each community kept pretty much to itself socially though they fraternised in business and religion."[26]

Back in Scotland, a dry goods merchant like George Elmslie would not have had Adam Fergusson's social standing. Fergusson and the many other affluent Scottish farmers who joined him were the ones with the "old Country" connections. But, irrespective of their differing backgrounds, it must be asked why wealthy people like Elmslie and Fergusson had renounced their comfortable lives in Scotland, only to submit themselves to the uncertainties and rigours of pioneer life. The usual motivations of escaping poverty and striving for better economic prospects do not apply. And how were they viewed by the majority of settlers, of very ordinary means, who had come to live in these settlements? The New World offered equality and the empowerment of ordinary people. Could Fergus do so, having so many people still wedded to their "old Country connections?"

At least it is known from the observations recorded by George Elmslie in his Diary that there were no obvious social divisions in Bon Accord. Writing of his relief that, in 1835, they were already "as one family," he contemplated their first winter:

"The winter was now approaching and the heavy rains and cold night gave indications of a severe one. With all our means and appliances and with abundance of warm clothing we were but indifferently prepared for it. The best that could be said of our houses and shanties was that they would shelter us from the violence of the storms, and that they were uncomfortable; our crops had perished and we had to weather another year on the interest of our little capital. Yet we were not discouraged: we had agreeable and intelligent society; and our new and isolated situation had increased friendship to attachment and attachment to love. There were no jealousies, no backbiting and no quarrels."[27]

1 *Farm Barn*	5 *Granary, St Andrews St*	9 *St Andrews Church* (on St George St.)	13 *Walker's house*	16 *Brewery*
2 *St Andrews hotel*	6 *Schoolhouse*	10 *Frame of barn.*	(baker in Provost lane)	17 *Provost Busts*
3 *Mill on Grand River*	7 *Houston's*	11 *Coopers shop* (St Andrews St.)	14 *Mennies house.*	18 *Owen Sound Road*
4 *Watt's house*	8 *James Morrisons (tailor)*	12 *Grant's house.*	15 *Home of Jas Edwards*	19 *A.D. Ferriers*

This sketch of Fergus in 1837 by an unknown artist was taken from "Belsyde," the residence of Alexander David Ferrier. Even though only four years had elapsed since its foundation, Fergus was already a substantial settlement with its own Church, schoolhouse and local businesses. *Metropolitan Toronto Reference Library J. Ross Robertson Collection.*

Elmslie puts his finger on Bon Accord's "agreeable and intelligent society." Fergus, too, was noted for its "reputation for intelligence," which was "far above most similar settlements" and for having exceptionally well educated men, many "being college graduates."[28] Alexander Dingwall-Fordyce, who settled at Fergus in 1835, is just one example. Coming from a wealthy Aberdeen business family, he had been educated at Marischal College (Aberdeen University). Other graduates of Marischal College who settled at Fergus include Arthur and James Ross, from a wealthy land-owning Aberdeen family, and the three sons of Alexander Cadenhead, an Aberdeen lawyer.[29]

These settlers wasted no time in building their first school and church. With funds raised in Scotland by James Webster, Alexander Dingwall-Fordyce, Alexander Ferrier and John Valentine, through their "Old Coun-

The Coat of Arms of the City of Aberdeen circa 1885, which displays the motto "Bon Accord." In 1834, Aberdeenshire emigrants named their settlement in Nichol Township, Upper Canada, Bon Accord to commemorate their roots. *Reproduced by permission of the City of Aberdeen.*

try connections," Fergus had the foundations of a school and church by December 1834, a year after the settlement had been formed.[30] And realizing that he was better suited to teaching than to farming, George Elmslie had taken charge of educational matters in Bon Accord. Initially managing the school from his own house, he later taught at a log schoolhouse built on his land.[31] By 1839 the School housed a Debating Society:

> "The settlement was not without some excellent amusement which was enjoyed by young and old. There was a Library, a Temperance Society …a Singing School and the…Bon Accord Mutual Instruction and Debating Society."[32]

While Fergus and Bon Accord attracted many well-educated and affluent people, its largest influx came from the ordinary farmers, tradesmen and labourers who were looking for better prospects. These settlements had a special attraction. Adam Fergusson and George Elmslie had been captivated by Upper Canada's excellent farming prospects. Acting as middlemen, they had purchased huge quantities of wilderness land in order to sell it on to settlers. Given their own connections in Scotland, the response came mainly from Aberdeenshire, Perthshire and the southern Lowlands. And so, emigrants with similar customs and geographical origins were brought together in Bon Accord and Fergus. For the first time in their lives, they would own their own land and get a direct economic payback from it while retaining their Old World traditions. And, as word spread of their success, wave after wave of emigrants would come and reinforce their distinctive cultural identity. Thus, it seems that it was idealism, a desire for self betterment and a belief in common values which brought these emigrants to Upper Nichol township. It was a harmonious blend of Old Country and New World values with entire communities striving for a common good. The Census Returns indicates that, by 1851, Scots could be found in a narrow but more or less continuous band stretched from one end of Wellington to the other. The highest concentrations were in Nichol and Puslinch townships, on either side of Guelph, which itself, had a sizeable intake of Scots mainly from manufacturing regions in the south of Scotland (Figure 5).[33] And while Scots in Nichol and Guelph townships had originated mainly from Aberdeenshire, Perthshire and the southern Lowlands, Puslinch's Scots came mainly from the Highlands. Thus there were clear links between regions of Scotland and Upper Canada.

Highlanders had shown a clear preference for the Huron Tract, located a short distance to the west of Wellington County. Owned by the Canada Company, it was the last great frontier, with near limitless quantities of wilderness land, which could be purchased on easy terms.[34] Duncan MacLennan, in Inverness and John Sutherland, in Wick, were its principal Highland agents. Their favourable reports of the good wages, work opportunities and land which could be purchased led large numbers of emigrants from the northeast Highlands to head west into Upper Canada, thus helping to create the large concentrations of Highlanders which eventually appeared in Perth, Huron and Middlesex counties (Figure 5).[35] But it was in Zorra, in Oxford County, just to the south of the Huron Tract, where Highland colonization would be most distinctive.

In 1820, two brothers from Sutherland, Angus and William MacKay, began clearing land which they had acquired in Zorra. Until this development, the steadily growing exodus from Sutherland had been directed principally at New Lairg and Earltown in Nova Scotia. But, by 1820, as both of these settlements ran out of available land, Sutherlanders had moved into Cape Breton, founding St. Anns, and had acquired a major foothold in Upper Canada. Working for nine years clearing their land in Zorra, the MacKay brothers returned home to Scotland then reappeared in Zorra in 1830 with their aged mother and a large contingent of Sutherland emigrants.[36] They were apparently "young and eager for adventure" having been "influenced by favourable reports from friends already settled." It seems that "many possessed property," while those who arrived in following year came with substantial amounts of "metallic currency."[37] And as was the case at Bon Accord and Fergus, no time was wasted on building a Presbyterian church:

"To say that our forefathers were a church-going people would be greatly to understate the truth…to attend its services they gladly travelled on foot over a winding path in the dense forest, 3, 6 or even in some cases 10 miles, returning the same day after the service was over."[38]

Thus the opening up of Zorra helps to explain the sudden growth, from 1830, in the numbers of Quebec-bound vessels which called for emigrants at Cromarty and Thurso (Table 3). Tenants whose homeland was being cleared to make way for sheep farms were relocating themselves with their compatriots in Upper Canada. They could do this by taking advantage of the regular succession of timber ships, which sailed close to Cromarty and Thurso on their way to crossing the Atlantic. One group arrived with capital of up to £7,000 to £8,000, even in the depression years of the early 1840s.[39] But by the time of the deepening economic crisis of the late 1840s and early 1850s, most had their travel expenses paid by their landlord, the Duke of Sutherland:

"I observe from an account in one of the Montreal papers that the Duke of Sutherland has chartered the *Panama* of Liverpool, and given a free passage to 287 persons, tenants and their wives and children residing on his estates in Sutherlandshire to Quebec, besides furnishing the whole with 10 weeks wholesome provisions for the voyage. The consequence was that they all reached Canada in good health, without a case of sickness or death occurring on board and last week the whole party I am informed have safely reached the township of Zorra in good health."[40]

In a period of around twenty years, large communities from the northeast of Scotland had re-established themselves in western Upper Canada. It had been the pull of family and community ties which drew Aberdeenshire settlers to Bon Accord and Sutherland settlers to Zorra. Neither place name survives but the sense of collective identity, which these settlers brought with them, can be seen in the strong Scottish traditions which persist in modern day southern Ontario. They had drawn strength as communities from their Presbyterian faith and belief in the value of a good education. Old World customs and traditions, what George Elmslie termed "an agreeable and intelligent society," had seen them through their formative years and beyond.

But the era of fast sailing, copper-bottomed brigs and ships which regularly plied the Atlantic was coming to an end. The steamship had arrived. As specialist passenger services run from Glasgow and Liverpool came to be established, Aberdeen's days as an emigrant port were numbered.

x. Steam Replaces Sail

"FOR THE INFORMATION OF EMIGRANTS
A large number of labourers are now required on the several railroads in
the course of construction in the province: The Quebec and Richmond
Railroad, The Montreal and Portland Railroad, The Prescott and Bytown
Railroad, The Toronto and Simcoe Railroad and the Great Western Railroad from Hamilton to Windsor. Wages from 4s. 6d. to one dollar per day.
  Wanted at Toronto: 5000 men on the Toronto and Sarnia section of
the Grand Trunk Railway. The highest wages will be given to masons,
bricklayers and labourers."[1]

This notice, issued by the Quebec Immigration Agent in 1853, her-
alded the new railways being constructed in Canada. Coupled
with this were the railway networks being extended in Britain.
And linking these two developments were the new steamships, which
offered much faster and more reliable Atlantic crossings. With their
arrival, sea transport entered a completely new phase. Because of their
great size and sophistication, steamships could only sail from a few major
ports. Increasing centralization around fewer ports brought in stricter
controls, and better enforceability and because they were no longer
dependent on the vagaries of the weather and wind direction, steamships
could depart on time and at a predetermined time. With their arrival, sea
transport entered the modern era. More and more emigrants opted for
their greater speed, safety, reliability and creature comforts, and by 1870
steam had replaced sail.

Aberdeen's role, both as an emigrant embarkation port and a source of Atlantic shipping services had been under threat, even before the arrival of steamships. From the 1840s, Aberdeen shippers had been competing with the Glasgow-based Allan Line, which ran ten ships a year regularly between Montreal, Glasgow and Liverpool. By 1852 the Allan Line completely dominated all passenger services between Scotland and Quebec. And by then, readers of the *Aberdeen Herald* were as likely to see notices of the Allan Line's "line of packets to Canada" as they were of locally run services.[2] While Aberdeen ships continued to do brisk business in the 1850s, the days when ships like the St. *Lawrence* of Aberdeen and the *Berbice* of Aberdeen, would set off for Quebec with emigrants were rapidly coming to an end. In 1860, just two passengers left from Aberdeen; in 1861, there were just 38 and from 1862 there were none.[3]

The railways brought emigrants to Glasgow and Liverpool and they also took them inland through Canada once they had arrived in North America. The Canadian Steam Navigation Company, established from 1853, ran regular services from Liverpool and Glasgow to Quebec and Montreal, twice a month in summer and once a month in winter. And linking its services with the railways, it offered emigrants an all inclusive fare for both sea and land transport during winter months. Thus, when the St. Lawrence was frozen over in the winter, emigrants could board ship at Glasgow or Liverpool, disembark at Boston then take a rail link from Portland, Maine to Montreal.[4] And, with the opening of the Great Western Railway, emigrants had no longer to dread the arduous and slow journeys west from Montreal, by river and lake, on boats and steamers. Now there were timetables, booking procedures, enforceable controls, interconnecting services and few delays.

The first half of the nineteenth century had been very different. The age of sail had no schedules and few controls. Atlantic shipping services were geared to trade, not passengers. Clearly, the choice of vessel and time of sailing were determined by the timber trade, not the needs of passengers. The involvement of Aberdeen, and other east coast shippers in this trade, meant that timber ships were taken past the northeast Highlands at a time when the zeal to emigrate was high. Thus, the large exodus from this one region owes much to the timber trade. But the emigrant's reliance on the timber trade also had its perils.

Going from east to west was fine since shippers had space to fill and offered cheap steerage rates. But going from west to east was an altogether different matter. Ships were packed with timber, restricting opportunities for travelling in the steerage. Consequently, the emigrant's cost of returning home to Scotland would have been far higher than his east to west fare. Not surprisingly, then, people went to great lengths to ensure that they considered every option and every difficulty before deciding whether to emigrate. George Elmslie and Adam Fergusson went out first to their chosen sites in Upper Canada to make sure that the best location had been chosen for the settlers who would join them. Norman MacLeod and Angus and William MacKay directed their Sutherland compatriots to regions of Cape Breton and Upper Canada where they thought they would flourish. And John Sutherland, the Highland emigration agent, took his message that good land was available in the Huron Tract, far and wide throughout the Highlands. The site location was carefully chosen and so was the sea crossing.

And what do we make of the much-documented terrors of crossing the Atlantic by sailing ship? Travelling steerage in a cramped, smelly hold was hardly going to be a pleasant experience. But this was the early nineteenth century when overcrowding, poor sanitary conditions and disease were facts of life. The evidence shows that, judged by the standards of the time, emigrants were offered the best available shipping. The owners provided good ships with long-serving captains, and were highly reputable. Theirs was a culture of stability and reliability.

The fast sailing copper-bottomed brigs and ships always got to their destinations and the emigrants usually arrived safely. "All in good circumstances" were words often used by the Quebec Immigration Agent to describe the emigrants who disembarked from Aberdeen ships. It seems that emigrants from the northeast of Scotland had been particularly well served by Aberdeen's maritime and business community. With safe crossings behind them, they could face the challenges of their new life in the Canadian frontier. They showed themselves to be extremely successful colonizers and excelled in every walk of life.

Appendix A

Characteristics of the Aberdeen sailing vessels which took Emigrants to British America

The Appendix covers all vessels that were used to take passengers from Aberdeen to British America during the first half of the nineteenth century. Although most vessels were registered at Aberdeen, some had unknown origins. For the sake of completeness these are included as well. The Appendix also gives details of the Aberdeen-registered vessels which took emigrants from Highland and Island ports to British America.

Passenger Data

Passenger totals are provided for each vessel listed. More detailed data, together with the documentary sources used can be found in Tables 1 to 3.

Passenger data are taken from a wide variety of sources. Some passenger totals are approximations and some are ambiguous. Uncertainties arise as to whether totals include all adults (not just heads of households) and children and infants. In some cases ships are known to have carried passengers but actual numbers are not given. Cabin passengers at this time may well have been business or recreational travellers and not emigrants. Accepting these limitations, the data reported in the Appendix provides the best available estimate of emigrant numbers taken by Aberdeen vessels during the sailing ship era.

Vessel Details

Information on the tonnage, vessel type, year built, place built and the Lloyd's Code have been taken from the *Lloyd's Shipping Register*. Vessel dimensions (length x width x depth), builder's name, and details of the owners and captains have been taken from the *Aberdeen Shipping Registers* (ACA CE87/11). The *Aberdeen Directories* have also been used to identify vessel owners.

Tonnage

This was a standard measure used to determine customs dues and navigation fees. Because it was a calculated figure, tonnage did not necessarily convey actual carrying capacity. Before 1836, the formula used to calculate tonnage was based only on breadth and length but after 1836 it incorporated the vessel's depth as well.

Vessel Type

The word "ship" can signify a particular vessel type as well as having a generic usage in denoting all types of sea-going vessels. Sailing ship rigs were many and varied. A major distinction was the alignment of the sails. There were the square-rigged vessels in which the sails were rigged across the vessel and the fore-and-aft rigs which followed the fore-and-aft-line of the vessel. The square rig was normally used on ocean-going vessels:

Brig (bg): a two-masted vessel with square rigging on both masts.

Snow (sw): rigged as a brig, with square sails on both masts but with a small triangular sail mast stepped immediately towards the stern of the main-mast.

Barque (bk): three-masted vessel, square rigged on the fore and main masts and fore-and-aft rigged on the third aftermost mast.

Ship (s): three-masted vessel, square rigged on all three masts.

Schooner (sr): fore-and-aft sails on two or more masts. Some had small square topsails on the foremast. They were largely used in the coasting trade and for fishing, their advantage being the smaller crew than that required by square rigged vessels of a comparable size.

Lloyd's Shipping Codes
These were assigned to vessels after periodic surveys according to their quality of construction, condition and age:

A: first class condition, kept in the highest state of repair and efficiency and within a prescribed age limit at the time of sailing.
AE: "second description of the first class," fit for safe conveyance, no defects but may be over a prescribed age limit.
E: second class vessels which, although unfit for carrying dry cargoes, were suitable for long distance sea voyages.
I: third class vessels only suitable for short voyages (i.e. not out of Europe).

The letters were followed by the number 1 or 2 which signified the condition of the vessel's equipment (anchors, cables and stores). Where satisfactory, the number 1 was used, and where not, 2 was used.
Failure to locate vessels in the *Register* does not in itself signify its exclusion from the Lloyd's classification system. To select the relevant vessel from the *Register*, it is usually necessary to know the tonnage and captain's name, information which is often elusive and problematic because of gaps in the available shipping and customs records. In all, codes were located for 82 of the 104 vessels covered in this study.
Taking just those 44 vessels which carried 60 or more passengers, codes were found for 36, and of these, 30 had first class rankings (see Table 4).

Vessel	Tons	Type	Year Built	Place Built	Dimensions	Lloyd's Code	Captain	Owners/ Agents
Aberdeenshire of Aberdeen	240	sw	1825	Aberdeen, by James Adamson	89 x 25.2 x 17	A1	James Oswald	Robert Catto

Yearly crossings from Aberdeen to Halifax 1827–35. From 1832–35 there were two crossings each year. Total passengers carried 246.

Vessel	Tons	Type	Year Built	Place Built	Dimensions	Lloyd's Code	Captain	Owners/ Agents
Aimwell of Aberdeen	232	sw	1816	Aberdeen	85 x 25.10 x 16.9	A1	John Morrison	Donaldson Rose

1816 crossing from Thurso to Halifax with 139 passengers. Crossings from Aberdeen to Halifax 1817–18 and 1832 with 89 passengers. Total passengers carried 228.

Vessel	Tons	Type	Year Built	Place Built	Dimensions	Lloyd's Code	Captain	Owners/ Agents
Albion of Aberdeen	266	bg	1826	Aberdeen, by Alexander Hall	94.2 x 25.6 x 17.2	A1	Alexander Leslie	Robert Duthie (1829–38); Alexander Stephen (1839–41); Alexander Cooper (1842–53)

Regular crossings from Aberdeen to Halifax 1829–53; twice yearly 1833,1837,1839,1840,1843,1850. Total passengers carried 582.

Alert of Aberdeen	177	bg	n/k	Foreign	82.9 x 22.8 x 12.6	E2	Andrew Johnston	William Johnston

A prize made free. One crossing in 1812 from Aberdeen to Quebec with 2 passengers.

Alexander Hall of Aberdeen	403	bk	1845	Aberdeen, by Alexander Hall	111.2 x 23.8 x 18.1	A1	Findlay	Donaldson Rose

One probable crossing in 1854 from Aberdeen to Quebec. Passenger numbers n/k.

Amethyst of Aberdeen	132	sw	1812	Aberdeen	n/k	A1	H. Greig	Greig & Co.

Crossings from Aberdeen to Halifax 1815–16 with a total of 65 passengers.

Amity of Aberdeen	312	bg	1825	New Brunswick	n/k	E1	David Rae	George Thompson Jr.

Crossing in 1835 from Aberdeen to Quebec and again in 1836. Total passengers carried 64.

Ann and Elizabeth	140	bg	1810	Sunderland	n/k	A1	John Gray	John R. Catto

3 passengers taken from Aberdeen to Quebec in 1816.

Annandale of Aberdeen	254	bg	1828	New Brunswick	91.10 x 25.2 x 17.3	A1	Alexander Anderson	Robert Catto (1831–32) Craig (1836)

Three crossings: 1831–32 and 1836 from Aberdeen to Quebec. Total passengers carried 91.

Vessel	Tons	Type	Year Built	Place Built	Dimensions	Lloyd's Code	Captain	Owners/ Agents
Atlantic of Aberdeen	216	sw	1824	Aberdeen, by William Stephen	84.6 x 24.2 x 16	A1	Alexander Lawson	n/k

2 passengers carried from Aberdeen to Quebec in 1826.

| *Augusta* of Aberdeen | 417 | s | 1828 | N. Brunswick | 114.5 x 28.4 x 5.11 between decks | E1 | William Rae | Neil Smith |

46 passengers from Aberdeen to Quebec in 1836

| *Aurora* of Aberdeen | 709 | s | 1843 | Miramichi, New Brunswick | 144.5 x 28.9 x 21 | AE1 | Alexander Morison | Alexander Cooper |

710 passengers taken from Aberdeen to Quebec in 1854–55.

| *Barbara* of London | 162 | bg | 1812 | British | n/k | E1 | William Epsom | n/k |

4 passengers carried from Aberdeen to Quebec in 1812.

| *Berbice* of Aberdeen | 340 | bk | 1847 | Miramichi | 107.8 x 23.4 x 17.2 | AE1 | James Elliot | Alexander Duthie (1848–54) Scott (1855) |

Regular crossings from Aberdeen to Quebec 1848–55, and generally twice yearly. Total passengers carried 1091.

| *Bolivar* of Aberdeen | 223 | sw | 1825 | Aberdeen, by William Stephen | n/k | n/k | Herman Ganson | n/k |

One crossing in 1835 from Aberdeen to Quebec with 7 passengers.

| *Bon Accord* of Aberdeen | 365 | bk | 1812 | Blyth | 101.6 x 28.10 x 6.4 between decks | AE1 | James Sim | Lewis Crombie |

One crossing in 1841 from Aberdeen to Quebec with 70 passengers.

Vessel	Tons	Type	Year Built	Place Built	Dimensions	Lloyd's Code	Captain	Owners/ Agents
Brilliant of Aberdeen	332	s	1814	Aberdeen, by Alexander Hall	97.2 x 28.8 x 19.3	AE1	Alexander Barclay	William Duthie (1830–32) Alexander Duthie (1833–36) James Elliot from 1836

Former whaling ship. Regular yearly crossings, often twice yearly, from Aberdeen to Quebec 1830–45. One of the 1833 crossings was from Dundee. Total passengers carried 1,343.

Vessel	Tons	Type	Year Built	Place Built	Dimensions	Lloyd's Code	Captain	Owners/ Agents
Cambria of Aberdeen	120	bg	1808	Aberdeen	n/k	A1	James Pirie, 1812 James Oswald, 1813 James Clayton, 1814 Alexander Lawrence, 1816 John Wilson, 1817	Peter Ritchie

Aberdeen to the Maritimes 1812 to 1816 and one crossing from Aberdeen to Quebec in 1817. The *Cambria* was rated as A1 from 1812–1814; however in 1815 it was rated as I2 and in 1816 as E2. Total passengers carried 120

Vessel	Tons	Type	Year Built	Place Built	Dimensions	Lloyd's Code	Captain	Owners/ Agents
Carleton of Aberdeen	404	bk	1834	New Brunswick	111 x 28.10 x 20.9	AE1	Alexander Anderson	Robert Catto

Crossings from Aberdeen to Quebec in 1835 and 1838. Total passengers carried 96.

Vessel	Tons	Type	Year Built	Place Built	Dimensions	Lloyd's Code	Captain	Owners/ Agents
Carolina of Aberdeen	170	n/k	n/k	n/k	n/k	n/k	Alexander Duncan	William White

Crossings 1815–16 from Aberdeen to Quebec. Total passengers carried 49.

Vessel	Tons	Type	Year Built	Place Built	Dimensions	Lloyd's Code	Captain	Owners/ Agents
Caroline of Aberdeen	393	bk	1839	New Brunswick	112.8 x 24.6 x 18.3	A1	James Marsh	Andrew Phillips

Two crossings (in 1840 and 1854) from Aberdeen to Quebec. Total passengers carried 25.

Vessel	Tons	Type	Year Built	Place Built	Dimensions	Lloyd's Code	Captain	Owners/ Agents
Centurion of Aberdeen	130	bg	n/k	n/k	n/k	n/k	James Morrison	Peter Ritchie

One crossing in 1811 Aberdeen to Halifax with 18 passengers

| *Circassian* of Aberdeen | 180 | bg | 1835 | Aberdeen, by William Duthie | 82.9 x 22.6 x 15.4 | A1 | Thomas Ritchie | William Duthie |

One crossing in 1836 from Aberdeen to Quebec with 117 passengers.

| *City of Aberdeen* | 260 | bg | 1826 | Aberdeen, by William Duthie | 90.4 x 25.9 x 17.1 | A1 | Alexander Duthie | William Allen |

Two crossings in 1826 and one in 1827 from Aberdeen to Quebec. Total passengers carried 14.

| *Douglas* of Aberdeen | 135 | bg | 1816 | Aberdeen | 69.10 x 21.9 x 12.8 | A1 | John Morrison | George Thompson. Jr |

One crossing in 1817 from Aberdeen to Halifax with 7 passengers.

| *Dove* of Aberdeen | 186 | n/k | n/k | n/k | n/k | n/k | Crane | n/k |

One crossing in 1801 from Fort William to Pictou with 219 passengers.

| *Earl of Dalhousie* of Aberdeen | 183 | bg | 1817 | Aberdeen, by James Adamson | n/k | A1 | John Levie | Peter Ritchie |

Regular crossings 1from Aberdeen to Quebec 1817–21. Total passengers carried 102.

| *Economy* of Aberdeen | n/k | n/k | n/k | n/k | n/k | n/k | James Frazer | n/k |

One crossing in 1819 from Tobermory to Pictou. Total passengers carried 285.

| *Emerald* | 200 | bg | 1800 | Peterhead | n/k | A1 | Alexander Anderson | n/k |

One crossing in 1806 from Aberdeen to Quebec with 7 passengers.

Vessel	Tons	Type	Year Built	Place Built	Dimensions	Lloyd's Code	Captain	Owners/ Agents
Emma Zeller	267	bg	1828	New Brunswick	n/k	A1	n/k	n/k

One crossing in 1832 from Aberdeen to Quebec with 9 passengers.

| *Emperor Alexander* of Aberdeen | 236 | sw | 1814 | Sunderland | 83.11 x 25.8 x 15.11 | A1 | Alexander Watt | Robert Catto |

One crossing in 1823 from Tobermory to Cape Breton and Quebec with 160 passengers.

| *Fairfield* of Aberdeen | 351 | s | 1795 | Whitby | n/k | E1 | James Morrice | n/k |

Crossings in 1810 and 1817 from Aberdeen to Quebec with 17 passengers.

| *Fame* of Aberdeen | 141 | bg | 1810 | Stockton | n/k | A1 | George Masson | Robert Duthie |

One crossing in 1815 from Aberdeen to Halifax with 4 passengers.

| *Fancy* of Aberdeen | 141 | bg | 1808 | Aberdeen | 72 x 22.4 x 13.2 | A1 | James Struthers | n/k |

One crossing in 1816 from Greenock to Quebec with 15 passengers.

| *Flora* | 147 | sw | 1812 | Aberdeen | n/k | A1 | James Work | David Milne |

One crossing in 1816 from Aberdeen to Quebec with 2 passengers.

| *Ganges* of Aberdeen | 208 | sw | 1800 | Aberdeen | n/k | E1 | Alexander Martin | n/k |

Used in wartime as a transport. One crossing in 1817 from Aberdeen to Saint John with 4 passengers.

| *Gem* of Aberdeen | 186 | bg | 1839 | Aberdeen, by Alexander Hall | 81.2 x 20.2 x 14.1 | A1 | P. Robb | James Nisbet & David Robertson |

One crossing in 1842 from Aberdeen to Quebec with 30 passengers.

| *Glentanner* of Aberdeen | 160 | bg | 1811 | Aberdeen, by James Adamson | 77.10 x 22.2 x 13.6 | A1 | James Laird | Robert Duthie |

One crossing in 1815 from Aberdeen to Halifax/Pictou. One crossing in 1820 from Tobermory to Cape Breton and Quebec with 141 passengers. Total passengers carried 158.

Vessel	Tons	Type	Year Built	Place Built	Dimensions	Lloyd's Code	Captain	Owners/ Agents
Good Intent of Aberdeen	159	sw	1816	Aberdeen	73.10 x 22.4 x 13.3	A1	Alexander Rodgers (1817) Hugh Thomson (1824)	n/k

Crossings from Aberdeen to Pictou/Quebec in 1817 and 1824 taking a total of 31 passengers.

Vessel	Tons	Type	Year Built	Place Built	Dimensions	Lloyd's Code	Captain	Owners/ Agents
Good Intent of Aberdeen	n/k	n/k	n/k	n/k	n/k	n/k	Robert Beverly (1816)	n/k

Crossings from Fort William to Pictou in 1801 and 1816. 69 passengers were carried on 1816 crossing.

Vessel	Tons	Type	Year Built	Place Built	Dimensions	Lloyd's Code	Captain	Owners/ Agents
Granite of Aberdeen	127	n/k	n/k	n/k	n/k	n/k	Alexander Scorgie	Donaldson Rose

One crossing from Aberdeen to Miramichi in 1816 with 6 passengers.

Vessel	Tons	Type	Year Built	Place Built	Dimensions	Lloyd's Code	Captain	Owners/ Agents
Halifax Packet of Aberdeen	185	sw	1814	Sunderland	76.8 x 24 x 15	A1	John Hogg	n/k

Crossings in 1814–15 from Aberdeen to Halifax with 10 passengers.

Vessel	Tons	Type	Year Built	Place Built	Dimensions	Lloyd's Code	Captain	Owners/ Agents
Harmony of Aberdeen	161	sw	1801	Aberdeen	n/k	E1	George Murray	n/k

One crossing from Cromarty to Pictou in 1822 with 125 passengers.

Vessel	Tons	Type	Year Built	Place Built	Dimensions	Lloyd's Code	Captain	Owners/ Agents
Helen	185	bg	1804	n/k	n/k	A1	James Moore	John Catto

One crossing in 1815 from Aberdeen to Halifax with 4 passengers.

Vessel	Tons	Type	Year Built	Place Built	Dimensions	Lloyd's Code	Captain	Owners/ Agents
Helen of Aberdeen	94	sr	1815	Newburgh	61.10 x 19.2 x 9.6	A1	George Legatwood	John Black of Newburgh

One crossing in 1816 with 11 passengers.

Vessel	Tons	Type	Year Built	Place Built	Dimensions	Lloyd's Code	Captain	Owners/ Agents
Helen of Aberdeen	366	bk	1826	n/k	n/k	E1	Anderson	George Thompson. Jr

One crossing in 1832 from Aberdeen to Quebec with 18 passengers.

Vessel	Tons	Type	Year Built	Place Built	Dimensions	Lloyd's Code	Captain	Owners/ Agents
Hercules of Aberdeen	250	bk	1781	Stockton in South Britain	88.6 x 26.2 x 6.3 between decks	E1 in 1831; not noted in 1841	Duncan Walker	William Duthie

Former whaling vessel. Crossings in 1831, 1834–1836 and 1840 from Aberdeen to Quebec. Crossing in 1837 from Stornoway to Cape Breton and Quebec with 112 passengers. Total passengers carried 653.

Vessel	Tons	Type	Year Built	Place Built	Dimensions	Lloyd's Code	Captain	Owners/ Agents
Heroine of Aberdeen	387	s	1831	Dundee	n/k	AE1	Duncan Walker	William Duthie

Former whaling vessel. Regular crossings from Aberdeen to Quebec 1840 to 1847. Crossing from Stornoway to Charlottetown in 1840 with 281 passengers. Total passengers carried 637.

Vessel	Tons	Type	Year Built	Place Built	Dimensions	Lloyd's Code	Captain	Owners/ Agents
Hibernia of Aberdeen	113	bg	1816	Aberdeen	n/k	A1	R. Lamb	n/k

One crossing from Stornoway to Quebec in 1816 with 42 passengers.

Vessel	Tons	Type	Year Built	Place Built	Dimensions	Lloyd's Code	Captain	Owners/ Agents
Highlander of Aberdeen	174	bg	1817	Aberdeen, by William Duthie	79.1 x 22.11 x 14.11	E1	Archibald Donald (1817) Fluckark (1836)	Robert Duthie

One crossing from Aberdeen to Saint John in 1817, one crossing from Leith to Halifax in 1833, and one from Cromarty to Quebec in 1836. Total passengers carried 223.

Vessel	Tons	Type	Year Built	Place Built	Dimensions	Lloyd's Code	Captain	Owners/ Agents
Hunter of Aberdeen	105	n/k	n/k	n/k	n/k	n/k	James Logan	n/k

One crossing in 1817 from Aberdeen to Halifax with 5 passengers.

Vessel	Tons	Type	Year Built	Place Built	Dimensions	Lloyd's Code	Captain	Owners/ Agents
Isle of Skye of Aberdeen	181	sw	1806	Aberdeen	n/k	A1	John Thom	n/k

One crossing in 1806 from Tobermory to Charlottetown with 37 passengers.

APPENDIX A

Vessel	Tons	Type	Year Built	Place Built	Dimensions	Lloyd's Code	Captain	Owners/ Agents
Jane Boyd of Aberdeen	387	bk	1843	Aberdeen, by Walter Hood	109.6 x 23.8 18.1	n/k	Herman Ganson	George Thompson. Jr

Regular crossings 1853–55 from Aberdeen to Quebec. Total passengers carried 245.

Jessie of Aberdeen	154	bg	1814	Spey	n/k	A1	James Thomson	Peter Ritchie

Two crossings 1816–17 from Aberdeen to Quebec with 29 passengers.

Juno of Aberdeen	150	bg	1819	Newburgh	n/k	A1	J. Henderson	n/k

One crossing in 1821 from Aberdeen to Quebec with 6 passengers.

Kincardineshire of Aberdeen	193	bg	1838	Cape Breton	n/k	AE 1	Goven	James Goldie

One crossing in 1839 from Aberdeen to Quebec with 55 passengers.

Lady of the Lake of Aberdeen	293	sw	1826	Miramichi	96.8 x 26.5 x 5.6	E1 between decks	Grant	George Thompson. Jr

One crossing in 1832 from Aberdeen to Quebec with 13 passengers.

Lord Metcalfe of Aberdeen	510	bk	1845	Quebec	120.7 x 26.1 x 18.3	AE1	Bain	George Thompson Jn.

Two crossings (1847–48) from Aberdeen to Quebec with a total of 82 passengers.

Lord Seaton of Aberdeen	440	s	1840	Quebec	114 x 24.5 x 18.5	A1	William Talbot	George Oswald & Co

Three crossings all to Quebec: In 1845 and 1846 from Cromarty and Thurso. In 1849, from Cromarty and Longhope (Orkney). Passenger data incomplete. Known passengers carried 41.

Vessel	Tons	Type	Year Built	Place Built	Dimensions	Lloyd's Code	Captain	Owners/ Agents
Louisa of Aberdeen	213	sw	1816	Aberdeen, by James Adamson	85.3 x 24.2 x 15.9	E1	James Oswald	Peter Ritchie

Regular crossings 1816–21 from Aberdeen to Halifax with 182 passengers. One crossing in 1819 from Tobermory to Pictou and in 1829 from Stornoway to Cape Breton together taking 290 passengers. Total passengers carried 472.

Vessel	Tons	Type	Year Built	Place Built	Dimensions	Lloyd's Code	Captain	Owners/ Agents
Malvina of Aberdeen	203	sw	1806	Aberdeen	n/k	A1	John Smith	n/k

One crossing in 1811 from Aberdeen to Quebec with 11 passengers.

Vessel	Tons	Type	Year Built	Place Built	Dimensions	Lloyd's Code	Captain	Owners/ Agents
Margaret of Aberdeen	226	sw	1818	Aberdeen	87.1 x 24.9 x 15.3	E1	James Troup	Robert Catto

One crossing in 1827 from Aberdeen to Quebec with 10 passengers.

Vessel	Tons	Type	Year Built	Place Built	Dimensions	Lloyd's Code	Captain	Owners/ Agents
Mary Ann of Aberdeen	221	sw	1819	Aberdeen	n/k	A1	Joseph Moore	n/k

One crossing in 1821 from Aberdeen to Quebec with 6 passengers.

Vessel	Tons	Type	Year Built	Place Built	Dimensions	Lloyd's Code	Captain	Owners/ Agents
Mary of Aberdeen	139	sw	1810	Aberdeen	73.1 x 21.6 x 12.5	n/k	James Morrison (1811–12) James Oswald (1815–16) James Clayton (1816–17)	Peter Ritchie

Regular crossings 1811 to 1815 from Aberdeen to Halifax. In 1816 a crossing from Aberdeen to Quebec and in 1817 from Aberdeen to Miramichi. Total passengers carried 142.

Vessel	Tons	Type	Year Built	Place Built	Dimensions	Lloyd's Code	Captain	Owners/ Agents
Minerva of Aberdeen	202	sw	1813	Aberdeen, by Alexander Hall	82 x 24.3	A1	W. Strachan	Catto

One crossing, in 1817 from Fort William to Halifax and Quebec with 26 passengers.

Vessel	Tons	Type	Year Built	Place Built	Dimensions	Lloyd's Code	Captain	Owners/ Agents
Monarch	216	bg	1819	Aberdeen, by William Duthie	n/k	A1	A. Martin	William Allen

One crossing in 1820 from Aberdeen to Saint John with an unknown number of passengers.

Vessel	Tons	Type	Year Built	Place Built	Dimensions	Lloyd's Code	Captain	Owners/Agents
Morningfield of Aberdeen	141	bg	1816	Aberdeen	n/k	AI	J. Perie (1816)	Peter Ritchie Laing (1819)

Two crossings: one in 1816 from Stornoway to Quebec and in 1819 from Tobermory to Pictou and Charlottetown. Total passengers carried 327.

Nautilus of Aberdeen	117	bg	1824	n/k	n/k	n/k	William English	n/k

One crossing in 1835 from Aberdeen to Cape Breton with 7 passengers.

Nestor of Aberdeen	364	sw	1802	Monk- wearmouth	100.11 x 29.8 x 6.6 between decks	EI	George	David Milne

Used in war-time as a transport. One crossing in 1822 from Aberdeen to Quebec with 5 passengers.

Norval of Aberdeen	188	sw	1818	Aberdeen, by William Duthie	83 x 23.2 x 14.8	n/k	Walker	n/k

One crossing in 1818 and again in 1821 from Aberdeen to Quebec Total passengers carried 10.

Pacific of Aberdeen	386	bk	1826	Nova Scotia	102 x 26.2 x 18.7	AEI	John Morrison	Alexander Cooper

Regular crossings from Aberdeen to Quebec 1835 to 1837. Regular crossings from Cromarty/Thurso to Quebec from 1841 to 1844. Total passengers carried 517.

Patriot of Aberdeen	98	bg	1811	Aberdeen	n/k	AI	Alexander Anderson	J. & R. Catto

Crossings in 1812, 1817 and 1819 from Aberdeen to Quebec with a total of 23 passengers.

Perseverance of Aberdeen	116	bg	n/k	foreign	4 x 20.10 x 11.6	n/k	Moncur (1814) J. Philip (1816)	Peter Ritchie

Crossings from Cromarty to Pictou/Halifax in 1814 and 1815, from Stornoway to Quebec in 1816 and from Skye to Pictou in 1818. Known passengers carried 202 (figures incomplete).

Vessel	Tons	Type	Year Built	Place Built	Dimensions	Lloyd's Code	Captain	Owners/ Agents
Phesdo of Aberdeen	245	bg	1815	Aberdeen	87 x 26.1 x 16.9	A1	Andrew Pennan	Alexander Duthie

Regular crossings 1815 to 1817 from Aberdeen to Halifax/Saint John with a total of 61 passengers.

Pilgrim of Aberdeen	170	bg	1828	Aberdeen, by William Rennie	75.6 x 22.10 x 14.3	A1	George Allan	Donaldson Rose

Crossings in 1835 and 1838 from Aberdeen to Quebec with a total of 130 passengers.

Pilot of Newburgh	114	bg	1818	Newburgh	68.6 x 20 x 12.7	n/k	John Law	John Black of Newburgh

One crossing in 1822 from Aberdeen to Miramichi/Saint John with 7 passengers.

Ploughman of Aberdeen	165	sw	1804	Berwick	n/k	A1	Alexander Yule (1811) James Main (1812–13) Alexander Duncan (1816)	Saunders & Mellis

Crossings 1811–13 and 1816 from Aberdeen to Pictou/Halifax with a total of 54 passengers.

Quebec Packet of Aberdeen	196	bg	1822	Aberdeen, by Nicol Reid & Co	82.10 x 23.11 x 15.4	A1	Alexander Anderson (1822–34) Stephens (1835–40)	Robert Catto

Regular crossings from Aberdeen to Quebec from 1822 to 1826 (twice yearly in 1823, 1825,1826) and in 1830, 1834, 1835 and 1837. One crossing from Cromarty to Quebec in 1840. Total passengers carried 181.

Renown of Aberdeen	311	bk	1842	Aberdeen, by Alexander Duthie	97.4 x 23 x 17	AE1	William Walker	William Duthie

Crossings in 1854 and 1855 from Aberdeen to Quebec with a total of 170 passengers.

Vessel	Tons	Type	Year Built	Place Built	Dimensions	Lloyd's Code	Captain	Owners/ Agents
Rob Roy of Aberdeen	243	bg	1819	Aberdeen, by James Adamson	90 x 24.8 x 15.7	A1	W. Nairn	Robert Catto

One crossing from Aberdeen to Quebec in 1819 with 7 passengers.

Robert McWilliam of Aberdeen	298	sw	1824	New Brunswick	95.7 x 26.8 x 18.7	AE1	Williamson	Robert Catto

Two crossings in 1835 from Aberdeen to Quebec with 31 passengers.

Rose of Aberdeen	253	bk	1843	Aberdeen, by Walter Hood	n/k	A1	James Gibb	Donaldson Rose

One crossing in 1843 from Aberdeen to Quebec with 94 passengers.

Ruby of Aberdeen	128	sw	1805	Aberdeen	67.9 x 21.5 x 11.1	A1 in 1816; E1 in 1822	Thomas Love (1815) J. Bodie (1822)	Alexander Gibbon

A crossing from Aberdeen to Halifax in 1815 with 2 passengers and from Cromarty to Pictou in 1822 with 125 passengers.

Sarah of Aberdeen	232	bg	1839	Aberdeen, by Alexander Hall	87.0 x 21.1 x 15.0	n/k	George Allan (1839–43) James Sim (1851–52)	Donaldson Rose

Regular crossings from Aberdeen to Quebec 1839–43 and crossings in 1851–52. Total passengers carried 390.

Sedulous of Aberdeen	226	sw	1840	Sunderland	82.6 x 22.6 x 15.6	A1	George Levie	James Nisbet & David Robertson

One crossing in 1843 from Aberdeen to Quebec with 8 passengers.

Vessel	Tons	Type	Year Built	Place Built	Dimensions	Lloyd's Code	Captain	Owners/ Agents
Seven Sisters of Aberdeen	170	bg	n/k	n/k	n/k	n/k	A. Brown	John Lumsden

One crossing in 1815 from Aberdeen to Halifax with 19 passengers.

Shakespeare of Aberdeen	179	sw	1825	Aberdeen, by Nicol Reid & Co	78.9 x 22.11 x 15	AE1	Rosie	Donaldson Rose

One crossing in 1836 from Aberdeen to Quebec with 84 passengers.

Sir William Wallace of Aberdeen	232	bg	1821	Aberdeen, by William Duthie	86.9 x 25.3 x 16.2	n/k	Daniel Anderson	Donaldson Rose

One crossing in 1833 from Aberdeen to Quebec with 28 passengers.

Sir William Wallace of Aberdeen	183	bg	1835	Aberdeen, by Alexander Hall	79.9 x 22.9 x 14.5	n/k	Daniel Anderson (1836–37) James Tulloch (1839) A. Andrews (1855)	Donaldson Rose

Crossings from Aberdeen to Quebec in 1836, 1837, 1839, 1843 and 1855 with a total of 164 passengers.

Sisters of Aberdeen	177	bg	1833	Aberdeen, by Alexander Hall	71.8 x 21 x 12.10	n/k	Hull	Donaldson Rose

One crossing in 1840 from Aberdeen to Quebec with 41 passengers.

Sprightly of Dundee	190	bg	n/k	Foreign	82.6 x 24 x 15.3	E2	Alexander Philip	J. & R. Catto

A Prize made free. One crossing from Aberdeen to Halifax/Pictou/Miramichi in 1816 with 20 passengers.

Spring of Aberdeen	109	bg	1810	Aberdeen	n/k	A1	Peter Grant	n/k

One crossing in 1811 from Aberdeen to Quebec with 15 passengers.

Vessel	Tons	Type	Year Built	Place Built	Dimensions	Lloyd's Code	Captain	Owners/ Agents
St. Lawrence of Aberdeen	352	bk	1841	Aberdeen, by Walter Hood	105 x 24.6 x 18	A1	James Tulloch	Donaldson Rose

Regular crossings from Aberdeen to Quebec 1842–55. Twice yearly crossings in 1847, 1849–54. Total passengers carried 1750.

| *Star* of Aberdeen | n/k | n/k | n/k | n/k | n/k | n/k | Alexander Blackett | n/k |

One crossing in 1818 from Aberdeen to Saint John with an unknown number of passengers.

| *Taurus* of Aberdeen | 184 | sr | 1841 | Aberdeen, by Walter Hood | 84.6 x 20.5 x 13.5 | A1 | John Martin | James Nisbet & David Robertson |

One crossing in 1841 from Aberdeen to Quebec with 134 passengers.

| *Thistle* of Aberdeen | 133 | sw | 1818 | Aberdeen, by William Duthie | 67.8 x 21.10 x 11.7 | A1 | Robert Allan | Alexander Machie |

One crossing in 1821 from Tobermory to Pictou and Quebec with 96 passengers.

| *Traveller* of Aberdeen | 195 | bg | 1819 | Aberdeen, by James Adamson | 82.10 x 23.7 x 15.1 | n/k | James Goldie | Peter Ritchie |

A crossing in 1819 from Tobermory to Quebec and in 1820 from Aberdeen to Quebec with a total of 163 passengers.

| *Union* | 173 | bg | 1813 | Sunderland | n/k | A1 | J. Ord | n/k |

One crossing in 1818 from Aberdeen to Quebec with 7 passengers.

| *Universe* of Aberdeen | 281 | bk | 1826 | Aberdeen, by William Duthie | n/k | A1 in 1828; AE1 in 1841 | Alexander Craigie | William Allen |

Crossing from Stornoway to Cape Breton in 1828 and from Thurso to Pictou and Quebec in 1841. Total passengers carried 588.

Vessel	Tons	Type	Year Built	Place Built	Dimensions	Lloyd's Code	Captain	Owners/ Agents
Venus of Aberdeen	80	n/k	n/k	n/k	n/k	n/k	Alexander Begg	n/k

Crossings in 1813 and 1821 from Aberdeen to Quebec with a total of 13 passengers.

Vessel	Tons	Type	Year Built	Place Built	Dimensions	Lloyd's Code	Captain	Owners/ Agents
Wellington of Aberdeen	211	bg	1815	Aberdeen	n/k	A1	Alexander Stephens	n/k

One crossing in 1815 from Aberdeen to Miramichi with 6 passengers.

Vessel	Tons	Type	Year Built	Place Built	Dimensions	Lloyd's Code	Captain	Owners/ Agents
William Glen Anderson of Glasgow	389	bk	1827	Richibucto, New Brunswick	n/k	AE1	Gillespie	Nicol & Munro

One crossing in 1842 from Aberdeen to Quebec with 152 passengers.

Vessel	Tons	Type	Year Built	Place Built	Dimensions	Lloyd's Code	Captain	Owners/ Agents
William of Aberdeen	172	bg	1815	Aberdeen, by James Adamson	n/k	A1	James Laird	Robert Duthie

One crossing in 1816 from Aberdeen to Halifax with 6 passengers. The *Pictou Advocate* (Nov. 20, 1815) probably incorrectly referred to the Brig *William* as the *Prince William*. If so then the *William* took 95 passengers from Cromarty or Thurso to Pictou in 1815 (See Table 3).

Vessel	Tons	Type	Year Built	Place Built	Dimensions	Lloyd's Code	Captain	Owners/ Agents
Ythan of Aberdeen	264	s	n/k	Newburgh	n/k	A1	Alexander Craigie	John Black of Newburgh

Two crossings (1816–17) from Aberdeen to Halifax/Miramichi with 23 passengers.

APPENDIX B

Passenger Lists

1. A List of Passengers who sailed on the *Ossian* of Leith, Captain Hill, from Cromarty to Pictou, June 1821 (*Inverness Journal* June 29, 1821)

"We have been favoured with the following list of the emigrants from Sutherlandshire who sailed from Cromarty, for Pictou, on Monday the 25th inst. per the *Ossian* of Leith, Captain Hill, with the particulars of the aid afforded to them from the fund raised by subscription in Bengal, and remitted by Messrs. Mac-Kintosh & Co. 'for Relief of the Expatriated Highlanders of Sutherland.'

Name	Aged	Family Adults	Under 14	Cash £.	S.	D.	Hat-chets	Spa-des	Pick-axes	Saws	Nails 1000	Gaelic Bibles	English Bibles	Tartan Yds	Barrels Pork
Jo. Sutherland, Miller	70	8	5	45	15	6	3	3	2	3	2	2	2	36	?
Dd. Suthd. M'Quarlish	50	4	5	5	15	6	2	2	1	2	1	1	2	20	?
Angus MacKay	40														
William Miller	36	4	1	10	0	0	2	2	2	2	2	1	2	24	?
Al. Suthd. M'Quarlish	50	3	5	20	9	6	1	1	1	1	1	1	1	15	?
Margt. Baillie, widow	55	8	1	39	7	6	4	4	2	2	2	2	2	36	?
Donald Sutherland	46	2	4	15	15	0	1	2	1	1	1	1	2	15	?
Robert McKay	70	7	1	30	0	0	1	2	1	1	2	1	2	18	?
William McDonald	55	5	5	31	0	0	2	3	2	1	1	2	2	24	?
George Baillie	46	4	5	26	15	6	2	2	2	1	1	2	2	25	?

Name	Aged	Family Adults	Under 14	Cash £.	S.	D.	Hat-chets	Spa-des	Pick-axes	Saws	Nails 1000	Gaelic Bibles	English Bibles	Tartan Yds	Barrels Pork
Mgt. McDonald, widow	60	4	0	18	18	0	2	2	1	1	1	2	2	12	?
Ann Sutherland, do.	55	4	0	14	14	0	2	2	1	1	1	1	1	12	?
Don. & Chr. Ross	19 & 20	2	0	9	9	0	0	0	0	0	0	1	2	6	?
Hugh McLeod	50	6	0	28	7	0	2	2	1	1	1	1	1	15	?
Donald Douglas	30	1	0	0	0	0	1	1	0	0	0	1	1	3	0
Norman Douglas	18	1	0	0	0	0	1	1	0	0	0	1	0	3	0
Jean Sutherland	22	1	0	0	0	0	0	0	0	0	0	0	1	3	0
Margaret Murray	30	1	0	4	14	6	0	0	0	0	0	0	0	3	0
Donald McDonald	16	1	0	4	14	6	0	1	0	0	0	0	1	5	0
Jean Murray	25	1	0	4	14	6	0	0	0	0	0	0	1	3	0
Alex. Grant, and	34														
Alex. McLeod	32	5	4	29	18	6	3	3	2	2	2	1	2	30	?

The *Ossian* was chartered to carry the Sutherland emigrants at the very moderate rate of Four Guineas and a Half for adults, and One Guinea and a Half for passengers under fourteen years of age. Her stores, of all descriptions, were laid in at Leith, of the best quality, at the sight of the Freighter."

2. A List of Passengers who sailed on the *Emperor Alexander* of Aberdeen,[1] Alexander Watt (captain), from Tobermory to Sydney, Cape Breton, July 1823. (*Inverness Journal* Jan 30, 1824)

"This is to certify that Mr. John McEACHERN, the steward on board the *Emperor Alexander*, of Aberdeen, for Mr. Archibald McNIVEN,[2] has done all manner of justice to us and all our fellow-passengers during out passage; and we further declare, that Captain ALEXANDER WATTS behaved to all his passengers with great humanity.
SYDNEY, CAPE BRETON ISLAND, 16th Sept. 1823"

Kintail

DUNCAN MACRA
GEORGE MACRA
ALEX. MACRA
DONALD MACCULLOCH
JOHN MACLENNAN
MALCOLM McCRIMMAN
JOHN McEARLICH
RODk. McLENNAN
ALLAN MACDONALD

S. Uist

his
ALLAN "X" MACDONALD
mark
his
DONALD "X" MACDONALD
mark
her
CHRISTIAN "X" MACDONALD
mark
his
RONALD "X" MACINTYRE
mark
his
JOHN "X" MACINTYRE
mark
her
EFFY "X" MACINTYRE
mark
her
MARION "X" MORISON
mark
his
JOHN "X" O'HEULY
mark

his
ALEX. "X" MACINTYRE
mark
his
ANGUS "X" MACINTYRE
mark
his
JOHN "X" CURRIE
mark
his
JOHN "X" STEEL
mark
his
NIEL "X" BEATON
mark
his
RANALD "X" O'HEULY
mark
his
ANGUS "X" O'HEULY
mark
his
ALEXANDER "X" STEEL
mark
his
JOHN "X" SMITH
mark

Benbecula

his
DUNCAN "X" MACINTYRE
mark
his
ANGUS "X" MACINTYRE
mark

Badenoch

ARCHIBALD MACDONALD

Arisaig

JOHN MACDONALD

Barra

his
MALCOLM "X" MACDOUGALL
mark

N. Uist

MALCOLM MACDONALD
ANGUS MACDONALD

NOTES

1. THE EXODUS TAKES SHAPE

1. Extract of a letter to the editor of the *Aberdeen Journal* (*AJ* Sept. 27, 1773).
2. *Scots Magazine,* vol. xxxv, 557.
3. The government investigated the factors behind the exodus of 1774–75. The passenger lists produced from this exercise have been reprinted in Viola Root Cameron, *Emigrants from Scotland to America 1774–1775* (Baltimore: Genealogical Publishing Co., 1965).
4. *Scots Magazine,* vol. xxxvi, 221, vol. xxxvii, 340.
5. Ian Hustwick, *Moray Firth, Ships and Trade during the Nineteenth Century* (Aberdeen: Scottish Cultural Press, 1994), 37, 42–43, 53–54.
6. For example, the *Bruce* in 1820 and the *Thistle* in 1821 which had both set off from Aberdeen, were being advertised as vessels which would stop to collect emigrants at Cromarty and take them to various ports in British America. *Inverness Courier,* June 1, 1820, June 22, 1821.
7. *Parliamentary Papers, Emigration returns for British North America, 1830–40; Colonial Land and Emigration Commissioners, Annual Reports, 1841–55.*
8. Emigrant transport legislation is discussed in Oliver Macdonagh, *A Pattern of Government Growth 1800–1860: The Passenger Acts and their enforcement* (London: Macgibbon & Kee, 1961) 80–9, 148–51, 216–9, 237–45, 337–49.
9. Dating back to the late eighteenth century, the *Lloyd's Shipping Register* offers a unique and highly reliable indicator of the quality of the individual vessels in use year by year. This source reveals that, with few exceptions, Aberdeen shippers provided emigrants with first class ships (i.e. rated A1 or AE1).
10. Lloyd's shipping intelligence was procured through paid correspondents in the main ports both in Britain and abroad. Initially, entries gave the vessel's date of departure, the port of departure, the Captain's name and destinations. Arrivals were recorded in the same manner. However, by 1812 *Lloyd's List* confined itself to only recording vessel arrivals. Ralph Straus, *Lloyds: A Historical Sketch* (London: Hutchinson, 1937).
11. While they are far from reliable or complete, the customs records for the main Scottish ports (SRO E.504 series from 1776 to 1830) often provide details of passenger numbers for individual vessels. Apart from the *Quebec Mercury,* which provides an invaluable and unique source of information on emigrant totals by vessel from the late eighteenth century, the other major statistical source is J.S. Martell, *Immigration to and Emigration from Nova Scotia 1815–38* (Halifax: PANS, 1942) which records data extracted

from customs records and local newspapers.

12. The space available between decks (horizontal platforms) was crucial to the comfort of passengers. Until 1842 the minimum legal limit was five and a half feet.

13. Data on the location of Scottish-born settlers is taken from the 1851 Census of Upper Canada, while ethnicity data for the Maritimes is taken from the Census returns for 1851, 1861 and 1871.

14. Elizabeth Ann Kerr McDougall and John S. Moir (eds.), *Selected Correspondence of the Glasgow Colonial Society 1825–1840* (Toronto: Toronto Champlain Society, 1994). The Quebec Immigration Agent's weekly reports are published as *Parliamentary Papers*. The Quebec Immigration Agent's Annual Reports commence as a series from 1831. They are published in the *British Parliamentary Papers* and are to be found under *Colonies, Canada* in the Irish University Press Reprints. The Immigration Agent's reports can give information on the geographical origins and destinations of emigrants and sometimes give details of their former occupations and economic status. For statistical data on the numbers of emigrants arriving in British North America from British ports see the *British Parliamentary Papers*: Emigration Returns (1830–1840) and the Annual Reports of the Colonial Land and Emigration Commissioners (1841–1855) which are to be found under *Emigration* in the Irish University Press Reprints.

15. Until Confederation in 1867, what we now call British North America consisted of separate self-governing colonies. The arrival of Loyalist settlers had an explosive effect on population, particularly in the Maritimes. Twenty thousand were added to the permanent population of Nova Scotia. New Brunswick province, created in 1784, took its population mainly from the 15,000 Loyalists who settled there. G. Wynn, "A Region of Scattered Settlements and Bounded Possibilities: Northeastern America 1775–1800" in *The Canadian Geographer*, Vol. 31 (1987) 319–21. Loyalists received free land with each family head being entitled to 100 acres. In addition, they could claim for provisions and other help under the British Loyalist assistance program.

16. David S. MacMillan, "Scottish Enterprise and Influences in Canada 1620–1900" in Cage, (ed.); *The Scots Abroad: Labour, Capital, Enterprise, 1750–1914* (London: Croom Helm, 1985) 63–64.

17. Former members of the Hamilton Regiment (the 82nd), who included both Lowlanders and Highlanders, also acquired land in Pictou, while men from the Fraser Highlanders (the 78th) also received land in Chatham. For the Glengarry settlements see Marianne McLean, *People of Glengarry 1745–1820: Highlanders in Transition 1745–1820* (Montreal: McGill-Queen's University Press, 1991) 102–14; for Pictou see Donald MacKay, *Scotland Farewell: The People of the Hector* (Toronto: Natural Heritage, 1996) 161–68; for Chatham in Lower Canada see Norman MacDonald, *Canada: Immigration and Settlement 1763–1841* (London: Longmans & Co., 1939) 478–80.

18. Jacqueline Rinn, "Factors in Scottish Emigration: A study of Scottish participation in the indentured and transportation systems of the New World in the seventeenth and eighteenth centuries," (Aberdeen University, unpublished Ph.D. thesis 1979) 387–95.

19. In 1775, a fifth of all British emigrants originated from the Highlands and Islands, second only to London as a source of immigrants. James Horn, "British Diaspora: Emigration from Britain, 1680–1815" in P.J. Marshall (ed.), *The Oxford History of the British Empire: The Eighteenth Century* (Oxford: Oxford University Press, 1998) 28–52.

20. Tacksmen were an elite class in the Scottish feudal system who acted as factors or farm managers under a laird. Lucille H. Campey, *"A Very Fine Class of Immigrants": Prince*

Edward Island's Scottish Pioneers, 1770–1850 (Toronto: Natural Heritage, 2001) 16–31.

21. R.H. Campbell, *Scotland Since 1707: The Rise of an Industrial Society* (Edinburgh: John Donald, 1985) 135–42; Helen Cowan, *British Emigration to British North America: The First Hundred Years* (Toronto: University of Toronto Library, 1961) 55–64.

22. Kelp is burnt seaweed which was formerly used in the manufacture of soap and glass. Production was primarily concentrated in the Outer Hebrides, in Skye and Mull, and in some Argyll coastal mainland areas. It was virtually wiped out by the 1820s as cheap imports of equivalent products broke into its former markets. Many of the people displaced by its demise settled in the Loch Lomond and Margaree regions of Cape Breton, the Uigg district of Prince Edward Island and in the Huron Tract of Upper Canada.

23. Eric Richards, *A History of the Highland Clearances: Emigration, Protest, Reasons* (London: Croom Helm, 1985) 286–87, 316–62. Initially most of the ships originated from Aberdeen, but in time vessels from Leith and other east coast ports were also involved.

24. Zorra in Oxford County was first colonized by Sutherland settlers in the 1830s, under the leadership of Angus and William MacKay. A major Scottish Presbyterian stronghold, it became one of the most highly concentrated Scottish clusters within western Upper Canada.

25. The 1851 Census reveals high concentrations of Scottish settlements in Huron, Perth, Oxford, Waterloo and Wellington counties. Marjory Harper, *Emigration from North-East Scotland* Vol. 1, *Willing Exiles* (Aberdeen: Aberdeen University Press, 1988) 215–24.

26. At this time, passenger accommodation for most consisted of crudely constructed berths in a ship's hold. Shippers had space to fill going from east to west and offered cheap steerage rates. But in going from west to east ships were packed with timber, thus restricting opportunities for travelling in the steerage.

II. EARLY ATLANTIC CROSSINGS 1774–1815

1. *Aberdeen Journal*, April 24, 1811. A roup is an auction.
2. *Inverness Journal*, May 27, 1814.
3. A prize is the name given to describe an enemy vessel captured at sea.
4. The *Perseverance* took emigrants from Stornoway to Quebec in 1816 and from Tobermory to Pictou in 1818 (E.504/33/3); George MacLaren, *The Pictou Book* (New Glasgow, Nova Scotia: The Hector Publishing Co., 1954) 119.
5. The one exception was the *Tweed* of Ullapool, a 75-ton sloop built in 1765 and owned by merchants in Loch Broom, which took 70 emigrants from Isle Martin (Ullapool) to Pictou in 1802 (HCA D217/20).
6. The punitive tariffs against Baltic timber never completely eliminated it from British markets. In the early 1840s it accounted for almost 20% of timber imported into Britain. Eric Sager, with G.E. Panting, *Maritime Capital: The Shipping Industry in Atlantic Canada 1820–1914* (Montreal: McGill-Queen's University Press, 1990) 38–46; Gerald S. Graham, *Sea Power and British North America 1785–1820: A Study in British Colonial Policy* (Cambridge, Mass.: Harvard University Press, 1941) Appendix C.
7. Rinn, "Factors in Scottish Emigration," 274–97.
8. *Aberdeen Journal*, June 5, 1775.
9. Public Archives of Nova Scotia MG7 Vol. 3A. Ian Adams and Meredyth Somerville, *Cargoes of Despair and Hope: Scottish Emigration to North America 1603–1803* (Edinburgh:

John Donald, 1993) 124, 217.

10. *Aberdeen Journal,* Jan 12, May 17, 1784.

11. Port Roseway, located near Shelburne, Nova Scotia, had, from the late eighteenth century, attracted large numbers of British Empire Loyalists and British ex-military personnel. *AJ* July 19, 1784.

12. The *John* was due to sail on to Philadelphia after leaving Nova Scotia. *AJ* Feb. 23, May 17, 1784.

13. The 1803 Passenger Act required more generous allocations of space and provisions than had been the case before. Macdonagh, *The Passenger Acts,* 54–62.

14. The *Dove* of Aberdeen and the *Sarah* of Liverpool together had taken some 570 souls from Fort William to Pictou in 1801. SRO RH 2/4/87; *Dictionary of Canadian Biography,* Vol. VII, 244–46.

15. Colin S. MacDonald, "Early Highland Emigration to Nova Scotia and Prince Edward Island from 1770 to 1853," *Nova Scotia Historical Society (Collections),* vol. xxiii (Halifax: Nova Scotia Historical Society, 1936) 44.

16. Public Archives of Prince Edward Island 2702; E.504/35/1.

17. *Quebec Mercury,* June 2, 1806; *Quebec Gazette,* Aug. 16, 1810.

18. *Aberdeen Journal,* Apr. 11, 1810.

19. Ralph Davis, *The Industrial Revolution and British Overseas Trade* (Leicester: Leicester University Press, 1979) 48–49. Duties increased from 25s. per load in 1804 to 54s. 6d. per load in 1811. Between 1814 and 1843 Baltic timber was sometimes shipped to North America and then back to Britain, as the saving of duty more than compensated for the double freight.

20. Scottish Record Office E.504/1/24.

21. They sailed on the *Barbara* of London and five Aberdeen-registered vessels: the *Ploughman, Alert, Mary, Patriot* and *Cambria*; QG May 30, 1812; *AJ* Jan. 29, Feb. 26, 1812.

22. Scottish Customs records show that, altogether, 35 passengers sailed in 1813 on the *Cambria, Ploughman* and *Venus* and 72 sailed in 1814 on the *Mary, Cambria* and *Halifax Packet* of Sunderland (SRO E.504/1/24, 25).

23. The vessels were the *Amethyst, Fame, Mary, Carolina, Halifax Packet* of Sunderland, *Seven Sisters, Phesdo, Wellington, Ruby, Glentanner, Helen* (SRO E.504/1/25; *NBRG* July 27, 1815; *IJ* May 5, 1815).

24. *Inverness Journal,* Feb. 12, 1813; *Lloyd's Shipping Register.*

III. THE TIMBER TRADE GROWS AND EMIGRANTS FOLLOW, 1816–30

1. *Aberdeen Journal,* Feb. 14, 1816.

2. In the British system, shipownership meant owning shares measured in 64ths. A typical merchant shipowner would own part shares in several vessels. Ownership of a particular vessel would often be widely dispersed amongst a business community, mainly comprised of merchants, sea captains and shipbuilders but also including lawyers, farmers, fishermen and tradesmen.

3. By 1816 only around 60% of the vessel crossings from Scotland to British America had originated from Clyde ports.

4. Measurements are taken from Aberdeen City Archives CE87/11/1, 2. The *Louisa* had an "E1" rating in the *Lloyd's Shipping Register.* See the Appendix for more details of

Lloyd's Shipping Codes.

5. E.504/1/24, 25. The E504 designation refers to the Customs Records for individual Scottish ports. They are held at the Scottish Record Office and list the goods which were imported and exported to and from each port.

6. E.504/1/26; *AJ* Feb. 14, 1816; *Lloyd's List.*

7. E.504/1/24; *AJ* Jan. 29, 1812.

8. E.504/1/26, 27.

9. E.504/1/25, 26; *NBRG* July 27, 1815; June 29, 1816. *IJ* May 5, 1815; *AJ* Jan. 3 1816.

10. Martell, *Immigration Nova Scotia*, 45; E.504/1/26.

11. *Aberdeen Journal*, May 8, 1817.

12. The *Patriot* took 14 passengers to Quebec in 1817. Its "E2" rating meant that the *Sprightly* was seaworthy, although of below standard construction. E.504/11/18; *DC* Jan. 17, 1817.

13. The *Phesdo* (245 tons) measured 87' long x 26.1' wide x 16.9' deep, the *Aimwell* (232 tons) 85' x 25.10' x 16.9' and the *Sprightly* (190 tons) 82.6' x 24' x 15.3'. The importance of hull design in influencing the choice of vessel used to carry passengers is discussed in Chapter 6.

14. Conditions in troop transports were usually very cramped. See the advertisement for the sale of the *Ganges* in *Aberdeen Journal* March 14, 1810, and for the *Nestor* in *AJ* March 17, 1810. The *Ganges* carried only 4 passengers in 1817 and the *Nestor* had 5 in 1822 (E.504/1/27; *QM* July 9, 1822).

15. The *Fancy* took two cabin and thirteen steerage passengers. E.504/15/112; *QM* Aug. 20, 1816.

16. E.504/1/26; *QM* June 7, June 25, July 23, 1816.

17. Official figures published in the *British Parliamentary Papers* are only available from 1825. Before 1825 emigrant numbers have had to be computed from a wide range of sources including customs records, newspaper shipping reports and miscellaneous archival and printed items. By their nature such sources will not necessarily include all passenger crossings and thus are likely to underrecord the numbers involved.

18. In 1820, Aberdeen had 374 vessels of 51,852 tons; Greenock came next with 338 vessels of 44,107 tons, while Leith was third with 213 vessels of 24,874 tons. Bruce Lenman, *An Economic History of Modern Scotland 1600–1976* (London: Batsford, 1977) 104–18, 123–24; Henry Hamilton, *The Industrial Revolution in Scotland* (Oxford: Clarendon Press, 1932) 214–15.

19. *Lloyd's List* shows that the vessels returned back to Aberdeen, while the Scottish Custom Records reveal that their return cargoes were predominantly timber.

20. E.540/1/26; E.504/7/5; E.504/33/3. Passenger numbers for Highland ports may on occasion include people who boarded ship at Aberdeen. For example the *Aimwell's* passengers who sailed to Halifax in 1816 included 74 who embarked at Thurso and 27 who embarked at Aberdeen.

21. E.504/7/5.

22. E504/35/2; *PEIG* Sept. 3, 1819; *QM* Sept. 14; Martell, *Immigration Nova Scotia,* 49.

23. *Aberdeen Journal*, April 24, 1811; the Lloyd's rating for the *Perseverance* could not be found and the presumption must be that she was never surveyed.

24. A galliot became the accepted term for a small Dutch trading vessel. The hull was built in a barge fashion with a rounded bow. David R. MacGregor, *Merchant Sailing*

Ships, Sovereignty of Sail 1775–1815 (London: Conway Maritime Press, 1985) 39–43; Keble Edward Chatterton, *Sailing Ships: The Story of their Development from the Earliest Times to the Present Day* (London: Sidgwick & Jackson Ltd., 1909) 303–04.

25. The *Perseverance* carried unknown numbers of emigrants from Cromarty to Pictou and Halifax in 1814 and 1815, 52 from Stornoway to Quebec in 1816 and 150 from Skye to Pictou in 1818. *IJ* May 27, 1814; Apr. 7, 1815; E.504/33/3; MacLaren, *Pictou Book,* 119.

26. A list of passengers for the sailing of the *Emperor Alexander* to Cape Breton (Jan. 30, 1824) appears in Appendix B (1).

27. E.504/35/2; *QM* Aug. 25, 1820; *QM* Oct. 7, 1823; Martell, *Immigration Nova Scotia,* 61–3.

28. Pictou County had attracted large numbers from Sutherland, Inverness-shire, Ross-shire and Perthshire in 1802–1803; National Library of Scotland MS 9646.

29. One hundred and eight people sailed on the *Ossian* of Leith, while the *Harmony* of Aberdeen and the *Ruby* of Aberdeen together took 250 emigrants E.504/17/9; IJ July 12, 1822. The *Ossian*'s passengers included 22 families and 72 adults. A passenger list appears in *Inverness Journal* June 29, 1821.

30. Thomas Dudgeon's letters, which were published in the *Scotsman,* were highly critical of the Sutherland clearances and attracted considerable controversy. The association attracted large numbers to its meetings but failed to raise much in the way of funds. NLS SP Dep 313/1468; *IJ* June 14, 18, 1819; Jan. 21, March 31, 1820; John Prebble, *The Highland Clearances* (London: Penguin, 1969) 117–29.

31. Lloyd's gave *Ossian* an A1 rating while the *Ruby* and *Harmony* had E1 codes. George Murray had captained the *Glentanner* of Aberdeen in 1820 when she carried 141 emigrants from Tobermory to Cape Breton and Quebec (E.504/35/2; *QM* Aug. 25, 1820). He was commended by his Lochalsh passengers on the 1821 crossing of the *Glentanner* to Quebec (*IJ* Nov. 23, 1821). The unknown sources in Bengal were probably people connected with the East India Company, suggesting that the emigrants' benefactors were in commerce and trade.

32. *Aberdeen Journal,* March 9, 1831.

33. The *Albion*'s steerage was said to be "comfortably fitted up with a stove" and to have "plenty of height" (*AJ, Ibid*).

34. Aberdeen City Archives CE/87/11/4 &5; MacGregor, *Merchant Sailing Ships,* 135, 285; Victoria E. Clark, *The Port of Aberdeen: A History of its Trade and Shipping from the Twelfth Century to the Present Day* (Aberdeen: D. Wyllie & Son, 1921) 134–5.

IV. UPPER CANADA BECKONS, 1831–55

1. *Aberdeen Herald,* Jan. 30, 1836.

2. *Aberdeen Herald,* March 5, 1836.

3. MacGregor, *Merchant Sailing Ships,* 77, 135.

4. The *Brilliant* was assessed at "AE1"; her age would have prevented her from being awarded the top "A1" rating. *AJ* March 9, 1831.

5. Included in this total are 84 emigrants who sailed from Dundee to Quebec in 1833. *QM* May 24, 1830; Oct. 1, 1831; May 17, 1832; May 15, Oct. 7, 1834.

6. An advertisement for "Quebec Timber Per Ship *Brilliant*" states: "As no pains have been spared by Captain Barclay who has had experience in the trade in selecting timber of the best quality, it will be found well worth the attention of those having

occasion to purchase" *AJ* July 12, 1826.

7. *Quebec Mercury*, May 15, Sept. 16, 1826.
8. *Quebec Mercury*, Aug. 1, 1833; *Dundee Courier*, May 3, 1833.
9. The *Hercules* had an "E1" rating; ACA CE/87/11/5.
10. *Quebec Mercury*, May 15, Sept. 20 1834; *AH* April 11, 1835; *QM* Aug. 27, 1836.
11. *Quebec Mercury*, May 28, July 19, Sept. 27, 1836.
12. *Aberdeen Herald*, March 26, April 23, 1836; ACA CE 87/11/9. The *Pacific's* dimensions were 102' x 26.2' x 18.7'.
13. Some of the *Albion's* passengers may have been people on their way to the United States. Shipping advertisements for the *Albion* often pointed out that there were "regular conveyances" from Halifax to ports in the United States and the distance was given as "only about two days sailing" (e.g. *AJ* Jan. 21, 1835).
14. *Quebec Mercury*, Aug. 19, 1836. The *Highlander* also took 41 emigrants from Leith to Halifax in 1833. Martell, *Immigration Nova Scotia,* 74.
15. *Quebec Mercury*, June 6, 1835, May 22, 1838.
16. The crossings were in 1831, 1832 and 1836. *AJ* July 13, 1831; *QM* Sept. 8, 1831, May 19, 1832, May 28, 1836.
17. L.C. Cornford, *The Sea Carriers 1825–1925: The Aberdeen Line* (London: Aberdeen Line, 1925) 24.
18. *Ibid,* 21–7.
19. Clipper is a generic term used to describe types of very fast sailing vessels.
20. *Quebec Mercury*, May 23, June 2, 1832; *QM* June 6, Oct. 29, 1835; *QM* June 4, 1836.
21. *Aberdeen Herald*, March 26, 1836.
22. *Parliamentary Papers, Annual Reports of the Immigration Agent at Quebec.*
23. J.M. Bumsted, *The Peoples of Canada: A Pre-Confederation History,* Vol. 1 (Toronto: Oxford University Press, 1992) 236–57.
24. Harper, *Emigration North East Scotland,* 130–34.
25. For example, James Tulloch had captained the *Sir William Wallace* in 1839 when she took 19 emigrants to Quebec. *QM* Aug. 24, 1839.
26. George Allan had been transferred from the *Pilgrim,* another Rose vessel. She had taken a combined total of 130 emigrants to Quebec in 1835 and 1838. *QM* Aug. 4, 1835; *QM* Aug. 19, 1838.
27. The *Sisters* had 41 passengers (*PP* w/e July 18, 1840) and the *Rose* 94 (*PP* 1844(181)xxxv). The *Rose* offered "upwards of 6 feet between decks" and an experienced captain in James Gibb; *EC* May 19, 1843.
28. The *Heroine* also took 281 emigrants from Stornoway to Prince Edward Island in 1840. J. Orlo, and D. Fraser, "Those Elusive Immigrants, Part 3," *Island Magazine,* No. 18 (1985) 34.
29. He was elected to Parliament (as a Liberal) in 1852, serving until 1857. Alexander Keith, *Eminent Aberdonians* (Aberdeen: Aberdeen Chamber of Commerce, 1984) 102–06.
30. Letter from George Thompson to the Colonial Office, 1848: PRO CO 384/ 79 261–65.
31. *Parliamentary Papers* 1847–48(964)xlvii, (971)xlvii; *AH* Jan. 14, June 10, 1854.
32. *Aberdeen Herald*, Feb. 4, June 7, 1854; *QM* June 19, Oct. 16, 1855.
33. Harper, *Emigration North East Scotland,* 45.

V. CROMARTY AND THURSO: HIGHLAND GATEWAYS TO BRITISH AMERICA

1. Public Record Office CO 384/28 517–18: Letter from Lewis Rose, Manse of Nigg by Parkhill, to the Colonial Office, 18 June 1831.

2. In his letter to the Colonial Office, Rose requested that public funds be made available to help 1,000 poor families emigrate to Upper Canada.

3. A guinea was worth 21 shillings (£1.05). Fares were roughly double this amount if the passenger's food provisions were supplied by the shipper.

4. The taxes collected were also used to help finance the costs of running quarantine stations. Cowan, *British Emigration to North America*, 152–53.

5. The *Corsair* and *Rover* had left from Leith, while the arrangements for the crossings of the *Industry* and *Cleopatra* had been made from Leith.

6. National Library of Scotland SP Dep 313/1468 60, 79–81.

7. *Inverness Journal*, June 29, July 12, 1821; E.504/17/9.

8. *Aberdeen Journal*, July 19, 1784. The *Mercury* would call at Cromarty to collect passengers for Nova Scotia and Philadelphia "if encouragement shall offer."

9. Peterhead is a short distance north of Aberdeen. *Inverness Journal*, April 7, 1815, April 26, 1816, *IC* June 28, 1816; E.504/7/5, E.540/1/26; Martell, *Immigration Nova Scotia*, 40, 43.

10. For example, James Campbell owned the *James and Isabella* of Inverness, the *Isabella* of Inverness and the *Mariner* of Inverness; HCA D217/4, 217/5. Vessel crossings were advertised in: *Inverness Journal*, April 7, 1815; Feb. 6, June 19, 1818; April 1, 1819; June 1, 1820; March 9, 1821; Feb. 22, 1822.

11. *Inverness Journal*, June 10, July 1, 1836; *JJ* July 1, 1836; *QM* July 19, Sept. 16, 1836; Martell, *Immigration Nova Scotia*, 84.

12. He may be the same Duncan MacLennan who was clerk to the Harbour Trustees of the Port of Inverness in 1860. *Slater's Royal National Commercial Directory and Topography of Scotland* (Manchester: I. Slater, 1860) 730.

13. *Inverness Journal*, Feb. 17, May 18, 1832.

14. *Inverness Journal*, Feb. 15, 1833.

15. Passengers boarded ship at Scrabster on the west side of Thurso Bay.

16. The 1851 Census reveals high concentrations of Scots in Huron, Perth, Oxford, Waterloo and Wellington counties—counties which fall within or adjoin the Huron Tract. The Canada Company's appeal to Scots would have been strengthened by the Scottish roots of John Galt, its principal founder. Galt, a well-known Scottish novelist, had a practical understanding of Scottish settler needs and pursued his role as Superintendent of the Company with great vigour. Accompanied in his activities by William "Tiger" Dunlop, another Scot and literary friend, Galt founded the town of Guelph in April 1827. The town of Galt (later to become part of Cambridge) was named in honour of John Galt.

17. The partners, John Sutherland and Duncan MacLennan, regularly extracted favourable reports of high wages and work opportunities for servants, labourers and tradesmen from the Canada Company's promotional literature and gave glowing accounts of emigrant successes in its townships.

18. See for example *Inverness Journal*, Jan. 15, 1841. Not all was necessarily as presented by the Canada Company, which sometimes gave an exaggerated picture of the quality of its land and services. One Robert MacDougall, originally of Perthshire and later of

Ross, having emigrated to Upper Canada's Huron Tract with his father and brother in 1836, returned to Glasgow in 1839 to write *The Emigrant's Guide to North America*. The book, written in Gaelic, presents MacDougall's authoritative voice "For I was there, and I saw it." Robert MacDougall (Elizabeth Thompson, ed.) *The Emigrant's Guide to North America* (Toronto: Natural Heritage, 1998) vii.

19. *Inverness Courier*, Aug. 5, 1840, *JJ* April 10, May 29, June 26, 1840.

20. *Parliamentary Papers* w/e Aug. 22, Sept. 12, 1840.

21. Church ministers supplied information in 1844 on the scale of emigration from Scottish parishes and the nature of any financial assistance received. *Report from the Commissioners appointed for inquiring into the Administration and Practical Operation of the Poor Laws in Scotland, 1844;* Answers to Questions 30 to 32 in the Appendices, 409.

22. *Ibid*, 403–405; T.M. Devine, *The Great Highland Famine: Hunger, Emigration and the Scottish Highlands in the Nineteenth Century* (Edinburgh: John Donald, 1988) 22, 177, 206, 323–26, 332. Eddrachilles, Farr and Tongue are the parishes in the County of Sutherland in which the Duke's tenants lived.

23. Public Record Office CO 384/77 ff. 461–69: Memorial to the Colonial Office from John Sutherland, Wick, 1846. The partners supplied 3 vessels in 1840 (369), 6 in 1841 (1037), 3 in 1842 (566), 3 in 1843 (416), 2 in 1844 (188) and 2 in 1845 (142). The numbers in parentheses are passenger totals.

24. *Pictou Observer*, Sept. 6, 1842; *John O'Groat Journal* article in *Inverness Journal*, July 1, 1842.

25. MacLaren, *The Pictou Book*, 104–05; SRO RH 1/2/908 *Mechanic and Farmer,* Pictou, Nova Scotia July 28, 1841; PANS MG 100 vol. 167 #8, *The Times*, Aug. 22, 1843.

26. *Pictou Observer*, Nov. 22, 1842.

27. In 1848, the *Ellen* of Liverpool sailed from Loch Laxford to Pictou with 154 passengers while the *Greenock* of Glasgow sailed to Quebec with 399 people. MacLaren, *The Pictou Book*, 108–10; PP w/e June 30. The *Scotia* also sailed that year from Loch Eriboll to Quebec with 196 passengers and, in 1847, the *Panama* took 279 emigrants from Loch Laxford to Quebec. *PP* 1847–48(964)XLVII; *PP* w/e July 8.

28. *John O'Groat Journal*, June 15, 1849.

29. *Ibid*, Sept. 25, 1840.

30. Frank Foden, *Wick of the North: The Story of a Scottish Royal Burgh* (Wick: North of Scotland Newspapers, 1996) 16, 458–9, 466–8.

31. Public Record Office CO 384/77 469. In considering his request to be appointed as an agent, the Colonial Office correspondence noted the support of Mr. Loch. In his letter to Mr. Traill, the M.P. for Wick, John Sutherland stressed the importance of having an agent who spoke Gaelic and could relate the advantages of life in British America.

32. The snuff box can be seen at the National Museum of Scotland in Edinburgh.

33. *John O'Groat Journal*, Sept. 26, 1851.

VI. THE ABERDEEN SAILING SHIPS WHICH CARRIED EMIGRANTS

1. *Aberdeen Journal*, Oct. 16, 1861.

2. *Quebec Mercury*, May 15, Sept. 16, 1826; May 5, 1827. *QM* May 17, 1833; May 15, Oct. 7, 1834; Oct. 13, 1835; *QM* June 4, Oct. 6, 1836.

3. William (1789–1861) established the firm and it went to his brothers Alexander (1799–1863) and John (1792–1880) in that order. *Day of the Clipper,* Textual record of the exhibition held at James Dun's House, 61 Schoolhill, Aberdeen, Nov. 2, 1979–March

25, 1980—Photo Panel 9.

4. The term clipper initially referred to the American-built schooners, which were known as Baltimore clippers.

5. Clipper ships which were sent from Britain to Australia to collect gold during the great gold rush beginning in the early 1850s, often carried emigrants. David R. Mac-Gregor, *Clipper Ships* (Watford: Angus Books, 1979) 110; Basil Lubbock, *The Colonial Clippers* (Glasgow: Brown, Son and Ferguson, 1948) 87, 118–20.

6. Clark, *The Port of Aberdeen*, 126–27.

7. *Ibid*, 140–42; Diane Morgan, *Villages of Aberdeen, Footdee and her Shipyards* (Aberdeen: Denburn Books, 1993) 41, 147, 165, 169.

8. David R. MacGregor, *Merchant Sailing Ships: Supremacy of Sail 1815–1850* (London: Conway Maritime Press, 1984) 111–12.

9. The *Hercules* was one of fourteen ships employed in Aberdeen's whaling industry in 1817 (Clark, *Port of Aberdeen*, 134–35). Two other ships amongst these, the *St. Andrew* and *Neptune*, were used in the 1840s to transport timber from the Maritimes to Aberdeen (see below). The *Heroine*'s use as a whaler is described in George A. MacKenzie, ed., *From Aberdeen to Ottawa in 1845: The Diary of Alexander Muir* (Aberdeen: Aberdeen University Press, 1990) 77. The *Brilliant* was one of two ships (the other being the *Don*) built in 1814 by Alexander Hall for the whaling trade. MacGregor, *Merchant Sailing Ships*, 135.

10. Gordon Jackson, *The British Whaling Trade* (London: A & C Black, 1978) 88–89, 130, 144–45.

11. MacGregor, *Merchant Sailing Ships*, 83–87. Sheathing consisted of thin copper plates secured to the bottom of wooden ships to give protection and help preserve the wood.

12. *Dundee Courier*, Feb. 7, 1834. It is not known whether the *Fairy* took passengers on her 1834 crossing. The advertisement for the crossing included a commendation supplied by James Soot from 30 to 40 passengers who travelled on this ship the previous year. Soot had interests in both the Dundee New Whale Fishing Company and the Union Whale Fishing Company (Dundee City Archives, CE70/11).

13. Even in 1834, only 121 emigrants left for British America from Dundee, representing a tiny fraction of the 1,800 who left from the Clyde and the 566 who left from Leith (*PP Emigration Returns*).

14. *Aberdeen Directory 1840–1841*. Clark, *Port of Aberdeen*, 134–5.

15. To ensure maximum profits, shipowners needed to set time limits on the use of their ships. Sailing times across the Atlantic were unpredictable, but strict time limits could be set on the time taken to load and unload cargoes.

16. Aberdeen University MS 2295/6.

17. *Ibid* 2295/3.

18. *Ibid* 129–31, 158.

19. Sager, *Maritime Capital*, 51–62.

20. A vessel sailing against the wind sails as near to the wind as she can. She does this when all her sails are just full of wind without any shivers in the sails. In a square-rigged vessel this is achieved when the wind coming over the bow fills the sails and draws the vessel forward.

21. MacGregor, *Merchant Sailing Ships*, 64–68.

22. Aberdeen City Archives CE87/11/2.

23. The *Perseverance* had a length to breadth ratio of 3.1 to 1 while the *Ruby*'s was 3.16 to 1 and the *Thistle*'s 3.1 to 1.

24. The *Mary*'s dimensions were 73' 1" long by 21' 6" breadth by 12' 5" deep. She had roughly the same proportions as a typical two-masted collier brig, with a length to breadth ratio of 3.4 to 1. See MacGregor, *Merchant Sailing Ships*, 57–59, 139–46. He shows a design of a collier brig giving 6 feet of headroom between the main and lower deck at the stern end.

25. *Aberdeen Journal*, March 17, 1810. Conditions on troop transports in the early nineteenth century were grim. J.M. Bumsted, *The People's Clearance: Highland Emigration to British North America 1770–1815* (Edinburgh: Edinburgh University Press, 1982) 102–3.

26. Schooners were fore-and-aft rigged vessels normally used in the fishing or coastal trade. E.504/1/26; *QM* Sept. 26, 1816.

27. E.504/1/26; *DC*, Feb. 5, 1829.

28. Their length to breadth ratio was in the range of 3.5–3.7 to 1, making these vessels thinner than average. At this time, most brigs or snows of 250 tons or less would have had a length to breadth ratio range of 3.1–3.6 to 1. See Sager, *Maritime Capital*, 61–2.

29. In 1826, the *Aberdeenshire* left Aberdeen for Halifax with a cargo which included bricks, linen, cotton, wearing apparel, beer, barley, oatmeal and haberdashery. The *Quebec Packet* left Aberdeen for Quebec with a cargo which included cheese, marmalade, barley, oatmeal, newspapers, seeds, wearing apparel, linen, cottons, woollens, leather and earthenware (E.540/1/31, 32).

30. MacKenzie, *The Diary of Alexander Muir*, 82.

31. MacGregor, *Merchant Sailing Ships*, 163–70.

32. *John O'Groat Journal*, June 26, 1840.

33. The ship was squared-rigged on all three masts while the barque was square-rigged on the fore and main mast but fore-and-aft rigged on the mizen. With the fore-and-aft rig, sails lie along the same plane as the vessel's fore and aft line.

34. Register tonnage determined a vessel's liability for customs dues and navigation fees. Before 1836 the formula used to calculate tonnage was based only on breadth and length, but after 1836 it included the depth as well. David R. MacGregor, *Fast Sailing Ships: Their Design and Construction, 1775–1875* (London: Conway Maritime Press, 1988) 283–85.

35. *Ibid*, 99–115.

36. The *Taurus* took 134 passengers from Aberdeen to Quebec in 1841. See PP w/e July 17. At 84' 6 " long by 20' 5" wide by 13' 5" deep, she would have had an unusually slim design.

37. Aberdeen City Archives CE87/11/1; *Aberdeen Journal* March 9, 1831.

38. Cowan, *British Emigration*, 149.

39. Macdonagh, *The Passenger Acts*, 150–51.

VII. EMIGRANT SEA VOYAGES: A GOOD OR BAD EXPERIENCE?

1. Extract of a letter "from an intelligent and respectable Aberdonian who emigrated to Upper Canada last Spring" printed in the *Aberdeen Herald*, March 26, 1836.

2. Highland Council Archives D207, James Fraser's reminiscences 10th July, 1867, London, Ontario. He describes the crossing of the *Diligence* in 1820 from Cromarty to Pictou with 130 passengers. The 107th Psalm contains the verses: "Others there are

who go to sea in ships and make their living on the wide waters. These men have seen the acts of the Lord and his marvellous doings in the deep. At his command the storm-wind rose and lifted the waves high.... So they cried to the Lord in their trouble and he brought them out of their distress."

3. *Ibid.*

4. *Aberdeen Journal,* June 29, 1836. The letter was signed by John Dickie, James Morrison, Joseph Elmsly, J.N. MacLean, William Primrose, John Duncan and George Nicol on behalf of 49 passengers.

5. James Elliot was captain of the *Molson* when she sailed with passengers from Dundee to Quebec in 1832 and 1833 (*QM* May 16, 1832; Aug. 1, 1833).

6. "Account of a Voyage from Aberdeen to Quebec," by William Shand, contained in a letter to his brother-in-law Alexander Ragg, in Dufftown, Banffshire, in MacKenzie, *The Diary of Alexander Muir,* 113–6. The original spelling has been modified to modern spelling where appropriate.

7. MacKenzie, *The Diary of Alexander Muir,* 19, 85.

8. For example, Alexander Leslie owned 8 out of 64 shares in the *Albion,* the same number owned by James Oswald in the *Aberdeenshire* and John Morrison in the *Pacific.* Alexander Anderson, in charge of Catto's *Annandale, Carleton* and *Quebec Packet,* held 4 out of 64 shares in the first two and 5 out of 64 in the third. ACA CE87/11/1, 2, 5.

9. Thomas Fowler, *Journal of a Tour through British North America to the Falls of Niagara containing an account of the cities, towns and villages along the route in 1831* (Aberdeen: Smith, 1832) 9–10.

10. MacKenzie, *The Diary of Alexander Muir,* 113–6.

11. Bumsted, *The People's Clearance,* 142–3.

12. *Emigration Select Committee,* 1826, A 1831–36.

13. A person who had sailed from Leith to Halifax offered advice to his friend in a letter which was later published in the *Inverness Courier,* July 8, 1819.

14. Public Record Office CO 384/6, 27–8: Letter from William Allan to the Colonial Office, May 10, 1820.

15. Public Record Office CO 384/8, 230–31: Letter from Dr. John MacRa, shipowner from Lochalsh to Lord Bathurst, Jan. 29, 1822.

16. In 1841, the law required emigrants to have 3 quarts of water daily and 2 1/2 lbs. biscuit, 1 lb. flour, 5 lbs. oatmeal, 2 lbs. rice, 3/4 lb. sugar and 2 ounces tea per week. Macdonagh, *The Passenger Acts,* 74–90, 148–51.

17. The 1855 Act, containing 103 different Clauses could not realistically be enforced nor could the previous legislation which had been passed in 1847, 1848, 1849 and 1852.

18. The term burthen expressed a ship's tonnage or carrying capacity.

19. National Library of Scotland MS 9646 f. 19: *"On Emigration from the Scottish Highlands and Islands attributed to Edward S. Fraser of Inverness-shire"* (1801–4); SRO RH 2/4/87 gives passenger lists for the *Dove* of Aberdeen and *Sarah* of Liverpool crossings in 1801. The controversy associated with these ship crossings is discussed in Bumsted, *The People's Clearance,* 88–92.

20. Scottish Record Office RH 4/188/1,2: *Prize Essays and Transactions of the Highland Society of Scotland (1799–1834)* Vol. III, 441–4, 475–92, 531–35.

21. Bumsted, *The People's Clearance*, 147–8; Macdonagh, *The Passenger Acts*, 57.
22. Some shipping advertisements made a special point of referring to the reduced fares which became available as a result of the relaxation in the tonnage to passenger number ratio. A typical fare for a passage from Cromarty to Pictou in 1819 was £10. 10s. in the cabin and £7. 7s. in the steerage (*IJ* 15 Jan, 3 March, 1819).
23. E.504/35/2; *PEIG* Sept. 3, 1819. One hundred people arrived at Charlottetown and 64 at Pictou.
24. E.504/1/26; E.504/7/5; Martell, *Immigration, Nova Scotia*, 40; *QM* Oct. 19, 1821; *QM* Oct. 7, 1823.
25. *Inverness Journal*, Jan. 30, 1824.
26. Martell, *Immigration, Nova Scotia*, 49; E.504/35/2.
27. These fares were for crossings from the Highlands to Cape Breton in the early 1820s. *Emigration Select Committee, 1826*, A 329.
28. Macdonagh, *The Passenger Acts*, 54–62.
29. Edwin C. Guillet, *The Great Migration: The Atlantic Crossing by Sailing Ships Since 1770*, 2nd ed. (Toronto: University of Toronto Press, 1963) 13–19.
30. *Inverness Journal*, March 29, June 7 1833; *QM* Aug. 29, 1833.
31. *Inverness Journal*, Feb. 22, 1833; *QM* June 4, 1833.
32. *Report from the Select Committee on the Passenger Acts* 1851, XIX, A911, A5054–5065.
33. *Moray, Nairn and Banff Courant*, April 28, 1837; *QM* July 27, 1837.
34. Steerage rates were £5 if food was supplied by the shipper. MacKenzie, *The Diary of Alexander Muir*, 83.
35. *Inverness Courier*, Aug. 5, 1840; *PP* w/e Sept. 12.
36. *John O'Groat Journal*, June 26, 1840.
37. Scottish Record Office GD 46/13/184: *Information published by His Majesty's Commissioners for Emigration respecting the British Colonies in North America* (London, Feb. 1832) 7.
38. Susan Longley (Morse) Flewwelling, "Immigration to and Emigration from Nova Scotia 1839–51," *Nova Scotia Historical Society (Collections)*, vol. xxviii (1949) 82–85.
39. *Parliamentary Papers* w/e Oct. 31, 1855.
40. Scottish Record Office GD 46/13/184, 6–7.
41. Macdonagh, *The Passenger Acts*, 150–51.
42. Aberdeen City Archives CE87/11/6,9; *AJ* April 20, 1836; *JJ* June 10, 1842.
43. Length to breadth ratios were now in the range from 4.2–5.0 to 1. Both the *St. Lawrence* and *Aurora* offered seven feet between decks (*AH* June 19, 1852; Feb. 4, 1854).
44. The *Lloyd's Shipping Register* is available as a regular series from 1775 apart from the years 1785, 1788 and 1817.
45. Still in use today and run by a Classification Society with a worldwide network of offices and administrative staff, the *Lloyd's Register* continues to provide standard classifications of quality for shipbuilding and maintenance. George Blake, *Lloyd's Register of Shipping 1760–1960* (London: Lloyd's, 1960) 1–7, 26.
46. The number of years that a ship could hold the highest code varied according to where it was built. In time, rivalries developed between shipowners and underwriters and this led to the publication of two Registers between 1800 and 1833—the *Shipowners Register* (Red Book) and the *Underwriters Register* (Green Book). Their coverage was similar but not identical. By 1834, with bankruptcies facing both sides, the

two Registers joined forces to become the *Lloyd's Register of British and Foreign Shipping.*

47. The Aberdeen-registered vessels which were used to carry emigrants were not unique in being of a consistently good quality. Vessels registered at other Scottish ports were of similar standard.

48. The *Dove, Economy, Mary, Traveller* and *Perseverance* were built relatively early and may never have been offered for survey in the first place. That, in itself, need not necessarily cast doubt on the quality of these vessel. The omission of the remaining three, the *Jane Boyd, Sarah* and *Sir William Wallace* can more easily be explained. They were the products of Aberdeen's finest shipyards. Alexander Hall built the *Sarah* and *Sir William Wallace* and Walter Hood the *Jane Boyd*. They would have been constructed to the highest of standards. Their owners, George Thompson and Donaldson Rose, ran large enough businesses to provide their own insurance and hence had no need to insure with Lloyd's.

49. The codes: A — first class condition, kept in the highest state of repair and efficiency and within a prescribed age limit at the time of sailing; AE — "the second description of the first class," fit, no defects but may be over a prescribed age limit; E — second class, although unfit for carrying dry cargoes were suitable for long distance sea voyages; I — third class, only suitable for short voyages (i.e. not out of Europe). These letters were followed by the number 1 or 2 which signified the condition of the vessel's equipment (anchors, cables and stores). Where satisfactory, the number 1 was used, and where not, 2 was used. George Blake, *Lloyd's Register of Shipping 1760–1960,* 12–13, 26–27.

VIII. NEW BRUNSWICK AND NOVA SCOTIA SETTLEMENTS

1. Extract of a letter from Reverend James Thomson to Mr. Alan Kerr, proprietor of a Glasgow shipping company, June 15, 1826, in McDougall et al. *Correspondence of the Glasgow Colonial Society,* 155–58.

2. A large group of Arran settlers went to New Mills in Restigouche County in 1830. See Public Record Office CO 384/22: Letter from Mr. M. Stewart to the Colonial Office, 12 March, 1829.

3. The French spelling is Boishebert. W.F. Ganong, "Monograph of the Origins of Settlements in the Province of New Brunswick," *Transactions of the Royal Society of Canada* 2nd series (10), sections 1–2 (1904) 150. In 1785, the Miramichi settlements consisted of scattered holdings stretching from the Bartibog River on the east to the point where the Miramichi River branches into northwest and southwest branches (at Beaubears Island). See Public Record Office MPI 297.

4. *Dictionary of Canadian Biography,* William Davidson: vol. IV, 195–97; *DCB* James Fraser: vol. V, 262–3. From 1812 the Glasgow merchants Pollock, Gilmour and Company were the dominant company on the north side of the Miramichi River.

5. *Dictionary of Canadian Biography,* Davidson, *Ibid.*

6. *Aberdeen Journal,* July 19, 1784.

7. The largest numbers were reported to have originated from or near Aberlour and Mortlach in Banffshire, Dallas and Duffus in Morayshire and Ardclach in Nairnshire. See Sir John Sinclair, *The Statistical Account of Scotland (1791–99),* 21 vols. (Edinburgh: M. Creech, 1791–99) Vol. XVI, 5, 327, 471, 493, 714.

8. The group was said to include an 83-year-old woman and some infants. *AJ* May 29, 1775.

9. For example, in 1774 the *George* of Greenock took 172 passengers, who included people from Strathspey, to New York. In 1775, the *Clementina* of Philadelphia took 211 passengers, who included emigrants from Morayshire and Nairnshire to Philadelphia. See Cameron, *Emigrants from Scotland*, 30–3, 81–5.

10. Scottish Record Office GD 1/620/84: Letter from Peter Clyde to Samuel Rogerson, 28 June 1830.

11. Ganong, *Settlements New Brunswick*, 123, 150, 152, 154.

12. Ganong, *Ibid*, 114–7, 175; Glasgow Colonial Society, *Seventh Annual Report of the Glasgow Colonial Society for promoting the religious interests of the Scottish settlers in British North America* (Glasgow: Glasgow Colonial Society, 1833) 12.

13. *Aberdeen Journal*, March 6, 1816.

14. Ganong, *Settlements New Brunswick*, 121,162–63.

15. Restigouche had the highest proportion of Scottish-born settlers within its early intake of population. People who could claim Scottish ancestry also made up a considerable percentage of the population of some Restigouche parishes, particularly the Colborne parish.

16. Reverend Christopher Atkinson, *An Historical and Statistical Account of New Brunswick, British North America* (Edinburgh: n.p., 1844). See especially pp. 45–55, 80–109, 230–43.

17. Harper, *Emigration North East Scotland*, 224–35; Ganong, *Settlements New Brunswick*, 134, 143. Glassville was named after the settlers' Presbyterian minister, Reverend Charles Gordon Glass. The "Scotch Colony" was also known as Kincardine.

18. The New Brunswick Census for 1851 reveals that the Irish far outnumbered all other immigrant groups, forming 71% of the total immigration and constituting about 15% of the total population of the Province. Next, in numeric terms came the Scots. Ganong, *Settlements New Brunswick*, 76.

19. Although Liddell's interests were mainly based on trade with Saint Petersburg, he also formed other companies. In all, he had co-partnerships with John Liddell (Halifax), John Clark (Miramichi), Edward Mortimer (Pictou) and Alexander Murison (Halifax).

20. *Dictionary of Canadian Biography*, Edward Mortimer, vol. V, 611–12. Mortimer obtained a 21-year lease for the entire Pictou coal mines in 1818. George Patterson, *History of the County of Pictou* (Montreal: Dawson & Bros., 1877) 250–68.

21. *Dictionary of Canadian Biography*, John Black, vol. VI, 60–61. MacMillan, *Scottish Enterprise*, 66–72.

22. *Ibid*, 303–8.

23. Andrew H. Clark, "Old World Origins and Religious Adherence in Nova Scotia," *Geographical Review*, vol. l (1960) 317–44. The communities founded by the first group of Highland Scots, who arrived on the *Hector* in 1773, are described in MacKay, *Scotland Farewell*, 135–68.

24. D.F. Campbell and R.A. MacLean, *Beyond the Atlantic Roar: A Study of the Nova Scotia Scots* (Toronto: McClelland & Stewart, 1974) 35–75; Patterson, *History of Pictou*, 222–75.

25. Patterson, *Ibid*, 276, 279; Campbell and MacLean, *Ibid*, 46; E504/9/9.

26. Richards, *Highland Clearances*, 316–43.

27. Robert Brown, *Strictures and Remarks on the Earl of Selkirk's Observations on the Present State of the Highlands with a view of the causes and probable consequences of emigration* (Edinburgh: Abernethy & Walker, 1806) Appendix; Patterson, *History of Pictou*, 236. Brown reported that 200 Sutherland emigrants travelled on two vessels from Ullapool, which had been arranged by a Mr. D. Roy from America.

28. National Library of Scotland SP Dep 313/1128/29: Letter from William Young to Earl Gower, May 1813. The word "run" refers to the Runrig method of farming used at that time in Scotland. Arable fields (the infields of a locality) were continually under cultivation while the outlying areas (or outfields) were only occasionally cultivated.
29. Donald McLeod, *History of the Destitution in Sutherlandshire* (Edinburgh: n.p., 1841) 6.
30. The group included men with service in the "local militia of Scotland," probably Lord Reay's Fencibles. Patterson, *History of Pictou*, 236; MacLaren, *The Pictou Book*, 100–01; PANS MG 100 vol. 226 #30: Memorial of emigrants who arrived on the brigantine *Prince William* from the shire of Sutherland and requested land in Pictou, 30 Sept. 1815.
31. McDougall and Moir, *Glasgow Colonial Society Correspondence*, 149–50. They crossed on the *Ruby* of Aberdeen, the *Harmony* of Aberdeen and *Ossian* of Leith. See Chapter 3.
32. Initially most of the vessels which called to collect emigrants originated from Aberdeen or the nearby port of Peterhead.
33. McDougall and Moir, *Glasgow Colonial Society Correspondence*, 149.
34. *Ibid.*
35. *Ibid,* 215–7. The Glasgow Colonial Society, formed in 1826, helped the Church of Scotland clergy establish Presbyterian congregations in British America.
36. Campbell and MacLean, *Atlantic Roar*, 71–75. A total of 78 people transferred to St. Anns in 1820. See Martell, *Immigration Nova Scotia*, 51. In 1853, Norman MacLeod went to New Zealand, along with other followers from St. Anns.
37. Martell, *Ibid,* 84; *IJ* June 10, July 1, 1836; *QM* Sept. 16, 1836.
38. Elizabeth, countess of Sutherland, who succeeded to the Earldom of Sutherland in 1766, married George Granville Leveson-Gower in 1785. Known then as Viscount Trentham, he became Earl Gower in 1786, holding that title until 1803. Having succeeded his father in 1803 as the second Marquess of Stafford, he was created Duke of Sutherland in January 1833. Following his death in July of that year, the title passed to his son George Granville Sutherland-Leveson Gower, who remained Duke until his death in 1861.
39. The 1847 group sailed on the *Serius* and the 1848 group on the *Ellen* of Liverpool. *Report from Commissioners, Poor Laws,* 403–05; Devine, *Great Highland Famine,* 324, 332; MacLaren, *Pictou Book,* 122.
40. Small numbers went on to Miramichi or Saint John, New Brunswick.
41. *Aberdeen Herald,* March 5, 1836. To the dismay of local administrators, both Halifax and Saint John, New Brunswick, came to be used as a gateway to the United States for those wishing to avoid American immigration taxes.
42. Campbell and MacLean, *Atlantic Roar*, 35–58.
43. Patterson, *History of Pictou*, 275–76; *Emigration Select Committee,* 1827 A 2391–2419.
44. *Ibid,* A 2418.
45. E.504/1/27; *QM* May 15, 1818; Martell, *Immigration Nova Scotia,* 45–6.

IX. SETTLEMENTS IN WESTERN UPPER CANADA

1. Extract of a letter from an "intelligent and respectable Aberdonian who emigrated to Upper Canada last Spring" in *Aberdeen Herald,* March 26, 1836.
2. "Notes of a Journey through part of Canada and the United States in 1834" by Thomas

NOTES

W. Valentine in A.E. Byerly, *Fergus or the Ferguson-Webster Settlement with an Extensive history of North East Nichol* (Elora, Ont.: Elora Express, 1932–34) 80.

3. The Huron Tract represented a large single area of unsurveyed land which consisted of just over one million acres; it eventually stretched across twenty-two townships in Huron, Perth and Middlesex counties. Cowan, *British Emigration,* 132–9.

4. Arthur E. Wright, *Pioneer Days in Nichol* (Mount Forest, Ont.: privately published, 1932) 49.

5. In 1832, emigrants would pay £6 and take about 6 days to get to York if they travelled from Montreal to Prescott by land; otherwise the cost of going the 550 miles from Montreal to York was £1.11s.6d. and the journey time was around 12 days. See Scottish Record Office GD 46/13/184 7–8.

6. Aberdeen University MS 2137–8 Reverend Patrick Bell, "Journals or Rather Observations made in Upper Canada during the years 1834–35–36 and 37" (1837) ff. 107–8.

7. *Ibid,* ff. 109. Reverend Bell had sailed from Liverpool to New York in 1833. The New York route was considered safer and faster than the Quebec route, but it was more expensive. Having arrived in New York, Reverend Bell would have gone up the Hudson River to Albany, where the Erie Canal commenced, and travelled along it to Buffalo on Lake Ontario. From there he would have travelled by land to Hamilton and then on to Guelph and Fergus.

8. Fergus comprised concessions XIV, XV and XVI in Upper Nichol township.

9. Bell, *Journals, Upper Canada,* 326–31.

10. Patrick Bell, a graduate of St. Andrews University, was a minister of the Presbyterian Church. A very distinguished man, he was the inventor of the world's first mechanized reaping machine. His 1828 invention was one of the earliest mechanization steps ever to be made in farming. Interestingly, he did not patent his invention, but gave it freely to the world.

11. Fergusson's *Practical Notes* in John Mathison, *Counsel for Emigrants, and Interesting Information from Numerous Sources concerning British America, the United States and New South Wales,* third edition with a supp. (Aberdeen, 1838) 118–9.

12. Harper, *Emigration North East Scotland,* 215–24. By 1839, the Hon. Adam Fergusson had been appointed a member of the Legislative Council of Upper Canada. His son, the Hon. Adam Johnston Fergusson-Blair, founded the Veterinary College at Guelph which was later taken over by the Ontario Board of Agriculture. A.E. Byerly, *Fergus or the Ferguson-Webster Settlement with an Extensive History of North East Nichol,* 40.

13. Harper, *Ibid,* 216–7.

14. According to tradition, "Bon Accord" was used as a password by Aberdonian supporters of King Robert Bruce when they attacked a garrison in the castle under the control of the English during the Wars of Independence (1306–28). The password was apparently then conferred on the city as its motto.

15. Wright, *Pioneer Days in Nichol,* 47–56.

16. Settled from 1824, New Aberdeen had 120 inhabitants by 1850. Byerly, *Wellington and Waterloo Counties,* 35.

17. *Parliamentary Papers* w/e June 6, 1835; *AH* March 5, 1836.

18. The numbers of passengers who left Aberdeen for Quebec were: 1837 (252), 1838 (147), 1839 (157), 1840 (194) 1841(354). See *PP, Annual Reports of the Immigration Agent at Quebec.*

19. Wright, *Pioneer Days in Nichol*, 46. Bon Accord comprised concessions XI, XII and XIII in Upper Nichol township. Although suffering less than most other parts of Scotland, Aberdeenshire did experience a severe enough depression by 1848 to cause large-scale unemployment. Harper, *Emigration North East Scotland,* 130–50.

20. *Ibid*, 223.

21. For example, *Parliamentary Papers* w/e May 16, 1840.

22. *Parliamentary Papers* w/e July 11, Sept. 23, 1843.

23. Wright, *Pioneer Days in Nichol*, 31–6.

24. *Aberdeen Herald*, March 12, May 19, 1836.

25. John R. Connon, *Elora,* (Waterloo, Ont.: Wilfrid Laurier University Press, 1930) 85.

26. Wright, *Pioneer Days in Nichol*, 51–5.

27. George Elmslie's Diary in Connon, *Elora,* 82. George Elmslie's Diary is preserved in the Wellington County Museum and Archives.

28. Connon, *Elora*, 103–4; Byerly, *Fergus*, 50.

29. Harper, *Emigration North East Scotland*, 215–24. Alexander Dingwall-Fordyce produced many early sketches of Fergus.

30. Byerly, *Fergus,* 50, 54, 262.

31. George Elmslie worked as a teacher for some 35 years at Ancaster, Hamilton, Guelph, Elora and Alma. Connon, *Elora*, 167.

32. *Ibid*, 103.

33. A.G. Brunger, "The Distribution of Scots and Irish in Upper Canada 1851–71," *Canadian Geographer*, vol. 34 (1990) 250–58. Guelph's "Paisley Block," created in 1828 and extended a few years later, probably takes its name from an intake of workers from this manufacturing area of Scotland. K.J. Duncan, "Aspects of Scottish Settlement in Wellington County," *Scottish Colloquium Proceedings, University of Guelph,* vol. 3, 1970, 16.

34. The Canada Company had been established in 1826 to encourage settlement by settlers able to fund their own emigration costs. The Huron Tract was a vast triangular-shaped area consisting of 1.1 million acres. Encompassing twenty-two townships, Goderich, located on the shores of Lake Huron, was the main population centre.

35. John Sutherland's *Inverness Journal* advertisement stated that he "was authorized to dispose of 225,000 acres of uncleared land at a cost from 7 s. to 15 s. per acre." *Inverness Journal*, April 5, 1844. The Huron Tract attracted its Scots from both the northwest and northeast Highlands, the Western Isles and from the Lowlands. J.M. Cameron, "A Study of the factors that assisted and directed Scottish Emigration to Upper Canada 1815–55" (Glasgow: unpublished Ph.D. thesis, 1970) 439–43.

36. Chapter 8 gives details of the growing exodus from Sutherland to British America during the first half of the nineteenth century.

37. *Inverness Courier*, June 23, Oct. 6, 1830; *IJ* Nov. 6, 1830; *AJ* July 13, 1831. Some early arrivals included Sutherland-born settlers from Pictou who migrated to Zorra.

38. A log church had been built by 1832–33. Reverend W.A. MacKay, *Pioneer Life in Zorra* (Toronto: William Briggs, 1899) 64,78.

39. *Parliamentary Papers* w/e Aug. 22, 1840; *Inverness Courier*, Aug. 5, 1840.

40. Scottish Record Office RH/1/2/612/8: Letter from Adam Hope to George Hope, Aug. 12, 1847.

X. Steam Replaces Sail

1. *Parliamentary Papers* w/e May 31, 1853.

2. For example, *Aberdeen Herald*, June 19, 1852.
3. Harper, *Emigration, North East Scotland*, 43–4.
4. Including the railway fare from Portland to Montreal, the first cabin fare was 20 guineas, the second cabin 13–15 g., with steerage at 7 g. *IC* Feb. 9, 16, 1854.

Appendix B (2)

1. The *Emperor Alexander* of Aberdeen sailed on to Quebec where a further 49 emigrants disembarked (*QM* Oct. 7, 1824).
2. Archibald McNiven was the principal Emigration Agent in the Hebrides from 1820 to 1840.

Index

1. The Duthies, from William to Alexander and John, and his son John Jr., were shipbuilders, shipowners, emigration agents and merchants.

BIBLIOGRAPHY

PRIMARY SOURCES (MANUSCRIPTS)

Aberdeen City Archives (ACA)
>CE87/11 Register of Ships, Aberdeen

Aberdeen University Library, Department of Manuscripts and Archives (AUA)
>AU MS 2137–8 Bell, Reverend Patrick, Journals or Rather Observations made in Upper Canada during the years 1834–35–36 and 37 (1837).
>AU MS 2295 William Penny Collection, 1842–43.

Dundee City Archives (DCA)
>CE 70/11 Register of Ships

Highland Council Archives
>D207 James Fraser's Reminisences, 10th July, 1867, London, Ontario.
>D217 Register of ships at Inverness Port

National Library of Scotland (NLS)
>MS 9646 "On Emigration from the Scottish Highlands and Islands attributed to Edward S. Fraser of Inverness-shire" (1801–4).
>SP Dep 313/1128/29 Letter from William Young to Earl Gower, May 1813.
>SP Dep 313/1468 Letter book of Francis Suther 1817–1819 relating to emigration from the Sutherland estates.

Public Archives of Nova Scotia (PANS)
>MG7 Vol 3A Log books, ships and shipping; ship names in *Nova Scotia Royal Gazette,* 1769–1797.
>MG 100 vol. 167 #8 *The Times,* Aug. 22, 1843.
>MG 100 vol. 226 #30 Memorial of emigrants who arrived on the brigantine *Prince William* from the shire of Sutherland and requested land in Pictou, 30 Sept. 1815.

Public Archives of Prince Edward Island (PAPEI)
>MSS 2702 Passenger lists, including *Isle of Skye* of Aberdeen, 1806.

Public Record Office (PRO)
>CO 384 Colonial Office Papers on emigration containing original correspondence concerning North American settlers.
>MPI 297 Place names and settlers on the Miramichi River, surveyed 1785.

Scottish Record Office (SRO)

   E.504 Customs Records, Collectors Quarterly Accounts, 1776–1830.

   GD 1/620 Rogerson Papers.

   GD 46/13/184 *Information published by His Majesty's Commissioners for Emigration respecting the British Colonies in North America* (London, Feb., 1832).

   RH 1/2/908 *Mechanic and Farmer*, Pictou, Nova Scotia, July 28, 1841.

   RH 1/2/612/8 Letter from Adam Hope to George Hope, Aug. 12, 1847.

   RH 2/4/87 Passenger Lists, *Dove* of Aberdeen and *Sarah* of Liverpool, 1801.

   RH 4/188/1,2 Prize essays and Transactions of the Highland Society of Scotland, Vol. iii, 1802–03.

Primary Sources (Printed)

Aberdeen Directory, 1840–1855.

Atkinson, Rev., Christopher, *An Historical and Statistical Account of New Brunswick, British North America* (Edinburgh, 1844).

Brown, Robert, *Strictures and Remarks on the Earl of Selkirk's Observations on the Present State of the Highlands with a view of the causes and probable consequences of emigration* (Edinburgh: Abernethy & Walker, 1806).

Glasgow Colonial Society, *Seventh Annual Report of the Glasgow Colonial Society for promoting the religious interests of the Scottish settlers in British North America* (Glasgow, 1833).

Fowler, Thomas, *Journal of a Tour through British North America to the Falls of Niagara containing an account of the cities towns and villages along the route in 1831* (Aberdeen: Smith, 1832).

MacKay, Rev., W. A., *Pioneer Life in Zorra* (Toronto: William Briggs, 1899).

MacLeod, Donald, *History of the Destitution in Sutherlandshire* (Edinburgh, 1841) [King collection in Aberdeen University Library].

Mathison, John, *Counsel for Emigrants, and Interesting Information from Numerous Sources concerning British America, the United States and New South Wales,* Third edition with a supp. (Aberdeen: John Mathison, 1838).

Lloyd's Shipping Register 1775–1855.

Sinclair, Sir John, *The Statistical Account of Scotland,* 21 vols. (Edinburgh: M. Creech, 1791–99)

Slater's Royal National Commercial Directory and Topography of Scotland (Manchester: I. Slater, 1860).

Parliamentary Papers

Annual Reports of the Immigration Agent at Quebec (1831–55).

Colonial Land and Emigration Commissioners, Annual Reports (1841–55).

Emigration Returns for British North America (1830–40).

Report from the Commissioners appointed for inquiring into the Administration and Practical Operation of the Poor Laws in Scotland, 1844; Answers to Questions 30 to 32 in the Appendices.

Report from the Select Committee on the Passenger Acts, 1851, XIX.

Reports from the Select Committee appointed to inquire into the expediency of encouraging emigration from the United Kingdom, 1826, IV; 1826–27, V.

Newspapers

Aberdeen Herald
Aberdeen Journal
Dundee Courier
Elgin Courier
Inverness Courier
Inverness Journal
John O'Groat Journal
Lloyd's List
Moray, Nairn and Banff Courant
Montreal Transcript
New Brunswick Royal Gazette
Pictou Observer
Prince Edward Island Gazette
Quebec Gazette
Quebec Mercury

SECONDARY SOURCES

Adams, Ian and Somerville, Meredyth, *Cargoes of Despair and Hope: Scottish Emigration to North America 1603–1803* (Edinburgh: John Donald, 1993).

Anon., *Day of the Clipper,* Textual record of the exhibition held at James Dun's House, 61 Schoolhill Aberdeen, Nov. 2, 1979–March 25, 1980—Photo Panel 9.

Blake, George, *Lloyd's Register of Shipping 1760–1960* (London: Lloyd's, 1960).

Brunger, A.G., "The Distribution of Scots and Irish in Upper Canada 1851–71," *Canadian Geographer,* vol. 34 (1990) 250–58.

Bumsted, J.M., *The People's Clearance: Highland Emigration to British North America 1770–1815* (Edinburgh: Edinburgh University Press, 1982).

Bumsted, J.M., *The Peoples of Canada, a Pre-Confederation History,* vol. 1 (Toronto: Oxford University Press, 1992).

Byerly, A. E., *Fergus or the Ferguson-Webster Settlement with an Extensive history of North East Nichol* (Elora, Ont.: Elora Express, 1932–34).

Byerly, A. E., *The Beginning of things in Wellington and Waterloo Counties with particular reference to Guelph, Galt and Kitchener* (Guelph: Guelph Publishing Co., 1935).

Cameron, J.M., "A Study of the factors that assisted and directed Scottish Emigration to Upper Canada 1815–55" (Glasgow: unpublished Ph. D. 1970).

Cameron, Viola Root, *Emigrants from Scotland to America 1774–1775* (Baltimore: Genealogical Publishing Co., 1965).

Campbell, D.F. and R.A. MacLean, *Beyond the Atlantic Roar: A Study of the Nova Scotia Scots* (Toronto: McClelland & Stewart, 1974).

Campbell, R.H., *Scotland Since 1707: The Rise of an Industrial Society* (Edinburgh: John Donald, 1985).

Campey, Lucille H., *"A Very Fine Class of Immigrants": Prince Edward Island's Scottish Pioneers, 1770–1850* (Toronto: Natural Heritage, 2001) 16–31.

Census of Canada, 1851, 1861 and 1871.

Chatterton Keble Edward, *Sailing Ships: The Story of their Development from the Earliest Times to the Present Day* (London: Sidgwick & Jackson Ltd., 1909).

Clark, Andrew H., "Old World Origins and Religious Adherence in Nova Scotia," *Geographical Review*, vol. 1 (1960) 317–44.

Clark, Victoria E., *The Port of Aberdeen: A History of its Trade and Shipping from the Twelfth Century to the Present Day* (Aberdeen: D. Willie & Son, 1921).

Connon, John R., *Elora* (Waterloo Ont.: Wilfrid Laurier University Press, 1975).

Cornford, L.C., *The Sea Carriers 1825–1925: The Aberdeen Line* (London: Aberdeen Line, 1925).

Cowan, Helen, *British Emigration to British North America: The First Hundred Years* (Toronto: University of Toronto Press, 1961).

Davis, Ralph, *The Industrial Revolution and British Overseas Trade* (Leicester: Leicester University Press, 1979).

Devine, T.M., *The Great Highland Famine, Hunger: Emigration and the Scottish Highlands in the Nineteenth Century* (Edinburgh: John Donald, 1988).

Dictionary of Canadian Biography, vols. IV–IX (Toronto, 1979–85).

Duncan, K.J., "Aspects of Scottish Settlement in Wellington County," *Scottish Colloquium Proceedings University of Guelph* (1970) 15–20.

Flewwelling, Susan Langley (Morse), "Immigration to and Emigration from Nova Scotia 1839–51," *Nova Scotia Historical Society (Collections)*, Halifax, N. S. vol. xxviii (1949) 82–85.

Foden, Frank, *Wick of the North: The Story of a Scottish Royal Burgh* (Wick: North of Scotland Newspapers, 1996).

Ganong, W.F., "Monograph of the Origins of Settlements in the Province of New Brunswick," *Transactions of the Royal Society of Canada* 2nd series (10), sections 1–2 (1904).

Graham, Gerald S., *Sea Power and British North America 1785–1820: A study in British Colonial Policy* (Cambridge Mass.: Harvard University Press, 1941).

Guillet, Edwin C., *The Great Migration: The Atlantic crossing by sailing ships since 1770* (Toronto: University of Toronto Press, 2nd edition, 1963).

Hamilton, Henry, *The Industrial Revolution in Scotland* (Oxford: Clarendon Press, 1932).

Harper, Marjory, *Emigration from North-East Scotland* Vol. 1, *Willing Exiles* (Aberdeen: Aberdeen University Press, 1988).

Horn, James, "British Diaspora: Emigration from Britain, 1680–1815" in Marshall, P.J. (ed.) *The Oxford History of the British Empire: The Eighteenth Century* (Oxford: Oxford University Press, 1998) 28–52.

Hustwick, Ian, *Moray Firth: Ships and Trade during the Nineteenth Century* (Aberdeen: Scottish Cultural Press, 1994).

Jackson, Gordon, *The British Whaling Trade* (London: A. & C. Black, 1978).

Keith, Alexander, *Eminent Aberdonians* (Aberdeen: Aberdeen Chamber of Commerce, 1984).

Kemp, Peter, (ed.) *The Oxford Companion to Ships and the Sea* (Oxford: Oxford University Press, 1988).

Lenman, Bruce, *An Economic History of Modern Scotland 1600–1976* (London: Batsford, 1977).

Lloyd's Register, Information Group, "*Lloyds Register*—Yesterday and Today," Infosheet No. 31 (Version 2 22.1.97).

Lubbock, Basil, *The Colonial Clippers* (Glasgow: Brown, Son & Ferguson, 1948).

Macdonagh, Oliver, *A pattern of government growth 1800–1860: The Passenger Acts and their enforcement* (London: Macgibbon & Kee, 1961).

MacDonald, Colin S., "Early Highland Emigration to Nova Scotia and Prince Edward Island from 1770 to 1853," *Nova Scotia Historical Society (Collections),* Halifax, N. S., vol. xxiii (1936).

MacDonald, Norman, *Canada, Immigration and Settlement 1763–1841* (London: Longmans & Co., 1939).

MacGregor, David R., *Clipper Ships* (Watford: Angus Books, 1979.

MacGregor, David R., *Fast Sailing Ships: Their Design and Construction, 1775–1875* (London: Conway Maritime Press, 1988).

MacGregor, David R., *Merchant Sailing Ships: Sovereignty of Sail 1775–1815* (London: Conway Maritime Press, 1985).

MacGregor David R., *Merchant Sailing Ships, Supremacy of Sail 1815–1850* (London: Conway Maritime Press, 1984).

MacKay, Donald, *Scotland Farewell: The People of the Hector* (Toronto: Natural Heritage, 1996).

MacKenzie, George A.(ed.) *From Aberdeen to Ottawa in 1845: The Diary of Alexander Muir* (Aberdeen: Aberdeen University Press, 1990).

MacLaren, George, *The Pictou Book* (New Glasgow, Nova Scotia: Hector Publishing Co., 1954).

MacMillan, David S., "Scottish Enterprise and Influences in Canada 1620–1900" in Cage, R.A. (ed.) *The Scots Abroad: Labour, Capital, Enterprise, 1750–1914* (London: Croom Helm, 1985) 66–72.

Martell, J.S. *Immigration to and Emigration from Nova Scotia 1815–1838* (Halifax: PANS 1942).

McDougall, Elizabeth Ann Kerr and John S. Moir (eds.), *Selected Correspondence of the Glasgow Colonial Society 1825–1840* (Toronto: Champlain Society, 1994).

McLean, Marianne, *People of Glengarry 1745–1820: Highlanders in Transition 1745–1820* (Montreal: McGill-Queen's University Press, 1991).

Morgan Diane, *Villages of Aberdeen: Footdee and her Shipyards* (Aberdeen: Denburn Books, 1993).

Morse, Susan Longley, "Immigration to Nova Scotia 1839–51" (Dalhousie, Nova Scotia, unpublished M.A. 1946).

Orlo, J. and Fraser D., "Those Elusive Immigrants, Parts 1 to 3," *Island Magazine,* Nos. 16–18 (1984–1985) 36–41 (Part 1), 32–7 (Part 2), 29–35 (Part 3).

Patterson, George, *History of the County of Pictou* (Montreal: Dawson Bros., 1877).

Prebble, John, *The Highland Clearances* (London: Penguin, 1969).

Richards, Eric, *A History of the Highland Clearances: Emigration, Protest, Reasons* (London: Croom Helm, 1985).

Rinn, Jacqueline, "Factors in Scottish Emigration: A study of Scottish participation in the indentured and transportation systems of the New World in the seventeenth and eighteenth centuries" (Aberdeen University, unpublished Ph. D. 1979).

Sager, Eric with G.E. Panting, *Maritime Capital: The Shipping Industry in Atlantic Canada 1820–1914* (Montreal: McGill-Queen's University Press, 1990).

Straus, Ralph, *Lloyds: A Historical Sketch* (London: Hutchinson & Co., 1937).

Wright, Arthur E., *Pioneer Days in Nichol* (Mount Forest, Ont.: the Author, 1932).

Wynn, G., "A Region of Scattered Settlements and Bounded Possibilities: Northeastern America 1775–1800" in *The Canadian Geographer*, Vol. 31 (1987).

INDEX

About the Author

Dr. Lucille Campey is a Canadian, living in Britain, with over thirty years of experience as a researcher and author. It was her father's Scottish roots and love of history that first stimulated her interest in the early exodus of people from Scotland to Canada. She is the great-great-granddaughter of William Thomson, who left Morayshire, on the northeast coast of Scotland in the early 1800s to begin a new life with his family, first near Digby then in Antigonish, Nova Scotia. He is described in D. Whidden's *History of the Town of Antigonish* simply as "William, Pioneer" and is commemorated in the St. James Church and Cemetery at Antigonish. Lucille was awarded a Ph.D. by Aberdeen University in 1998 for her researches into Scottish emigration to Canada in the period 1770–1850.

This is Lucille's second book on the subject of emigrant Scots. Described by the *P.E.I. Guardian* as "indispensable to Islanders of Scottish ancestry" her first book, *"A Very Fine Class of Immigrants": Prince Edward Island's Scottish Pioneers 1770–1850* (Natural Heritage, 2001) gives the most comprehensive account to date of the Scottish influx to the Island. Her second book, on the Aberdeen ships which carried emigrant Scots to Canada, is the culmination of many years of research. It interweaves material from her doctoral thesis with entirely new research into shipping patterns and emigrant settlements.

A Chemistry graduate of Ottawa University, Lucille worked initially in the fields of science and computing. After marrying her English husband, she moved to the north of England, where she became interested in medieval monasteries and acquired a Master of Philosophy Degree (on the subject of medieval settlement patterns) from Leeds University. Having lived for five years in Easter Ross while she completed her doctoral thesis, she and Geoff returned to England, and now live near Salisbury in Wiltshire.